British & Irish Hunts & Huntsmen

VOLUME I

British & Irish Hunts & Huntsmen

VOLUME I

J.N.P. Watson

B.T. Batsford Ltd, London

By the same author

Biography
*Captain-General and Rebel Chief, the Life of
James, Duke of Monmouth* (George Allen &
Unwin, 1979)

Field sports
The Book of Foxhunting (Batsford, 1977)
*Victorian and Edwardian Field Sports from Old
Photographs* (Batsford, 1978)

Other sport
The World of Polo (Rolex, 1981)

Anthology
The World's Greatest Horse Stories (Paddington
Press, 1979)

Frontispiece The author

© J.N.P. Watson 1982
First published 1982

ISBN 0 7134 2169 X

Filmset in Monophoto Ehrhardt by
Servis Filmsetting Ltd, Manchester

Printed in Great Britain by
The Anchor Press Ltd
Tiptree, Essex
for the publishers B.T. Batsford Ltd,
4 Fitzhardinge Street, London WIH OAH

Contents

Acknowledgments

The material contained in this volume has been developed from the series of articles on British and Irish hunts which *Country Life* has been publishing under the author's name since 1970 and is reproduced by kind permission of the Editor.

The Author and Publishers would like to thank the following individuals and organisations for permission to use their photographs. *Country Life*, 5, 6; The Press Association Ltd, 8, 9; John Tarlton, 11, 44, 51, 72; Jim Meads, 12, 13, 14, 18, 20, 21, 26, 27, 28, 29, 30, 32, 34, 39, 41, 42, 43, 45, 46, 49, 56, 57, 61, 63, 64, 68, 79, 80, 81, 83, 84, 85, 89, 91, 92, 96, 97, 98, 99, 100, 102, 104, 105, 107, 108, 109, 110, 111, 112, 114, 115, 116, 117, 119, 120, 124, 126, 128, 132, 138; Marshall P. Hawkins, 15; John F. Hughes, 19, 24, 87; The Paul Mellon Centre for Studies in British Art (London) Ltd, 22, 23; Stanley Hurwitz, 36; Central Press Photos Ltd, 55; Roger Robinson, 48; Leslie Lane, 50; A.H. Paul, 53; Roger M. Smith, 59; John Keene Studio, 65, 76, 77; George Williams, 66; John Williams, 67; Robert Chapman, 74, 75; Seán Hagerty, 93, 94, 95, 121; Sport & General Press Agency Ltd, 101; Fox Photos, 122; R. Clapperton, 125; David Hope, 127; John Angus, 129; Charles Fennell, 133, 134; Peter Sweetman, 135; and Doonmoon Photographs, 137.

The maps are by Colonel W.F.N. Watson.

Foreword

By His Grace the Duke of Beaufort, KG, GCVO, PC, MFH

The four original volumes under the title *British Hunts and Huntsmen*, which were produced by the Biographical Press during the Edwardian era, marked a major milestone in hunting literature; for they contained the first complete accounts of all the principal fox and stag hunts in Britain and Ireland. But they did not include hare hunts, and since they came from a great variety of local personalities in the hunts concerned, they lacked a central style and theme.

However, the volumes which Batsford are here publishing under that title not only bring the records up to date, but they also come from the same pen, that of the hunting correspondent to *Country Life*.

The excellent accounts of the hunts included in this first volume, all of which were published in the magazine between 1969 and March 1976, give comprehensive histories, together with descriptions of countries, organisations and hound-breeding and of the author's day out with the foxhounds, staghounds, harehounds and bloodhounds of the hunts concerned.

Since John Watson continues to visit, ride with (or run with, as the case may be) a dozen or so different packs each season for *Country Life*, he has now recorded well over one hundred and thirty. So work on the third volume, which Batsford hope to bring out in a few years' time, is well under way.

I have pleasure in recommending *British and Irish Hunts and Huntsmen*, as the new and principal reference library on these subjects, for all those in Britain and Ireland who follow hounds, whether by horse or foot.

Beaufort

1 Peter Beckford, Dorset Master of the late 18th century, pioneer breeder of hounds and author of the classic *Thoughts on Hunting*.

Introduction

The title *British Hunts and Huntsmen* was first given to four volumes published by the Biographical Press between 1908 and 1911. Organised on a regional basis and written by local specialists, these contained brief histories of fox and stag hunts of England, Scotland, Wales and Ireland, with biographical notes on the Masters and other leading personalities. Each volume was prefaced with dissertations on different aspects of the general history of hunting, the evolution of the hound and the horse and the natural history of the fox and the stag.

This book is intended as a sequel to my *Book of Foxhunting* (Batsford, 1977). It is designed not only to bring the old *British Hunts and Huntsmen* up to date with a more homogeneous presentation, and the addition of hare and bloodhound – and mink, too – as well as fox and stag hunts, but also to produce more accurate and comprehensive hunt histories, coupled with a visitor's impression from a day out with each of the packs concerned during the 1970s and 1980s.

These volumes are the fruit of twelve seasons' enjoyment as hunting correspondent to *Country Life*, an assignment I was lucky enough to secure on joining the editorial staff of that magazine in 1969. My brief from the Editors (first Mr John Adams, then, from 1973, Mr Michael Wright) has been to take a day's hunting with a particular pack once every two weeks or so throughout the season, and to write an article comprising some two-thirds history, and the remainder a description of the day's sport, the hound-breeding and the country. At the time of my appointment, these articles were confined to foxhunts, and were illustrated simply with photographs of the day spent. But I extended the scope to cover harehunts, and went on to include firstly pictures to support the historical aspect, and then maps showing the whereabouts of the relevant country in relation to its adjacent hunts, and – in the case of an adventurous day's hunting – the lines taken by hounds.

A great many people enquire as to how I arrange my programme. As the magazine's senior feature writer, I devote the rest of my journalistic year to the preparation of articles on wildlife conservation, animal welfare, hound shows and the Game Fair, animal and sporting art exhibitions, rural museums and other centres, and – between late May and early August – to reports on the high-goal polo matches. At the conclusion of the polo season I select a dozen or so hunts, spread as evenly as possible across the map, and then write to the respective senior joint-Masters, asking if they would be kind enough to let me have a day with their hounds, with a view to a *Country Life* article. I suggest a date (not forgetting to state my riding weight) and enclose a couple of previous articles to show the magazine's approach.

Masters of hounds are nearly all co-operative and hospitable people, and I have much to thank them for. But there are those who believe hunting correspondents are equestrian geniuses, whose principal aim is to lead the field from start to finish. I will give two examples. I was once lent a horse in the Midlands which reared and bucked so furiously at the meet that it took me several minutes to get on his back. Hounds found straight away and off we went like a rodeo. He made no real attempt to jump the first fence, but turned upside down in the ditch preceding it, then scrambled to his feet and careered away across the field beyond, with me plodding over the plough behind. A young farmer caught the horse and, as I was reunited with it, a generous woman suggested I take hers and that she should ride the Wild One. The farmer looked at her aghast: 'Oh no you won't, Mary!' he said, '*this* is a well-known *killer*!' and turning to me, he added, 'I think they were interested to know whether a really *experienced* horseman could manage it. . . .'

The second incident was in the far north, when an impeccable thoroughbred mare, with oiled feet, spit-and-polish coat, plaited mane and beautiful manners was waiting at the meet for me. We spent the day on heather-moors, intersected by narrow sheep-drains, many of which were overgrown and blind. Local hunt horses stepped over these little obstacles faultlessly, and, doubtless, they could have done so blindfold. But not mine. On several occasions she put her foot straight in, sinking to the knee, and, twice, I went over her head, smearing my hat with peat.

'How are you getting on with that horse?' asked a kind enquirer at about 1.00 p.m.

'Oh, she's a fine blood-horse, a lovely ride! . . . But she doesn't seem to know the hill very well', I replied.

'Know the *hill*', commented the kind enquirer

2 Hugo Meynell, Master of the Quorn from 1753 to 1800 and 'founder of the modern foxhound'.

not necessarily involve a postponement of the visit; in spite of them I usually still keep my date to stay in the country and produce an article. On a couple of occasions, however, my proposed expedition had to be cancelled owing to hunts being afflicted with political and domestic problems. Then, in order to fulfil the magazine's schedule, I have been obliged to negotiate, at short notice, with an alternative hunt.

But a hunting correspondent must take the rough with the smooth, and the smooth can be paradisial!

As I have mentioned, my main business is the history, and I make sure of reading all the historical references I can lay my hands on before each visit. Many of the famous hunts boast most comprehensive classics of their own, and nearly all of these are in the collection left to the London Library by a colourful American foxhunting bibliophile, Henry Higginson, who was Master of the Cattistock in the early 1930s. Most of the pamphlets written by those four hard-working chroniclers, Ralph Greaves, Jack Fairfax-Blakeborough, William Scarth-Dixon and William Fawcett are to be found on the same shelves. In addition there are the potted accounts in the Edwardian *British Hunts and Huntsmen*, of which volumes I have a set at home.

I do most of the picture research in advance, too. Prints of the important relevant historical pictures are frequently contained in these old books, and these are readily copied; but quite often I hear of significant paintings (of which no photographs are available) hanging in a house in the country concerned. In which case I contact the photographer who is to cover the day's hunting and ask him to bring his lamps and other indoor equipment.

Then there is the map. Before leaving the country of my visit, I rough out a sketch of the perimeter and the hunt's most important meets, the other landmarks and the adjacent hunts. On return I hand this to *Country Life's* free-lance cartographer, who draws the final version.

Hunting people with little feeling for history often ask me why *Country Life* lays so much emphasis on the past. What on earth is the relevance of all those old chronicles? The answer to that is that the preservation of a rich heritage, provided it does not hinder wise progress, is a pearl of great value to almost any organisation. For example, in the armed services in general – and in ships, regiments and Air Force units in particular – corporate pride, strong morale and aspiration to high standards are, in great measure, founded on tradition. As between schools, universities and municipalities so between hunts of long standing a healthy rivalry exists. And from the

incredulously; 'oh *no*. She's never been up here before. But we thought, as you spent your winters going round strange countries riding strange horses, you'd be just the fellow to break her in for us. . . .'

There are other, more natural hazards, ice and snow, for example, floods and swine fever. These do

3 George Osbaldeston, great Master and hound breeder of the early 19th century.

4 Lord Henry Bentinck, Master of the Old Burton from 1842 to 1862. He was described by Henry Chaplin, a later Master of that hunt and himself a distinguished hound man, as 'possibly the finest brain ever given to the breeding of hounds'.

ancient traditions of the hunting-field stem its beautiful spectacle and its sounds, the finest pageantry of the British and Irish countrysides.

And here is another reason. In these days of intensive agriculture and exorbitant land prices, if it were not for this heritage which reaches back in many cases more than ten generations, it is most unlikely that the hunts would have access to the land over which they ride and run. Hunting is something which most British and Irish landowners and farmers have lived with for two centuries. Since their forbears saw it as an integral part of British rural life, they themselves are prepared to make sacrifices, and to accept a modicum of damage, too. And all this is now made much easier by the fact that the present generation of farmers, having more time for recreation, are much more widely represented in the hunting-field than were their forefathers.

The evolution of British hunting is a fascinating study in its own right. Up to the middle of the seventeenth century the deer was the favoured quarry. But by the end of the Civil War the forests had been decimated for timber and fuel for iron-working, to such an extent that, as one Cavalier put it, 'nothing remains but rabbits and Roundheads'.

Following the Restoration, harehunting grew in popularity and during the late seventeenth century the hare came to be regarded as the 'queen of all venery'. But already under the later Stuarts, some of the nobility were beginning to appreciate the sporting potential of foxhunting. The future James II was recorded as 'going a-Fox Hunting' from the 1660s; at the same time the Duke of Buckingham was hunting the fox in Yorkshire; Charles II's eldest son, the Duke of Monmouth and his friend, Lord Grey of Werke, both kept packs entered to fox, under Squire Roper at Charlton, near Chichester, in Sussex. So did Lord Arundell on the borders of Hampshire and Wiltshire.

The eighteenth century saw more and more of the squirarchy turning from hare to fox: the 3rd Earl of Darlington, the 5th Duke of Beaufort, Sir Richard Puleston, the Earls of Berkeley, the 3rd Duke of Rutland, Charles Pelham and the 1st Lord Yarborough; and in Leicestershire, the birthplace of modern foxhunting, Thomas Boothby. But all these early foxhunters, like their harrier friends, set out at dawn, their hounds following the fox's overnight drag to the kennel where he slept off his meal. Then with their slow low-scenting southern-mouthed hounds, they pursued him to his earth and dug him out.

In the early 1750s one or two Masters were looking for the means of greater pace. Hugo Meynell, who succeeded his grandfather, Thomas Boothby, in the Mastership of the Quorn in 1753, John Smith-Barry in Cheshire, and John Warde, in Northamptonshire, started to hunt their foxes, fresh and alert in the middle of the morning, and make them 'fly or die'; but, by and large, their ponderous hounds failed to catch them in the open.

Hugo Meynell, knowing that a hound cannot run faster than its scenting power, began to breed for *drive*. He took some of the best of the light-boned Northern hounds, and crossed them with exemplars from the outstanding kennels breeding the lower-scenting deep-voiced Southern hounds, to produce fox catchers with a good turn of speed and a nose to match it. Soon Brocklesby and Belvoir were the kennels finding the tap-roots of the foxhound blood

5 From dog-cart to sidesaddle as hounds arrive at the meet *c.*1900.

6 Taking a thorn fence in the 1890s.

7 19th-century fell huntsmen; their country is comparatively unchanged.

8 and 9 Royal foxhunters of the 1920s and 30s, HRH The Princess Royal and HRH The Prince of Wales.

we know today, and Osbaldeston Furrier and Brocklesby Ralleywood were acknowledged to be the foundation-stones of the stud book.

In the second half of the eighteenth century – and through the times of the Napoleonic wars – came changes in the countryside. Better drainage for richer grazing meant crisper, more resilient turf. Wider acreages were put under the plough and divided into plots. Largely as a result of Robert Bakewell's experiments in breeding, cattle and sheep were properly penned; and a series of Enclosure Acts, producing a pattern of thorn and cut-and-laid fences, added the thrill of jumping to the thrill of pace. At first many of the young bloods indulging in the new sport thought they could gallop where they liked. But, in 1809, they were sharply corrected. One anti-hunting landowner was the Earl of Essex. In that year he sued his brother, the Rev. the Hon. William Capel, for taking hounds across his land, adding that 'the destruction of a noxious animal was not the real reason for the trespass'. The case went

against Capel, and thereafter no-one could hunt across another's land without permission; and hunt boundaries began to take shape. This stricture had an admirable effect on hunting; and farmers, consequently shown increasing respect, followed hounds, too.

With the march of the Industrial Revolution many more changes influenced the sport: the macadamisation of the roads rendered the better countries more accessible and driving to meets much easier; the building of hundreds of miles, first of canals, then of railways, seemed at first to threaten the very existence of foxhunting; but, as it transpired, neither hindered the sport too badly. Railways indeed proved a boon. (As Surtees's character, the cockney grocer, John Jorrocks pointed out: 'My offices in Great Coram Street are close to the two best covert hacks – the Great Northern and Euston stations'.)

With the improvement of the shotgun in the mid-nineteenth century pheasant-shooting became more

10 Sir Alfred Munnings's conception of the apogée of
Leicestershire elegance in the 1930s: *Two Busvines and a
Cutaway.*

popular; keepers began destroying the fox – then a
comparatively rare wild animal – on an alarming
scale; so the need for close co-operation between the
hunting and shooting fraternities began early. But it
was barbed-wire, seen more and more in the hedges
from the 1880s onwards, and then motor cars and
tarmac roads, which did more than anything else to
bring the golden age of foxhunting to an end.
(Though it should be noted that for foxhunting on
the Lakeland Fells this golden age has never ceased.
There – where the tradition is older than in the 'low'
countries and hounds are followed on foot – the
character of the country has scarcely changed at all.)

By the Edwardian period, with women and
children as much in evidence in the hunting-field as
men, and a much wider spectrum of society involved
throughout Britain and Ireland, the sport saw a
heavier following than ever. Then came the devas-
tation of the Great War. And, in the post-war years,
while some of the big estates were broken up,
smallholders, many of them opposed to hunting,

11 His Grace The Duke of Beaufort, President of the
Masters of Foxhounds' Association and Master or joint-
Master of his own hounds since 1924.

many indifferent, tended to put a brake on the sport, though, for the most part, foxhunters were still welcomed everywhere. Cars replaced horses, grooms became mechanics, and the social and economic revolution which followed the war rendered the running of hunt countries more complex and difficult. However, hunting survived all that – and Hitler's war, too – with remarkable verve.

But some jealous and non-comprehending townsmen, of a sort who always stood against hunting, then endeavoured to put an end to the sport on the grounds of cruelty. In 1951 they were temporarily silenced by a Government board, the Scott Henderson committee, 'enquiring into practices or activities which may involve cruelty to British wild mammals'. This committee – composed of vets, naturalists, zoologists and ethologists – judged that the control of foxes by shooting, gassing, trapping and poisoning all entailed greater suffering and that hunting with hounds was at once the most effective and the most natural method of culling so far devised. (The first four pages of Chapter 18 of my *Book of Foxhunting* discuss the issues involved.)

Meanwhile the Masters of Foxhounds' Association revised a number of their rules to ensure the proper conduct of the sport and the least possible suffering to the fox; and the British Field Sports Society worked, as they continue to do, with great success to win more and more hearts for hunting's cause. The foundation of the hunt supporters' clubs – the foot, car and bicycle brigade, who raise money and lend their services in a variety of ways – has contributed as much as anything to broadening the base of the sport.

These volumes are concerned with foxhunts, harehunts, deerhunts and draghunts. Of these the foxhunts, with 204 packs in Great Britain and 34 in Ireland, have the largest following. But the harehunts are not far behind. Of the total of 171 of these in the British Isles, there are 24 of harriers in Britain and 25 in Ireland; and 92 of beagles and bassets in Britain and 30 in Ireland. The Holcombe, a Lancashire pack tracing its lineage to the seventeenth century, is the oldest of the harrier hunts, but the flat and open tracts of East Anglia comprise the chief strongholds of that branch of venery.

Modern beagling is a late-comer on the sporting stage. Its history dates from the late 1820s when Parson Honywood, of Coggeshall, Essex, just down from Oxford, crossed some of his rabbit-beagles with harriers to produce the ancestors of the modern foot-beagle. Beagling had been quite popular among the English gentry until late Tudor times, after which the sport was neglected until the nineteenth century. Although the Royal Rock, whose country is the Wirral of Cheshire, have the best claim to antiquity, it was in Surrey – after Honywood and Col. Thornton and others had shown what the 'miniature harrier' could do – that the great revival took place, the packs emerging there, from the late 1830s to the Edwardian period, being the Epsom and Ewell, Worcester Park, Buckland, Surbiton, West Surrey, Horsell and Guildford and Shere (all of which are now condensed in the Surrey and North Sussex).

The 1970s despite many difficulties, continued to see good sport nearly everywhere. The previous decade had been notable for the shrinkage of huntable country – a factor largely responsible for the merging of the Hertfordshire, Old Berkeley and South Oxfordshire into the Vale of Aylesbury, and the amalgamations of the Meynell and South Staffs and the Garth and South Berks; of the Newmarket and Thurlow with the Puckeridge, and of the Surrey Beagles with the North Sussex. Nor, with the continuing programme of M-ways and other main road construction, the completion of the electrification of the railways and the continued growth of suburbs and housing estates, has the situation improved. The following hunt fusion was the Cowdray with the Chiddingfold and Leconfield, and the next (1978) between the Hambledon and the Hursley.

The recent decade has also been one of relatively unkind climate, of late harvests, dry autumns and muggy winters – with the happy exception of the 1974–5 and 1977–8 seasons – until 1978–9 when foxhunters suffered a winter so severe that they lost more days owing to snow and frost than in any season since 1962–3. Throughout these years the threat of rabies loomed higher on the horizon. As the disease has swept through northern France to the channel ports, hunting people have been increasingly alarmed at the prospect of an outbreak in this country. But the MFHA are, on the one hand, confident that it can be kept out, and, on the other that, if it comes they can handle the situation.

The seventies were marked, too, by growing violence from the abolitionists, notably the Hunt Saboteurs' Association, which has been responsible

12 Capt. R.E. Wallace, Chairman of the Masters of Foxhounds' Association and Master or joint-Master of the Eton Beagles (1936–8), the Ludlow (1944–8), the Cotswold (1948–52), the Heythrop (1952–77) and the Exmoor since 1977.

13 Mr John Kirkpatrick, Hon. Secretary and Hon. Treasurer of the Masters of Harriers and Beagles Association. He has also been a joint-Master of Foxhounds (Heythrop 1977–8).

for assaulting and poisoning hounds, terrifying horses, trespassing on private land and doing much damage to private property. The League against Cruel Sports has caused a number of problems to its neighbours in Somerset by buying up Exmoor farms.

If only the misguided fox protectionists were to lend their weight in the one sphere which has caused *real* suffering to the species. I refer to the pelt trade which – owing mostly to the demand on the Continent (by males more than females) for fox-fur coats – has run like a festering sore through many parts of rural Britain. Foxes have been trapped in very large numbers and frequently with the most cruel implements (which throws into relief again the fact that hunting with hounds is the most humane method of fox control).

Meanwhile the Socialists' Home Policy Committee proposed to include a resolution to ban all forms of hunting with hounds as part of their policy; but, although this was rejected by their Executive, coursing and staghunting were earmarked for abolition in the 1979 Party Manifesto. As a result the League made a present of £80,000 to the Labour Party for its General Election Fighting Fund. Labour has promised that if and when it is returned to power, it will set out to have all forms of hunting with hounds abolished.

In 1977 the British Field Sports' Society concluded its Fighting Fund, far exceeding the target of £250,000. But, tragically, just before the objective was reached, the chairman of the committee raising the money, Major Robert Hoare, died. He was a former Master of the West Norfolk, the Cottesmore and the South Notts and a most gifted amateur huntsman; and to his buoyant and stimulating personality much of the campaign's success must be accredited.

14 Judging the class for two couples of bitches at Peterborough.

15 The author (right) with Mr William W. Brainard Jr in the Old Dominion country, Virginia, USA. Mr Brainard has for many years been a familiar figure in Britain and Ireland, both in the hunting-field and at hound shows.

Despite heavier economic pressures than at any time since the Second World War, the 1970s showed more people than ever following hounds, with a higher proportion of hunting-field candidates from the Pony Club too, and ever-widening membership of that invaluable echelon, the hunt supporters' clubs. Doubtless this fresh swelling of hunting's ranks was given impetus by the participation of Their Royal Highnesses the Prince of Wales and Princess Anne, whose grandfather's and great-uncles' enthusiasm gave the sport such a fillip during the 1930s. Prince Charles, who has proved a most

ardent devotee, expressed his ambition to hunt with more packs than his great-great-grandfather, Edward VII, followed as Prince of Wales, and with (at the time of writing) 43 to his credit, he has already overtaken that score. Both he and Princess Anne presided at the Royal Foxhound Show at Peterborough during the 1970s, Prince Charles doing so for the show's centenary in 1978.

The 1970s saw a greatly increased interest in hound-breeding and hound shows, and the standards have been consistently high, with the Duke of Beaufort's and the Heythrop (under the guidance of their Master Capt. Wallace, who is also Chairman of the MFHA) predominating in the foxhound classes. But the pundits are looking for new blood; and finding it, too, as witness the wide use of Sir Newton Ryecroft's Anglo-Welsh broken-coated Medyg. In most countries now there is very little holding scent and it is astonishing how well the foxhound has adapted to modern conditions.

Also on the credit side has been the imaginative work, in 1972–3, of the fox/pheasant project under the auspices of the Game Conservancy and the BFSS, in which trials were carried out on two shooting estates, the Heythrop being the demonstration pack. Mr Terence Blank, of the Game Conservancy, commented that the coverts 'received as thorough a stirring-up as any pack of hounds is ever likely to hand out', and concluded that 'while hunting and shooting people may not agree on the optimum number of foxes present during the breeding season, in the shooting season, given full co-operation over dates, there should be little cause for friction'.

Another splendid feature of the period under review has been the Beagling Festival, staged annually in Northumberland and now attended by a great many of the foot packs.

Thus the scene keeps changing, and so the history of these sports – foxhunting, harehunting and staghunting – is being made continuously. We, the chroniclers, can look forward with optimism to the remainder of the 1980s.

A little before the 1979–80 season I sent copies of these articles to the Master of each hunt described, asking them to bring the history up to date. In the cases where no postscript is given I was advised that there had been no changes in those regimes.

The East Midlands

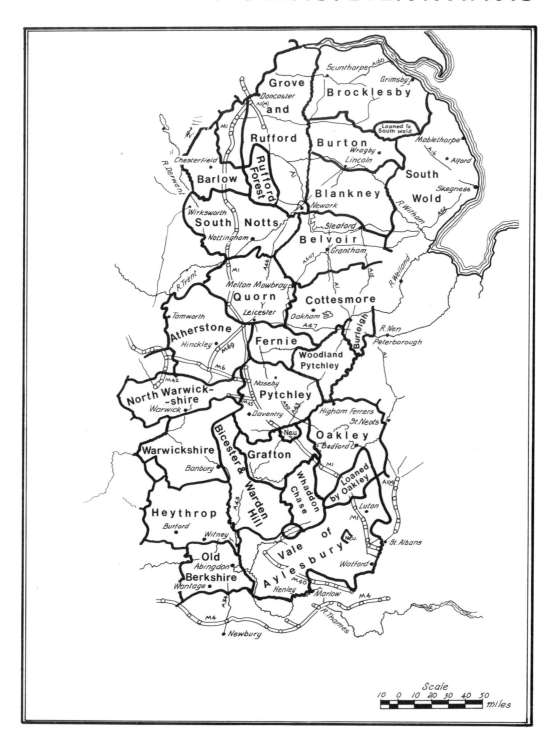

The Atherstone

SASSOON'S TIP-TOP COUNTRY

The fog was so intense when we steered north from the M1 to the A5, then crawled between Leicester and Coventry, into the Atherstone country on the evening of Friday, 14 November, that it seemed impossible to expect hounds to meet in the morning. But, emerging from a hunt supporters' fund-raising party, near Ashby de la Zouch, at midnight, we saw that it had almost cleared. When we got on our horses at the kennels at Witherley at 11.00 next morning, we were thankful to be in nothing more than a downpour of rain.

Hounds were under Tony Beeney, a very energetic and successful young huntsman, who whipped in to the Fitzwilliam for five seasons, and the Puckeridge and Thurlow for another five, before coming here as kennel-huntsman to Mr Kenneth Beeston in 1973. Mr Bill Winter (who was good enough to mount me), turned hounds for him, and the field, about 80 of us, were duly led away by Messrs Travers Lisney and Graham Arm (joint-Masters since 1972 and 1973, respectively). We were going to spend the day in the centre of the 24-by-18-mile country, some of the Atherstone's best, and it was good to get the feel of this part of the grassy, open Midlands: wide pastures of ridge and furrow, bordered by blackthorn hedges, with a ditch one side or both, and not much afflicted by wire; small, thick coverts; and a minor proportion of ploughland, which – to people coming from a clay country – seemed as light as the grazing.

They soon had a brace away from Mr Garland's Witherley Osiers, found the line of one of them – following an animated chorus of *holloas* from mounted followers, impatient for the first pipe-opener – and killed him 15 minutes later, at a pile of sticks on Mr Dawson's land, with those Atherstone sportsmen pointing their horses on a broad front at a succession of some 12 stout hedges before they galloped up to Beeney and his shrill *who-op!* No matter that hounds were no longer running, they did not go for the gates, but jumped the thorn fences several abreast, while the huntsman trotted westward to draw the good fox-holding drain and the roadside rough at Trivett's. Mr Trivett is one of at least 100 farmers up there who find little use for wire; and still riding in the first flight, at 68, he can look back to nearly 60 years of Atherstone hunting – **almost** to the days of Mrs Inge, widow of an Edwardian master, who followed Norman Loder (Sassoon's Denis Milden who was killed in action). Assisted by her daughter and Sam Morgan and the great Jack Molyneux (then a mercurial whipper-in) and 'a first-class stud of hunters' – as Molyneux said in his *Memoirs* – throughout the First World War Mrs Inge kept this large country open, whose cavalcade of great names stretches over two centuries.

Let us turn back the clock and bring the Atherstone Masters on stage. First to appear before the footlights are two noblemen in frock coats, thigh boots and tricorne hats, the Marquess of Donegal and, a little behind him, Lord Talbot, of Ingestre Hall; then another, wearing one of the first stove-pipes and flanked by hunt servants in a famous orange livery, Lord Vernon of Sudbury; and three more, Sir Richard Puleston, of Shropshire, the Rev. the Hon. G. Talbot (a 'once-a-week parson') and Major Cook, holding up a copy of his well-reviewed *Observations on Foxhunting*. At this point the curtain drops for a moment, then rises before an empty stage, on to which trots a tough, stocky figure, who looks as though he would ride into hell if the stakes were worth it. He is the founder of the Atherstone Hunt Club, of the kennels at Witherley, and virtually of the hunt we know today. His name is Squire Osbaldeston. But he is a fleeting figure, for he had only two seasons here (1815–17) and with the wave of a fox's brush about his head and a scream of *tally ho!* he careers away eastwards towards the Quorn, with his long-suffering whippers-in, Tom Sebright and Dick Burton, in his wake.

The Squire's place in the footlights is filled by another five-day-a-week man, Sir Bellingham Graham, a tall and elegant figure in scarlet swallow-tails, and long-winged collar, with, half a horse's length behind him, brave Kit Anderson, the thong of whose whip dangles towards a beautifully matched pack of hounds. Bellingham Graham begins to relate some of his two-hour runs, but finds there is not time, so claps on his spurs, following Osbaldeston to the Quorn. Then comes Lord Anson, afterwards Earl of Lichfield, who now, for ten seasons (1820–30), deserts his Shugborough Hall, near Stafford, each winter to hunt from Witherley. Sir John Gerard, who was also 'his own huntsman' steps in behind, then Messrs Applethwaite and Colvile.

16 and 17 Atherstone Masters: William E. Oakley (1871–91) in bronze, and Mrs Inge (1914–20).

After these comes a lofty figure, who rides and speaks like an officer of heavy cavalry; we shall see him twice more, for he had three Masterships here in between seasons at the helm of his native Fife: Col. Anstruther Thomson. And here, briefly, comes Mr Selby-Lowndes – slim and wiry, with black mutton-chops – before turning south towards fame with the Whaddon, and giving way to Viscount Curzon; then Anstruther Thomson again, with Mr Oakley. Anstruther Thomson leaves the stage, this time for the Pytchley; but Oakley, who was Master of the Atherstone for 20 years (1871–91) remains under the floodlight for a few minutes with his hunt servants, Stephen Dickins and George Castleman, to show off three couple of his Welsh cross-breds (he was ahead of his time on that score). Now comes Mr W.F. Inge and Mr Gerard Hardy, with his brilliant huntsman, George Whitmore, whose arms, covered in rosettes, are loaded with Peterborough cups.

Hardy steps off stage for the Meynell, while Whitmore stays there with Mr Munro, who has carried the horn for ten years in Sussex, and the Midlands too. At this juncture the figures 1908 appear above the stage, and on to it strides a new Master, the Earl of Huntingdon. He is succeeded by Tommy Bouch, who goes on to make a name for himself with the Belvoir. Then comes Norman Loder from the Southdown, accompanied by his Sussex

18 Tony Beeney with his hounds out cubhunting.

friend, who, with a poetic lilt, recites from a book he has written called *Memoirs of a Foxhunting Man*: 'The Packlestone (Atherstone) . . . appeared to be a paradise of jumpable fences, and compared with the well-wooded Ringwell (Southdown) region, it was a tip-top country. For the first time in my life I was able to sit down and jump a dozen clear fences without pulling up. . . .' Sassoon and Loder are in khaki and the curtain goes down for the Great War. . . .

So we return to the vivid personality of Mrs Inge, resplendent in sidesaddle habit and silk hat. In 1920, when she spoke of retirement, 1000 farmers, so wrote the hunt historian of the 1930s, requested her

to carry on in their interest. But, because of ill-health, she resigned, and Major Hawkins came forward to succeed her. In 1922, Major W.E. Lyon (who was well known until quite recently as an author of books on equitation) took the Master's cap, and he was joined in the following season by Mr B. Hardy. This Mastership lasted until the 1924–5 season, when Capt. Edward Ramsden took office.

The hunt was divided in 1930 into North and South, because, as a contemporary wrote, 'it was found that the old area was too big in these costly, overtaxed days to hunt with one establishment as heretofore.' But 20 years later, when Mrs J.S. Atkins was Master of the southern area and Miss Inge of the northern, there was a reunification under Capt. Brian Parry. And with that dedicated houndsman,

19 Followers at a hedge near Atterton, Leicestershire, during the author's day with them.

Col. Eric Morrison, at the helm, between 1953 and 1967, the working qualities of the hounds at Witherley were supreme. And the lines that Morrison guarded (to Brocklesby Ranter 1842, Lord Vernon's Rhapsody 1804 and Lord Abingdon's Virgin 1753) are guarded still.

Leaving the farm of Mr Trivett, who remembers the Great War, but still goes so well, we pointed down Green Lane towards Atterton, found a brace and a half in Mr Hidderley's kale, marked one to ground by the A444, changed to second horses by the roadside at 1.45 p.m., and pressed on towards Upton Park, the home of Mr Graham Arm. Here hounds surprised an outlier, pushed him through a wood called Eleven-acre, and – with 50 followers still helping themselves to those black hedges – on to Shenton where he shook them off in the village. Beeney cheered them into the canal covert next (a leash of seven were once found there), but hearing a *holloa* behind, he quickly lifted them to Greenhill. For the first time in the day scent was really strong, and with a terrific cry, they packed up tight on the line, only to be cheated of their prize by a big, new earth half a mile south. The rain was coming down hard now, it was 3.50 p.m. and getting dark. So Tony Beeney blew 'home', and we hacked to Shenton Hall, where Mr Peter Hall, the hunt chairman, provided cover for the horses, while the boxes were summoned from Witherley; and we went in to Mrs Hall's tea with the same impression of 'Packlestone' acres as Sassoon had 62 years ago: tiptop.

There are sinister plans for it: a new motorway, due to be completed in 1978, to link the M1 and M6, and further north, on about the same parallel, a dual carriageway to bypass Tamworth and Ashby de la Zouch. But, whatever happens, one cannot see those hard-riding Atherstone foxhunters allowing anything to reduce their ration of sport by very much.

(14 November 1975)

In 1977 a new Mastership, composed of the Hon. Mrs J. Russell and Mr N.G. Maddock, was appointed, and they were joined, in 1979, by Mr R.J. Lampard.

P. Barry succeeded A. Beeney in 1979, and Mr W.T. Winter then came in as amateur whipper-in.

The Bicester and Warden Hill

FOXHOUNDS OF FOUR COUNTIES

Within a minute or two of the Bicester hounds moving off from Mr Hugh-Smith's meet at Grendon Underwood, Buckinghamshire, on Wednesday, 3 February, there was a *holloa!* from Dr Preston, who had spotted a roaming brace of foxes on a stream bank to the west of the village. Unhesitatingly, Mr Anthony Younghusband, the Master and huntsman, jumped his horse out of the road and over the hedge, cheering his hounds to the yell, with the field of 70 following suit, galloping full tilt and flying the dark thorn fences of the Bicester south country, with all the panache for which this hunt has been so consistently famous for the past 200 years.

For the dashing reputation that Mr Younghusband and his followers bring up to date so convincingly began in the mid-eighteenth century with hard-riding Lord Foley, who kennelled a pack of foxhounds at Oxford and hunted all of what are now the areas of the Heythrop and Bicester South. But it was that most able of Masters, John Warde – widely known as 'The Father of Foxhunting', described by Surtees as the most perfect example of an old English gentleman and, according to a later historian, one who 'left his mark upon the history of the chase as few save Meynell and Osbaldeston have done' – who put the Bicester on the map. Giving up his hounds in Normandy, in 1778, establishing kennels at Bainton, near Bicester, and hunting six

20 Mr Tony Younghusband (joint) Master and huntsman (1967–72) and Mr John Sumner, a former joint-Master and chairman of the hunt committee.

days out of seven in Buckinghamshire, Oxfordshire, Northamptonshire and Warwickshire, Warde founded this long (35 miles north to south, 20 miles wide) stretch of the south Midlands that came to be known in 1800 – when Sir Thomas Mostyn took over – as the Bicester and Warden Hill.

Sir Thomas was a character who provoked a mixture of opinions. One recorder tells us that 'he was a good old sort but had no ear for hound music and, in fact, bred his hounds to run mute'. His contemporary, Nimrod, insisted 'there are few better qualified to be at the head of a pack of foxhounds than Sir Thomas; his attention to his kennels is great, and in the field he is a pattern for all Masters', while Goodall, his second huntsman, complained that 'he was a good, but most provoking man, for you could never judge from his face whether he was pleased or angry with the day's sport'. At any rate all agreed with Nimrod that 'Sir Thomas's hounds have had the advantage of three celebrated huntsmen – 'Gentleman' (complete with private income and retinue) Shaw, Stephen Goodall and Tom Wingfield. . . . Goodall (5 feet 5 inches and 18 stone), in my opinion had the speediest pack in England; he had such a name as a hound breeder and breaker that he could get 15 guineas a couple for his drafted hounds. As for Tom Wingfield, any true lover of sport would ride 50 miles to see him hunt these hounds. . . .'

Eulogising on the Bicester, 'The Druid' rightly pointed out that they were blessed with only three Masters in 72 years (1779–1851): Warde, Mostyn and Thomas Tyrwhitt-Drake, a universally respected Master from 1829–51, and again from 1857–62, who was followed by his son. During the interregnum (1851–7), however, Col. Anstruther Thomson took command, and '. . . found all not happy at the kennels. Cross, the huntsman, suffered from a softening of the brain, Mrs Cross became a heavy gin-addict, and the kennelman absconded, so that the colonel was obliged to act as kennel-huntsman beside hunting the hounds for a season. . . .' But the Bicester affairs were soon on an even keel again. Drake was succeeded by 'that greatest of men to hounds', Lord North (1866–70), and there followed – as one historian described it – 'a brilliant succession of Masters': Sir Henry Peyton (1870–72), Viscount Valentia (1872–5), the 3rd Lord Chesham (1885–93) who was afterwards killed hunting with the Pytchley, Mr Colville-Smith (1893–5), the Earl of Cottenham (1895–9), Major J.P. Heywood-Lonsdale (1899–1922), the 4th Lord Chesham (1922–5), Mr H.M. Budgett (1925–31), Col.

Heywood-Lonsdale and his son (1931–3), and Major R.E. Field-Marsham (since of Eridge fame), Brig-Gen. A. Courage and Col. R.V. Buxton (1936–42).

For the first few years after the last war the country was hunted in two parts, the Bicester South and Warden Hill, coming together again in 1948 under Mrs Lloyd-Mostyn and Mr M.V. Courage. Mr R.A. Budgett, son of the 1920s' Budgett, joined Capt. Miles Gosling from 1954–60. Mr and Mrs John Sumner (he is now chairman) held office from 1963–4, and Mr R.P. Cooper from 1964–7, while Mr R.C. Smith-Bingham, who had been hunt secretary for 14 years (the post now filled by Mrs Peter Hodgson, Capt. Gosling's twin-sister) shared the Mastership with Mr Cooper and Mrs R.F. Haworth, and subsequently with Mr Younghusband, who now holds the command on behalf of the committee.

Considering the closeness to London and the very extensive area, the Bicester have, for the most part, been lucky enough to escape the growth of amenity. No dual carriageways or main line railways pass through the country, and the south – at any rate – enjoys wonderful stretches of pasture land with negotiable fences. Brian Pheasey hunts the bitches on Tuesdays and (in the northern Warden Hill sector) on Saturdays, while Mr Younghusband takes a mixed pack to the southern meets on Mondays and Thursdays. (The Grendon meet was arranged last Wednesday due to the hunt jumble sale being held on Thursday.)

It is a happy and effective arrangement. They kill an average of 75 brace of foxes a season, thus vigorously maintaining the Bicester tradition. Will Cox, who was huntsman for a quarter of a century (1895–1920), throughout Col. Heywood-Lonsdale's first tour, is said to have killed over 3000 foxes, an average of 65 brace a season. Clarence Johnson had a similar record: during his alliance with Major Field-Marsham, 100 brace a season were killed in each of the three seasons before the war, and his equally popular son Charlie (1947–64) comfortably fulfilled the same average. Much of this success is due to the long tradition of the Bicester's selective hound-breeding, which was begun by Sir Thomas Mostyn in 1800, the famous Lady '01, whose monument still stands close to the old Bainton kennels and whose line is still strong, being matron to his pack. A hundred years later Charles Cox bred the highly influential brood-bitch Fearful '06, which went back to Belvoir Weathergauge through Blankney Benedict. Now the prominent influences of Mr Younghusband's kennels at Stratton Audley have

21 Capt. Ian Farquhar, who has been acting joint-Master and huntsman since 1973. He is the son of Lt-Col. Sir Peter Farquhar, pioneer breeder of the modern foxhound.

come from the Heythrop, Beaufort and Whaddon.

Harking to Dr Preston's *holloa!* by Grendon Underwood on 3 February, and enjoying the wonderful scent for which this country is famous, the Bicester hounds soon showed their mettle, with Friar, a dog of Whaddon breeding, and Saracen, a Beaufort-Heythrop product, usually a fraction ahead of the others on the line. They came over the Gallows Bridge road on to Sharp's Hill where Mr Smith's tight fences gave us much fun. With their resounding chorus, they then raced on to Ham Wood, but returned on the heel line of Dr Preston's second fox, to the Closes. Taken back to Ham Wood, they started another over the Woodham Lane to Knapp's Hook, puzzling out their line over Mr Hall's wheat and up to Grendon Wood. And there, failing to shake off his trail among the numerous fresh foxes, after 100 minutes spent circuiting this massive forest, their fox was broken up in the density of the trees. We changed to second horses in the afternoon; three hunts finished with one fox to ground and two lost in buildings. Then a fourth run of 35 minutes on Mr Wood's farm at Twyford gave an exhilarating end to this magnificent day.

Almost impeccable grassland, combined with Mr Younghusband's rare huntsman's instinct and relentless drive and his very high-quality pack of hounds, have given Bicester Thursdays a sporting reputation that would be hard to beat anywhere.

(3 February 1971)

Mr Younghusband went to hunt the Mendip Farmers in 1972. Capt. Ian Farquhar (son of that very famous amateur huntsman and houndsman, Lt-Col. Sir Peter Farquhar) took the Mastership and the horn in 1973. His joint-Masters (since 1978) have been Mrs M.H.D. Barlow, Miss S.H. Budgett and Mr A.C.R. Preston. At the time of writing Brian Pheasey continues as kennel-huntsman and first whipper-in.

The Brocklesby

YARBOROUGH BLOOD, THEN AND NOW

The meet for 21 February was at one of the lodges of Brocklesby Park – Newsham, only ten minutes' ride away; so it was not until 10.30 that we set off from Lord Yarborough's great stables, which were built by Charles Pelham, the founder of the hunt, in 1720. By this time the fog had long vanished, to allow a clear, warm day, and as we left, the hounds came trotting by, 23 couple of them – under Cooper Atkinson, their huntsman – with the sun sparkling on their backs.

To see the Brocklesby hounds for the first time is an enviable experience: in the first place they sport the strong, old-fashioned tricolour, which makes your image of most modern packs seem wishy-washy; then there is that silky quality about them, coupled with their beautiful match; their conformation is all you have been told a foxhound's ought to be; your eye is at once caught by their perfect necks and shoulders, and by their gentle eyes, set in exquisite heads, much as Stubbs portrayed the Brocklesby Ringwood 1788. There, trotting the lane to Newsham Lodge, was the net result, you knew, of two-and-a-half centuries' experience of catching foxes with consistent style and success in North Lincolnshire.

About 120 mounted followers, led by Mr Lawrence Kirkby, Lord Yarborough's joint Master, stood below the Lodge walls to honour them. Being half-term there were some 40 children, and of the remainder, a large proportion were farmers and their wives, some of them tenants of Lord Yarborough, whose estate, if much reduced over the generations, still amounts to 30,000 acres.

The history of the hunt is in large degree a history of the Pelham family. The first family house at Brocklesby was established by Sir William Pelham, a distinguished military commander of Elizabeth I, who retired to his Lincolnshire manor when he fell into temporary disfavour, but returned to fill a high command under Essex for the Zutphen campaign, and died in action at Flushing. Doubtless the park and home farmland over which we rode on 21 February, rang to the cry of hounds throughout the sixteenth and seventeenth centuries, but the ancestors of the pack we know today came with Sir William's great-great-grandson, Charles Pelham, who succeeded to the family estates in 1691 and, soon afterwards, combined with his neighbours, Sir

John Tyrwhitt and Robert Vyner, to establish foxhounds at Brocklesby. That joint-Mastership was short-lived, Charles Pelham soon carrying on alone until he died in 1763. The hound-lists which he began in 1746 have been kept without a break by his descendants.

Having neither sons nor brothers, Charles Pelham's estates went to his sister, Mrs Francis Anderson, and it was her grandson, Charles Anderson-Pelham, who became 1st Lord Yarborough, Master of the Brocklesby in succession to his great-uncle and the breeder of some of the most famous foxhounds of all time: Neptune 1785 and Ringwood 1788, for example, and Ranter 1790. It was not long before such names appeared in pedigrees all over England. Lord Yarborough's Mastership endured for 53 seasons. His hounds had the reputation of drawing widely, with speed and fearless vigour. The hounds in the present Brocklesby kennels are the same. On my day they roused their first fox from the briars of Newsham Lodge within five minutes of moving off and, in a flash, formed their quick tricolour ribbon behind him, careering through the coverts of the Chase and Spur Plat, on south past the Home Farm and Blue Gate Wood and finally up to his earth – a brand-new one – close to the family mausoleum, a fine round Palladian edifice, standing high on the site of an ancient tumulus. That was about three miles as hounds ran.

Not once in that very active day did we leave the park. Cooper then drew north through Mausoleum Woods, until another fox was *holloaed* as he entered them from Pamela Paddocks, but in the catchy scent of that warm climate, they were too far behind to trace his line. A brace from Milner's Wood gave us a gallop with lots of good timber-jumping up to the same woods and back again via Bell Pits. The huntsman then drew blank through Rough Pastures, Carr Leys and Thomas and Major Woods, but hounds found in Newsham at 2.00 p.m., and killed in the water-meadow just below – with the whole field up to see it – making another 'nose' to help build up the famous Brocklesby collection.

Cooper Atkinson, who was huntsman to three other packs before he came to Brocklesby (and now believes it is a dreadful pity that Welsh blood ever infiltrated English kennels!), holds an office which

22 Ringwood, painted by Stubbs.

was filled by some of the great experts in the history of the sport. One begins with the Smith dynasty, with Tom Smith the elder, serving Charles Pelham, and after a term of 59 years handing over to his son, Tom, early in the reign of the 1st Lord Yarborough. Then his son, Will, who carried the horn to the first Earl (Master 1816–46), and under whose eye Rally-wood '42 was born and bred, the hound which is said to have 'made' the Belvoir and from which half the foxhounds in England are descended. After Will's life ended over a fence, hunting hounds in 1845 (with a shout of 'Look out for Ranter, don't lose

sight of Ranter!' on his lips), his son, another Will, went on as huntsman to the 2nd Earl ('Yarborough the Good', Master during 1846–62). Will's son, Tom Smith III, who saw out that Mastership, made way for his father's second spell for the 1863–4 season, early in the reign of the third Earl (1862–75).

After the Smiths' 150 years came the highly talented Nimrod Long (a son of Will Long, who had served at Badminton under no fewer than four Dukes of Beaufort). In his 1322 Brocklesby days, Long killed 1026 foxes, with 490 to ground. He carried on for two seasons under the acting Master-ship of the 3rd Earl's widow, Victoria, Countess of Yarborough (1875–80), and hunted the bitches,

23 Tom Smith the Elder and (*to the left*) his son, Tom, with the hound, Wonder, also by Stubbs.

while her second husband, John Maunsell Richardson (the rider of two National winners and reputed to be 'the finest horseman of his generation'), hunted the dog-pack. Long was succeeded, in 1877, by his first whipper-in, Alfred Thatcher (the member of another celebrated family of hunt servants) who held office just long enough to see the 4th Earl come of age and assume the Master's cap, which he was to wear for 56 seasons.

After three memorable years with George Ash, the 4th Earl appointed Will Dale who, with his immense gift for horsemanship and for breeding and hunting hounds, showed 12 seasons' sport such as even the Brocklesby had rarely seen. It was under him that the fine stallion, Belvoir Weathergauge, was used with such success. When Lord Yarborough was obliged to sell his dog-pack in 1896, Dale went on as huntsman to the Duke of Beaufort, handing over at Brocklesby to his first whipper-in, Jim Smith (no relation to the earlier Smiths). In 1921, Sir Charles Wiggin came in as joint-Master and amateur huntsman with the 4th Earl, until 1925, when Lord Conyers – the future 5th Earl, who inherited his first title from his mother, Marcia, Countess of Yar-

borough – joined his father, and the horn was carried for the first time by the great Alf Peaker (brother of Fernie Bert Peaker and Worcestershire and Cheshire Tom).

In 1928, Capt. A.H. Jaffray arrived as joint-Master – and to hunt the bitch pack – until 1932, when hunting days were reduced to two a week, Peaker then carrying the horn, with his great verve, on both days, till 1951. And so the tradition continued – and continues – into the reigns of the 5th Earl (1936–48), the 6th Earl (1948–66) – partly with Lady Yarborough and Messrs Mark Patrick and Lawrence Kirkby – and the present Earl, who took over when he succeeded in 1967. There is no hunt committee. Lord Yarborough owns the hounds and – with the help of Mr Kirkby in the field and in the background, and his agent's wife, Mrs Michael Glover, as senior joint-secretary, and others – governs the hunt and takes full responsibility for the hound breeding just as his ancestors had always done.

Special mention must be made of Ronald Harvey, who was huntsman from 1951–71. Starting as a kennel-boy Harvey was riding second horseman to the Brocklesby in 1932, being appointed second whipper-in in 1936 and first whipper-in (to Alf Peaker) in 1937. On the outbreak of war he joined

24 Victoria, Countess of Yarborough. She acted as Master during the minority (1875–80) of the 4th Earl.

the Sherwood Rangers as orderly to the 5th Earl and was captured by the Germans in Crete. He returned to Brocklesby when the 6th Earl inherited in 1948, relieving Peaker as huntsman in 1951. There were many who believed this very popular servant to be every bit as good as Peaker and he was widely mourned when he died of cancer in 1971.

There are 58 couple in kennels now, and this year's beautiful young entry comprises 20 couple. The problem is to find good fresh outcrosses. From the beginning their blood has been shared mostly with the Belvoir, with whom they have always nicked best, and who, indeed, are still using their blood. But there are very few lines left, the Hurworth, the Muskerry, and the Puckeridge and Thurlow, being now the only other kennels to supply them. The Brocklesby are by no means exclusive: Lord Yarborough pointed out to me, among others, his best stallion hound, Schemer '71, which has recently been used by the Old Surrey and Burstow, the Puckeridge and the North Staffs.

There is no lack of foxes, for another excellent tradition there is that hunting and shooting must live in harmony. On his highly successful shoot, Lord Yarborough forbids the destruction of foxes. And – encouraging sight – among the mounted field on 21 February was Jim Clark, his head keeper. After that kill at Newsham at 2.00 p.m., we were given a fast, twisty run from Roxton to Iron Gate, with the 80 remaining followers looking very contented with their sport. The Brocklesby Hunt is surely one of the best examples in the world of an ancient and a thriving tradition, built up and maintained with such care and devotion that it is far too precious for its guardians ever to allow it to be tarnished or diminished.

(21 February 1976)

Mr C.D. Dawson, of Grainthorpe, joined the Mastership in 1978, and Mr Kirkby resigned in 1979.

The Fernie

EXCLUSIVELY LEICESTERSHIRE

Knowing the very superior and independent character of the Fernie today, it is astonishing to remember that the Quorn gave birth to this hunt – and with labour pangs that lasted half a century.

It all began with Sir Richard Sutton. 'I have only one hobby' (he declared in 1852, dismissing some objection when hunting six days a week as Master of the Quorn): 'it costs me £10,000 a year, and *I go where I like*'. But by then he had hunted the Burton country for 18 years, the Cottesmore for five and the Quorn for another five; he was in his fifties, and the southern – Billesdon – portion of his country was a long hack from Quorn Hall. His territorial fancies had shrunk; he was looking for an excuse to abandon that sector. 'Here, I'm sick of having my hounds over-ridden by you,' he is said to have told his son Dick the following year, 'you'd better clear off with 20 couples and break your neck over those Skeffington ox-fences'. And, from that moment, the fate of what would become Mr Fernie's country hung delicately in the balance.

Young Dick neglected the Billesdon sector, while the Earl of Stamford, who had taken over the Quorn at 28, drew its coverts only very occasionally, so that hunting men of Billesdon, Harborough and Skeffington were soon complaining: 'If our country is left long without a Master, the coverts will be ploughed, foxes destroyed and large sums of money diverted from the neighbourhood'. It was then, in 1856, that William Ward Tailby – 'probably the most highly respected figure in Leicestershire at that period' – came forward, secured approval to hunt the areas of both the south Quorn and the Cottesmore woodlands, signed on Tom Day, of Quorn fame (by then aged 60), acquired '20 couples of Mr Colyer's, a very blood-like lot' and, at Billesdon, built himself 'one of the most lavish kennels in England'. During Tailby's 22 years of Mastership, Stephen Goodall, followed by Dick Christian, then Richard Summers, were Tom Day's successors. With such a command in such a country, Tailby could scarcely fail.

Such was the Billesdon's reputation that 1000 horsemen were frequently seen out on the famous Tailby Thursdays, and as that keen observer of the Melton scene, Capt. Pennell-Elmhirst put it: 'surely if ever Fortune lavished her favours on a Master of

25 Mr C.W.B. Fernie, who gave his name to the hunt. He was Master from 1888 to 1919.

hounds she has done so with Mr Tailby; there is no time to be dallying or coffee-housing when his brilliant lady-pack are at work; nor are the Tailbyites content with waiting'. Among the Quornites, however, jealousy and suspicion prevailed: 'Mr Tailby holds those regions of the Quorn and Cottesmore on sufferance', wrote a cynic in 1866, 'and for that reason, I suppose, his men flaunt the Quorn button'. It was said, with good evidence, that 'the goings-on of the Quorn were, in hunting circles, comparable to the fate of the Government in general public'. So, in 1878, when Col. Lowther of the Cottesmore and Mr Coupland, the Quorn's new Master, demanded the return of their respective sectors, passions ran high. The matter was referred to the Foxhounds' Committee (precursors of the MFHA), who sat at Boodle's Club. Tailby – who by this time 'had ruled in High Leicestershire for 21 seasons, and ruled superlatively well' – first shrugged and took no notice ('I simply found a derelict country and picked it up'); then he became very irascible, refusing to conciliate.

Tailby resigned and in 1879, amid an overcurrent of disharmony, it was agreed that Sir Bache Cunard should hunt the country. 'For two years,' said the Quornites. 'Till he wished to resign', said the Billesdonites. While the pundits of Boodle's continued to pontificate. 'Who are they to decide our fate?' asked a yeoman; 'Can Boodle's stop an action for trespass or cause wire to be removed?' demanded a second; 'Who *is* this Boodle anyway?' the farmers wanted to know.

But Sir Bache Cunard, who had built new kennels at Melbourne, outlasted Mr Coupland, and when he handed over to Charles Fernie, of Keythorpe Hall, in 1888, the Quorn, weary of the 40 years' battle, virtually surrendered their Billesdon sector. That year the hunt secretary was pleased to record in his minutes, 'there was little argument about the name, South Quorn was approved; Mr C.W.B. Fernie proposed South Leicestershire, finally it was agreed Mr Fernie should hunt in his own name'. Charles Fernie arrived at Keythorpe with his doctor's assurance that he had only a few years to live. He defied his doctor – he was Master for 31 seasons. So successful was he, that in 1909, a permanent settlement was negotiated for the hunt and, when he died 10 years later, he left his hounds to the country on condition that the Quorn relinquished any claim to it. 'Mr Fernie's Hounds' became 'the Fernie Hunt'.

Steered into the twentieth century under the aegis of such great sportsmen as Tailby, Cunard and Fernie, this now firmly established hunt – and the only one to operate solely in Leicestershire – was unlikely to be short of a succession of influential and dedicated men and women willing to take the Mastership. Having held this alone during the 1919–20 season, Mrs Charles Fernie was joined by Mrs Faber – with the clever Arthur Thatcher as huntsman – till 1923, when they handed over (new kennels having been built at Great Bowden) to Lord Stalbridge, who had been hunting the South and West Wilts. Still acting as huntsman, Stalbridge was joined by Capt. (later Major-Gen. Sir Harold) Wernher as Master until 1928, when the colourful Mr Charlie Edmonstone replaced him; and that very fine natural huntsman, Bert Peaker, received the horn, retaining it until 1948, having also served Commander F.J. Alexander, Lady Zia, wife of Capt. Wernher, Capt. (afterwards Lt-Col.) J.D. Hignett, now chairman of the committee, and Col. P.H. Lloyd.

Taking over from Peaker, Walter Gupwell, a similarly gifted huntsman, carried the horn for the Masterships of Col. Lloyd, Major Currie and Capt. Gillinan, and for the first season of Lt-Col. G.A. Murray-Smith, who came in 1960 and was himself the Fernie's amateur huntsman until 1966, when Bruce Durno, formerly kennel huntsman, took over. Now Col. Murray-Smith shares the Mastership with Mr Archibald Clowes, who is to be relieved next season by Capt. B.R.W. Bell, who comes from the Cotswold to be joint-Master and huntsman, Bruce Durno reverting to kennel-huntsman.

Ever since the era of Tailby's 'very blood-like 20 couples', the consistent quality of the Fernie hounds has been widely acknowledged. Certainly in Fernie's time the pack contained some of the best blood in the country, while Maxim, the famous stallion which Lord Stalbridge brought with him from the South and West Wilts, has been a spectacular influence right up to the present. Col. Murray-Smith, who is surely one of the most experienced and able masters in the shires – he was Master of the Quorn for six seasons before coming to hunt the Fernie – goes mainly to the Heythrop, and has bred a swift and staying hound which has little difficulty in negotiating the tight Harborough fences. He sets great store by music and, to build up the melody of his pack, he has also bred from a Maryland bitch, Green Spring Valley '59, producing a beautiful tenor note in the chorus.

If any day was set for a hound exam it was Ash Wednesday, 24 February, when the meet was at Gumley in the best of the Fernie's grass country with strong sunshine and a breeze on the ground,

26 Lt-Col. G.A. Murray-Smith. A former Master of the Quorn, Col. Murray-Smith has been Master of Fernie's since 1960. He carried the horn during 1962–5.

dubious weather for hunting, though a lovely day for a ride. But the Fernie cry, if intermittent, was no less melodious for the poor scenting conditions. In Gumley covert their song came like the choir's burst in a cathedral; then running close and fast over Col. Murray-Smith's pasture, with Holloway on their right, the song faltered as they wheeled left-handed under Barford House, over the Laughton Hills and back to Gumley, where they ran their first fox to ground after a 45-minute spectacular race on this faint line.

Bruce Durno, the huntsman – with his father Percy, the celebrated ex-Heythrop huntsman, acting as whipper-in – then rode west again to draw John Ball, one of the Fernie's time-honoured fox-holding coverts. Sure enough, one led us immediately over Major Cowan's good fences to Shaddington Lodge, and north again to Fleckney, where he shook them off, having passed through a flock of ewes with lambs, after 30 minutes. Back east now – after changing to second horses at Mowsley – for Gumley Wood, and another fox away by Gartree Prison – and a happy audience of warders – to the myriad of ruins on the disused airfield beyond; and there he had to be given best. But all day the bad weather conditions served to accentuate the tenacity of this

27 Bruce Durno (*right*) with hounds. He has been kennel-huntsman or huntsman since 1962.

handsome pack: wherever the scent revived, the sudden music and purpose returned like an electric current. This hound sureness, joined with the elegance of the followers and the general quality of their horses, gives the Fernie that stamp which is only to be expected of a hunt whose domain is exclusively Leicestershire.

(24 February 1971)

Capt. Bell duly joined Col. Murray-Smith in 1971, but, after one season, he went on to the Warwickshire; and in 1972 Mr J. Cowen joined the Mastership. At the time of writing, Bruce Durno continues as huntsman.

The Grafton

PERFECTIONISTS OF THE SHIRES' SOUTHERN FRINGE

Hunting with the Grafton from Brackley Grange last Saturday reminded me that the world of foxhunting loses one of its most respected professional figures at the end of this season: Joe Miller, who joined the hunt as a whipper-in from the Craven in 1937, was promoted huntsman in 1953, and who is soon to retire. And, since his success story is due in great measure to Col. N.P. Foster, Wheedon-trained Household Cavalryman, formerly commander of the Northamptonshire Yeomanry, senior joint-Master of the Grafton since 1950 and one of the outstanding men to hounds in Britain today, I remembered, too, that this hunt's long history is particularly rich in the names of prominent huntsmen owing their fame to the patronage of Masters who were really dedicated and talented houndsmen.

Happy indeed the hunt servant who made his mark with the Fitzroys, the Dukes of Grafton, 200 years and more ago, when those Dukes hunted from kennels at Croydon in Surrey, and Euston Hall, Norfolk, as well as Wakefield Lodge, Stony Stratford, at the centre of their Northamptonshire property. Blessed were the huntsmen, reviled those that were slow to co-operate. 'The old [2nd] Duke used to complain bitterly', we read in the *Sporting Magazine* of February 1793, 'of the interruption he met with in crossing the Thames at Westminster for the delay and inattention of the ferrymen, by which he lost several hours of a fine morning before he arrived at Croydon. To remove this inconvenience he projected a bridge at Westminster and brought a bill into Parliament for its erection which was completed in the year 1748. . . .'

Joe Smith, huntsman to the 2nd and 3rd Dukes, who rode to hounds till he was 89, and who watched the building of Westminster bridge for the benefit of foxhunting, was succeeded by the colourful Tom Rose, who was born two years after its completion and hunted the Grafton, for the 3rd and 4th Dukes, for 50 seasons. 'Who can ever forget old Tom Rose's rattling holloa when coming away from Whistley Wood?' asks Robert Vyner in his *Notitia Venatica* (1842). 'I fancy I still see his fine old white locks flying in the wind'. Nimrod, in his reminiscences goes further: 'I saw little alteration in that father of huntsmen, old Tom Rose. His white locks, to be sure, formed a striking contrast to his black velvet

cap, but they were still more at variance with anything like a white feather in his tail, for he rides to his hounds at 75 with all the courage and animation of youth'. Tom's motto, too, remained constant to the end: 'Every fox I hunt, I mean to kill'.

The 3rd Duke bred up his pack with the help of Lord Egremont's sires at Petworth and we know from such diary entries as the following, what an ardent hound-lover Smith and Rose served: 'Nov. 23, 1786: I did not see a single thing done wrong by any hound . . . young Juniper and Drummond appeared equal in power to any of the older ones. . . . Jan. 26, 1788: a bad-scenting, unsatisfactory day. I wished I had not taken them out at all, for no day could have been more uncomfortable to me than this one was. I every day feel the want of poor old Trouncer, who is dying. . . .' And visitors to Euston Hall can still read this gravestone inscription against a wall of the house: *1788 – TROUNCER – Foxes rejoice! – Here buried lies your foe.*

His son, the 4th Duke, was no less a trainer of huntsmen. 'The Duke of Grafton's system of hunting,' Robert Vyner records, 'is to have everything done as quietly as possible . . . when a hound from behind is running for the head, the Duke holds that this is not skirting, but what every good hound ought to do. When Tom Rose or the Duke are forward with the leading hounds, the whipper-in's great attention should be turned to get up the tailhounds. The Duke would have the huntsman alone, if he is up, speak to the hounds, while trying at fault. . . .'

The 4th Duke confined his hunting to his Wakefield estates, of which Whittlebury Forest was the greatest foxholding tract. 'Here', says *Fore's Guide to the Hounds of England* (1849), 'the celebrated Tom Rose, his son Ned, and afterwards George Carter . . . cheered the Grafton hounds to death and glory – immortal names in the records of Dian. In the latter years of Carter's reign, when Stevens and Dickens played second fiddle to him, the music in Whittlebury Forest was second to none. Forty minutes was the term vouchsafed to a fox, when he was handsomely found by these artists. . . . No pack in England stood in higher repute than the Grafton when hunted by the above trio. . . .'

When, in 1842, the 4th Duke handed over his country to Lord Southampton (head of another

28 A group commemorating Col. Foster's presentation on his retirement from the Mastership, after 27 seasons, in 1977. *Left to right*: Capt. Richard Hawkins, Mrs Hawkins, Col. Neil Foster, Mrs Ward, Mrs Foster, Mr Rodney Ward and Major Charlton.

branch of the Fitzroy family, and Master of the Quorn from 1827–31) and sold his hounds to Assheton Smith, who was about to establish his family pack at Tedworth, Hampshire, George Carter went with the hounds and 'remained with Mr Assheton Smith for many seasons' so we are told. Lord Southampton, another perfectionist, who bought Osbaldeston's pack for £2000, found six successive huntsmen below par before George Beers joined him from the Oakley, in 1848. Beers held office until 1862, when Lord Southampton sold the bulk of his pack to William Selby-Lowndes, whose Whaddon country had been part of the Grafton. The Mastership then reverted to the 6th Duke, but it was his brother-in-law, Col. Edward Douglas-Pennant, afterwards 1st Lord Penrhyn, who hunted the country, and who bought for this purpose the pack

belonging to Mr John Hill, of Pickering, a close friend of Osbaldeston. And since Hill had free access to Osbaldeston's kennels, Douglas-Pennant's purchase matched nicely with what were left of Lord Southampton's.

It was Frank, George Beer's son, whom Douglas-Pennant chose to hunt these highly valuable hounds, which were now presented to the 6th Duke. Of this classic huntsman, the Victorian sporting writer Brooksby (Capt. Pennell-Elmhirst) wrote: 'It may be said of him, as of Tom Firr, that in whatever sphere of life he had found himself, he would have surely made his mark. . . . To see him work out a run, and bring his fox to hand at the end was ever a delightful and instructive experience'. While the Rev. C.F. Sams urged:

Confess it, ye thrusters, squires, parsons or peers,
No huntsman e'er showed better sport than Frank Beers.

Frank Beers came into his zenith under the universally popular 2nd Lord Penrhyn who, in 1882, took on the Mastership from the 6th Duke. And, as one recorder states: 'The pack were now beautifully bred with the old Osbaldeston strains sedulously guarded and many successful outcrosses to Belvoir, Oakley and Lord Fitzwilliam's. The bitch pack, "the beautiful Grafton ladies", hunted with amazing dash and élan as only a bitch pack can. . . .' After Beers, Tom Smith filled in two seasons with the Grafton (1892–4), before the great Tom Bishopp came on the scene. A most successful hound-breeder, he was responsible, in particular, for the famous stallion Grafton Woodman '92, whose line is still strong in many kennels, notably the Puckeridge – Edmund Barclay's Wiseman, by Woodman, being his most influential sire.

In spite of more than two full centuries' worth of history, the Grafton's list of Masters and huntsmen is remarkably short. Mr Charles Fitzroy McNeill, a great-grandson of the 1st Lord Southampton, who had made a great name for himself with the North Cotswold, took over from his kinsman, the 4th Lord Southampton, in 1907. He hunted the Wednesday and Saturday country himself, with Bill Batchelor carrying the horn on the more fashionable Mondays and Fridays. Then, in 1913, came Major Henry Hawkins, father of the contemporary joint-Master, Capt. Richard Hawkins; to be followed in 1920 by Lord Hillingdon, who continued in office until the first season after the last war, his only breaks being when Major V.D.S. Williams, of British Horse Society fame, took over for three years at the end of the twenties, and when Lord Cadogan stood in for two seasons immediately before the war. During this period only William Freeman (brother of Frank) and Will Pope, whom Joe Miller understudied for 15 years, carried the horn.

Last Saturday, Joe, aged 58 and never one to be easily defeated, cleared the five-bar gate he had been rated for jumping as a young whipper-in in 1937. Not that he enjoyed an exciting day. As has been the case for much of this muggy winter, conditions were more or less scentless. But Col. Foster, always in search of the impeccable, and a great admirer of Capt. Wallace's work, is the very artist of a hound-breeder. This is one of the most elegant and stylish packs the author has seen for a long time, and there were a few fascinating, if snatchy, periods last Saturday when one could watch the pack pick out the faintest traces, notably after they had found in some rough grass by the disused railway line adjacent to Whistley Wood, where they later lost him among the whiff of five other foxes.

'Who can ever forget old Tom Rose's rattling halloa, when coming away from Whistley Wood?' remarked Vyner. And not many of the present generation will forget Joe Miller's.

(15 January 1972)

Mr Rodney Ward joined the Mastership in 1976. In 1978, Col. Foster, who had been in it since 1950, stood down. His place was filled by Mrs Richard Hawkins.

Capt. Hawkins, who first entered the Mastership for the single season with Col. Foster in 1953–4, returned to it in 1961 and is still serving.

The Grafton has also been fortunate in being served by three fine chairmen since the war: Col. Richard Agnew, Col. William Beddington and now Major John Charlton.

Tom Normington relieved Joe Miller as huntsman before the 1972–3 season, and Capt. Hawkins tells me that 'he is brilliant in kennels . . . the best hound man you could hope for.'

The High Peak Harriers

CRESTING THE HIGH TOPS OF DERBYSHIRE

If there is a Utopian hare country it is sheep pasture, sound and verdant, wrapped upon limestone and shale, with stretches of heather and longer grass, white and windswept, that often converges with the stooping cumulus, so that the hares are running, as it were, against the sky. Add to this, for the sake of the harrier-follower, plenty of drystone walls to jump, but include as little human habitation and as little wire as can be. Such an elysium lies between Bakewell and Buxton in Derbyshire, and is fittingly hunted by the most celebrated pack of harriers in central England: the High Peak.

Anyone who has hunted hare-hounds, and made a close study of the quarry, will sympathise with Mr Pole-Thornhill of Stanton for giving up, in 1848, no less a distinguished pack of foxhounds than the

Warwickshire, in order to hunt hares in the uplands of his native Derbyshire. For surely the hare was conceived, not to be trapped or poisoned or shot, but to be *hunted*. Apart from her being verminous, she invites it. Sometimes, as you approach, she waits till the last moment before springing from her form; sometimes she trots towards the huntsman's voice, literally enticing his hounds; then she soars across the downland as fleet and spry as Pegasus and plays such tricks – some apparently flirtatious, some that would put a Machiavelli to shame – with her pursuers, as only a creature born to be hunted would play. Pole-Thornhill was not a man to resist her challenge.

With 22 couples of 18-inch hounds bought from Lord Stafford, he hunted that lovely 30-mile stretch of high Derbyshire for 11 years, showing consistently fine sport before handing over to his great friend Robert Nesfield of Castle Hill, Bakewell, agent for the Duke of Rutland's 30,000-acre Derbyshire estates. Nesfield hunted these hounds for 32 seasons, changed the name from the Stanton to High Peak, killed 1000 hares in 1234 days and remains the greatest name in the hunt's history.

If the breeding of the High Peak lacks a constant thread, it certainly owns a powerful tradition of seeking hound perfection; first by Pole-Thornhill who bred the strain that gave birth to a most outstanding performer – Sampler, whose blood remains strong in many harrier kennels today; and, secondly, by Nesfield, who experimented with the Duke of Rutland's Belvoir blood, with the best of Sir Thomas Boughey's blue-mottled pack, with Col. Fane's attractive harriers, and with the Badsworth whose Master was Nesfield's son-in-law, that great Victorian hound expert, C.B.E. Wright. A few years after Nesfield's retirement, however, interest was lost and the High Peak hounds dispersed.

But, in 1901, a fine natural huntsman of fox and hare, Col. Robertson-Aikman, attracted to Derbyshire's grassy mountains from the hunting-fields of Lanarkshire – rather as Pole-Thornhill was drawn to them from the Warwickshire – revived the High Peak, with kennels at Shutts Bakewell, where they have since remained. He brought his own pack of stud-book harriers from Scotland, and set about breeding a different stamp, heavier and showing much foxhound blood. In 1910 there was an exchange of Masters and packs, Col. Robertson-Aikman going to the Dove Valley harriers and Mr Walter Tinsley bringing 14 couples of the Dove Valley to the High Peak. In 1920 Tinsley presented his pack to the committee and, thereafter, the High

Peak hounds were bred entirely from harrier strains.

Between the wars the name Baillie predominated. Lady Maud Baillie, a formidable judge of hound and horse, and a daughter of the 9th Duke of Devonshire, whose Chatsworth estates march with the Duke of Rutland's, was already steeped in the High Peak heritage when she took over the Mastership in 1922, with her husband, Capt. the Hon. Evan Baillie, as huntsman.

Lady Maud continued in office until 1947. Then, in 1948, the Misses Violet and May Wilson, twin-sisters of Major Wilson (who was Master of the Barlow for half a century) took over. In 1956, Ernest Wiltshire, whose previous career was spent with the Barlow and the Southwold, became kennel-huntsman and carried on in that post under Mr Henry Stephenson (since chairman of the Masters of Harriers Association), whose father, Col. Sir Henry Stephenson, had been joint-Master with Lady Maud Baillie.

Wiltshire has now completed 15 seasons, and in company with Mr Bernard Swain, the present Master and huntsman, who came from the Grove and Rufford, has exercised much influence in the breeding of this pack. They go mainly to the Cambridgeshire, the Windermere and the Rockwood. Though predominantly black-and-tan, the High Peak are classic-looking harriers, the dog-hounds standing 20–21 inches at the shoulder and the bitches 19–20 inches. It was their silky quality and the fine aspect of their heads which particularly struck me on seeing them for the first time when they met at the fifteenth-century Bull i' the Thorn inn, midway between Ashbourne and Buxton on the A515, at 11.30 last Saturday, 27 March, for their last meet of the season.

Looking all about from the inn last Saturday, I saw the Peak District at its loveliest, a magnificent harmony of green and grey beneath a hot spring sky: the green offered by miles of sheep-nibbled turf as sound and smooth as Newmarket; and the grey by clumps of naked ash and sycamore, and by the drystone walls which break it up like ashen check-lines on green tweed. After Mr Gilbert Hinckley, the secretary and treasurer, had collected £50 for the British Field Sports' Society, Mr Swain moved west with his 16½ couples. They cast over the disused mineral line on Sparklow Hill, where they pushed their first hare northwards towards Earl Sterndale, giving us a grandstand aspect as they raced across the hills in close column, with their quarry a length or two in front, so lightly skirting the sunlit grass that you saw her darting shadow larger than herself.

29 Mr John Hine over a post-and-rails. He has been a joint-Master since 1976 when he left the South Notts foxhounds.

Three hares were broken up and many more hunted as we struck east across the A515, over Flagg race-course and Chelmerton, to re-cross the road farther north by a limeworks. We never stopped till we loosened our girths at the Duke of York's at 2.30 p.m. Within ten minutes, we were casting and hunting again, over the race-course towards Monyash, circling back to the Bull i' the Thorn at 3.30.

Mr Swain gave ample evidence that day of the strong rapport that exists between himself and his obedient pack. With him hunting hounds you are always on the move, constantly jumping, presented with ever-changing views of those lovely undulations. It was said we travelled 25 miles and crested some 160 drystone walls before last Saturday's hunt (and the High Peak's 1970–71 season) came to a close. They knew it that evening in the Bull i' the Thorn!

(27 March 1971)

Mr Adlington took over the Mastership from Mr Swain in 1974 and stayed for two seasons. Messrs Hine and Sutherland were in command for the next two; then Mr Sutherland stood down and a new partnership was formed – of Mr John Hine and Mr M.E. Salmon. Mr Hine hunts hounds. R. Deakin took over from E. Wiltshire as kennel-huntsman in 1980.

The South Notts

ON THE SHIRES' NORTHERN FRINGE

When the South Notts met at the Lime Kiln, Cropwell Bishop, last Thursday, thoughts turned to a legendary Victorian run of 35 miles, and three and a half hours: for it was almost exactly a century ago (on 16 February 1872) that $17\frac{1}{2}$ couples belonging to John Chaworth Musters, the name most strongly connected with this tract on the shires' north fringes, met at Cropwell Grove and found in Harlequin Gorse to make their most celebrated find, and thus to be immortalized:

From the Harlequin Gorse he was hallooed away,
'Ere the dew left the grass on this thrice-famous day . . .

Their challenger led them south-west over the Nottingham-Grantham canal, over the Fosseway by Stanton and Widmerpool, and 17 miles on to Hoton before turning north-east almost to Kinoulton, where they pulled him down in the open. 'Mr Parr of Nottingham and I were reduced to walk', recalled Chaworth Musters in his book, *The Great Run*, 'and the third field from Row How my horse stood still' (he had ridden three and was astride his second again); 'and as I looked over the fence, the hounds brought their fox round a haystack towards me, and ran into him close to the buildings.'

. . . In sight of but five of the numerous field,
His breath and his brush he at length had to yield.

In the nineteenth century this was indeed a fine area to hunt, in spite of Osbaldeston's verdict. 'It is a very bad country', wrote the Squire, who came to hunt it from the Old Burton for two seasons around the time of Waterloo; 'and very inconvenient for hunting, as the Trent, which divides it, is so wide and deep that hounds and horses must be taken over in a boat to go to covert. . . . The hazel, ash and other trees form good holding for foxes, but these extend to so many miles and are so full of earths that the foxes only run a large ring, skirting the gorse and other coverts, before returning to the wood-clad banks of the river, where they endeavour to go to ground. . . .' But Osbaldeston was prejudiced. He took over from another John Chaworth Musters, grandfather of *The Great Run* Master, who, for good reasons, when he left to hunt the Badsworth, refused the Squire the use of his house and kennels, so that a hunting-box had to be rented and new kennels built for a mere two years.

'The handsomest man of his day, of great assurance and very imposing address, he was a great favourite with the ladies,' Osbaldeston derided Chaworth Musters; 'but as a sportsman and Master of hounds, he was less successful. . . . When he found the fox had beaten him, he used to cast in all directions in search of a rabbit-hole or drain, and having found it, would take his hounds near, get off his horse and look into the hole, when the hounds at once began to bay. He would then observe to the field that hounds could not carry the scent further than this rabbit-hole. . . .' Contrast this with the verdict of another contemporary, Robert Vyner: 'Mr Chaworth Musters is decidedly the most skilful amateur huntsman that has ever cheered a hound, and can draw forth the hidden powers and capabilities of the animal on a bad scenting day, to a greater degree than any man in England.' Another chronicler believed that 'the secret of his success was his amazing gift for gaining the confidence of his hounds; he appears, indeed, to have been one of those rare people to whom all animals show an instinctive affection.'

So the great Osbaldeston was jealous of the man who first achieved sporting fame in South Nottinghamshire with ten couples given him by Hugo Meynell, and who went on to become the record-holding vulpicide of Lincolnshire and to be one of the Pytchley's most successful Masters. Osbaldeston came into a country brightly lit by a family of whose prestige as a whole he was envious – the family that founded this hunt. It was this John Chaworth Musters' father who, in 1775, formed the first recorded pack of foxhounds in the county. And it was the founder's great-great-grandson, author of *The Great Run*, who, in 1862, established a new pack based on four Bicester couples of Tom Tyrwhitt-Drake's; and who, a South Notts observer tells us, 'had the same happy knack of gaining his hounds' confidence as his grandfather; he had but to speak and they flew to him, and he would place them where he liked.' He gave up the Mastership of the South Notts in 1876, having 're-established the hunt on a prosperous basis from which it never receded.'

It is a South Notts tradition to find men that combine very competently the offices of Master, huntsman and breeder of hounds; men like the 8th Earl of Harrington, who did so for 35 seasons, from

30 The late Major Robert Hoare, joint-Master and huntsman, lifting hounds to a *holloa* over heavy plough.

1882 till his death in 1917, with German Shepherd and, subsequently, Fred Earp, as kennel-huntsman; like his grandson, Lord Petersham, who kennelled at Elvaston Castle; Mr Filmer-Sankey (who also rode so successfully under rules between the wars); Mr W.E. Seely, who fulfilled these three roles from 1935 until the war, and his brother, Major James Seely from 1944 to 1954. Last season the South Notts could certainly have taken no better step to further this tradition than to secure Major Robert Hoare. He hunted the West Norfolk from 1937 to 1940 and, after returning from war service with the Leicester-shire Yeomanry, carried that hunt's horn again until 1958, when he went to the Cottesmore for a decade; so that he is now in his 30th season as a Master and huntsman. And he stands today as one of the principal figures of British foxhunting.

Major Hoare is happy enough with the quiet compact fields of the South Notts after the great congregations of the Cottesmore. Only 52 sup-porters, mostly farmers, followed him last Thursday when he led hounds beneath a thinly falling snow from the Lime Kiln to draw the banks of the Grantham canal. Afterwards he declared that, in half a century's hunting, it was the worst scenting day he had ever known. Notwithstanding the snow, it was apparently too warm; you could almost feel such scent as there was lifting head-high as soon as it was laid. Albeit there were three foxes in the Old Gorse, and although they hunted one south-east beyond Colston Bassett over the Belvoir boundary, it was impossible to get on terms.

Given the best conditions, could 'The Great Run' ever be repeated in the South Notts country? Since Chaworth Musters' and Osbaldeston's day, the Fosseway has become the lethal A46, while a close complex of other roads have sliced up the country. The area to the west of Nottingham, comprising Derbyshire's pleasant hills, with stone walls and springy turf, is largely unspoilt; but here, to the south-east side of the Trent, there is a good deal more arable and wire than they would wish for. Now, at 1.30 p.m., moving westward across what

Major Hoare calls 'good, honest plough country', they drew Blanche's and Winifred's blank. Then Langar Lane covert. Here they found again, and sticking close as could be on the fresh scent, they coursed along the stream back to Colston Bassett, only to lose him a little short of the Belvoir's Kaye Wood.

What a pity the climate prevented one seeing more of this swift and elegant two-day-a-week pack, that has just accounted for 12 brace of cubs in a singularly dry autumn. Major Hoare brought most of these hounds with him when he handed over the Cottesmore kennels to Capt. Clarke in 1969. Clearly they are a great improvement on their predecessors in the kennels at Epperstone. For then there was trouble with whelps, and the South Notts was simply a conglomeration of drafts from local packs. Now the carefully bred inmates of Epperstone are nursed with great devotion by Mick Carnell, formerly kennel-huntsman with the Galway Blazers, with Tom Potts, the second whipper-in, supporting him.

At 3.00 p.m., Mr John Hine, the new field Master, led us down to Owthorpe fish ponds, where a fox was surprised and chased past the point-to-point course and right-handed along the canal, eventually being lost on the great mounds of waste at the gypsum works. Half an hour later, with his characteristic thoroughness and buoyant style, Major Hoare drew the two bramble-thick coverts at Dobbin's Gorse. There was no joy to be had there. It had been a scentless day, it remained a scentless evening. But this did nothing to demoralise the South Notts followers. They are a true-hearted, unspoilt lot, of whom the good Jorrocks would have approved without reserve. You sense a particularly strong sense of brotherhood here and a ready instinct that this hunt belongs to them, much more than in name. And when they bade the Master 'Good-night', you knew from their exuberance that they were abundantly glad to be out with him, sport or no sport.

(18 November 1971)

The late Major Hoare retired from the joint-Mastership in 1973 and Mr Hine in 1974. Mr S.A. Blyth carried on alone in 1974–5 after a single season in dual command with Mr Hine. Then in 1975 Major Vallance was joined by Mr Strawson and Mr Arm. Capt. S.O.S. Wynn joined the Mastership in 1980.

David Anker was huntsman from 1976, showing excellent sport. Mick Carnell returned to relieve him in 1980.

The East

The Cambridgeshire Harriers

ILLUSTRIOUS REIGN OF A LADY MASTER

Cambridgeshire hunting folk in search of variety have a choice of four local packs: apart from Mrs Hugh Gingell's celebrated Cambridgeshire harriers, whose empire spreads into six counties – Essex, Suffolk, Cambridgeshire, Huntingdonshire, Bedfordshire and Hertfordshire – there is the University drag, the Trinity Foot beagles and the Cambridgeshire foxhounds. Last Saturday, considering the weather, there is no doubt that the harriers were the ones to be out with. Driven by a remorseless east wind, quite unchecked in this flat arable country by ridges, tree belts or hedges, slender knitting-needles of rains, interspersed with snow, spiked horizontally on your face and brought a total numbness to the fingers – discomfort that might well have preoccupied you if beagle-plodding through the plough, or waiting at covertside, or even galloping at the teeth of it behind a drag-line.

But, with the harriers ever casting forward and changing direction as they puzzled out a line, you were always on the move, yet always confronted with this distraction from the elements. It was rotten climate for scent – as we 60 followers discovered soon after leaving the lawn meet given by the Master's cousin, Mr John Marriage, QC, at South End House, Bassingbourn. For although Mrs Gingell's 20½ couples found their first hare within seconds of spreading themselves on the ploughs to the north of the Royston-Baldock road, the rain not allowing the scent to diffuse they could only hunt her in view.

Circling right-handed over Mr Hunter's land, under Ashwell village, north over Ashwell Street and on to the Old Aerodrome, it was absorbing to watch what New Zealand and American experts have described as 'Britain's premier harrier pack' cast itself in hard driving spurts across the tacky plough, undaunted by acres of powerful-smelling sprouts. And then, reflecting Cambridgeshire's ancient harehunting tradition, you realised what a contrast the sport must have been when half this country was wasteland; and eighteenth-century squires, although riding over comparatively good scent-holding ground, stood immobile and cold half the time while their old Southern-type harriers, slow and snuffling and deep-throated, worked out their ponderous line.

In 1745, it seems, one of those squires, no longer able to hunt, handed over his hounds to a clique of spirited hunting farmers. And it was these men who founded the Cambridgeshire harriers on a trencher-fed basis. They and their descendants remained at the helm until Mr (later Sir) William Austin, whose hare-hunting days began at Ampleforth College, went up to Trinity Hall, Cambridge, in 1891, and made the farmers an offer they could not resist: to take over and kennel the hounds with all expenses paid. Although Austin kept on excellent terms with the farmers across whose land he and his fellow-undergraduates careered for the next decade, the Cambridgeshire came to be regarded as a University pack. And a school for future Masters of foxhounds, too, when it produced such successful houndsmen as B. Hardy, who went on to be Master of the Atherstone and of the Meynell, and Hugh Gray-Cheape of Berwickshire fame.

The undergraduates' affection being transferred to the Trinity Foot beagles when they were re-established, after being many years in suspended animation, the local farmers took control again. So began what might be described as the 'Towler dynasty', for the brothers James and John Towler, landowning farmers, put in 20 seasons as Masters, covering six periods between 1902 and 1942. And it was John Towler who, to end this period in the austere summer of 1942, handed over the remaining four and a half couples kennelled at his home, Tunbridge Hall, Bottisham, to Mrs Hugh Gingell.

Betty Gingell is and always was a perfectionist. There was never any doubt about her ambition: she wanted to breed the best pack of harriers in the world. Regularly setting forth with her four and a half couples during the 1942–3 season, she studied the huntsman's art for all she was worth, and even accounted for a few hares. Daughter of a breeder of cattle – a pioneer with Friesians – and having an instinct for genetics, she spent her spare time in the summer of 1943 visiting every harrier pack in England. Eventually deciding to cross the Towler blood with some of the Lartington (a now long-redundant Durham hunt, then privately owned by Mrs Norman Field) and a Clifton Foot dog-hound, she built up a wonderful level quality pack of 35 couples of 21-inch hounds, with noses to match the sticky plough, stamina to traverse it non-stop four or five hours a day, and the sweetest of music.

31 Miss Betty Marriage (afterwards Mrs Hugh Gingell) on 'Poppy' at the Essex Show in 1923.

Breeding five or six litters and drafting four or five couples every year, she keeps a lofty standard, and, since the 1955 Peterborough, has shown 13 champion dog-hounds and nine champion bitches. She also exports to the USA and to New Zealand, where, between them, her Pointer and Conrad have won half a dozen barrier championships.

It proved a happy omen last Saturday when they chopped an inattentive hare just east of Steeple Morden, because just then the rain stopped, scent was strengthening and, despite far too many hares to make for consistent line-holding, they really showed us the stride and drive for which they are so well known. For, just by the chopped one, they roused a stout customer who gave them the run – and us the spectacle – of the day. I was well up (on Mr Frank Starling's champion Windsor and Royal heavyweight hunter, El Bruce) to see their hare dash for Abingdon Piggotts, bend left-handed for Steeple Morden and head straight down the lane west of the Old Aerodrome.

Taking the plough once more above Ashwell Street she changed course for Litlington, and then, as she swung towards the Brook, they bowled her over in the muddy ridge and furrow. 'On that note,' smiled Mrs Gingell, 'we'd as well call it a day.' She spoke too soon. A few yards away up sprang the next

32 Mrs Gingell leading off to the first draw when the author was out in January 1973.

one to give them another unfaltering 20 minutes' circling, before they lost her among a bevy of fresh hares close to Litlington. And there, at 3.00 p.m., Mrs Gingell blew 'home'.

That night Hugh Gingell, the field Master, and his wife, with the organising assistance of Mr Ernest Edwards (who has himself completed nearly 30 years as honorary secretary), gave a dinner for the hunt members to celebrate this her thirtieth season. For those who knew her well it was an occasion for memories: memories of Betty Gingell as a horse-woman of life-long dedication, who has produced many fine show hunters and who is in constant demand as a judge of horses and ponies as well as hounds; of one, indeed who has set an impeccable standard with her own hunt horses; and of a greatly admired woman with a unique message of sympathy and encouragement in particular for young people.

John Marriage, who spoke on behalf of the members, voiced the hunt's huge debt of gratitude over three decades. And that went, one felt, for the world of hounds and equitation at large.

(20 January 1973)

Mrs Gingell has since bred a further four dog-hounds and three bitches which have been champions at Peterborough.

The Essex

HERITAGE OF A PLOUGH COUNTRY

Tom Watchorn, whose hunting career began with the Belvoir in 1932 and has only been broken once – by war service (mostly in Burma with the Gunners) – went as huntsman to the Essex 25 years ago. Between 1935 and 1937 he was with the Berkeley, where his father-in-law, Jack Scarratt, had served under both Lords Fitzhardinge and Berkeley. Hanging in his house by the kennels, near Harlow, are two very nice original Lionel Edwards' prints of those yellow coats in action by the Severn, legacies of his wife's; and a bit of a mist comes into Tom's eyes when he talks about 'those oceans of Gloucestershire grass and the best scenting country in Britain'. Afterwards he knew such fine pastures as those of the Meynell, Blackmore Vale, Craven and North Cotswold, so the ploughs of Essex must have seemed particularly heavy and flat when he first rode across them in 1950.

But he soon found them such an irresistible challenge that he would not now exchange them for any paradise, however green. Nor can there have been many days in which he found conditions more challenging than 24 January, when – excellently mounted by one of the two joint-Masters, Mr William Bullman – I joined the Essex at Roxwell, in their Saturday country. The mugginess of mid-week had been blown away by a sharp north-east wind and replaced by 20 degrees of frost; but the drought was so longstanding that when our impressive column of ninety mounted followers – as well turned out a field as I have seen for some time – left Roxwell Green at 11.00 a.m. and struck out behind Tom on the ploughed fields' edges for Boyton Cross and Newland Brook, despite the frigid surface, they created as much dust as cavalry in August. Whereas what the Essex need for scent is rain, rain, and more rain.

So one was not surprised to see hounds draw Newlands Osiers blank, and the same, around midday, with Chalk End, Skreens Wood, Hardy's plantations and the nearby Beechwood. It was not until about 1.00 p.m., when we were standing along the lane leading south to Bushy Hayes, that a fox, lying snugly in a bone-dry drain near Torrell's, felt hounds too inquisitively close for his comfort, and bolted across the cold and dusty arable, setting his mask towards Rowes Wood, to give us the run of the day. And as those Essex foxhunters shortened their reins and glanced for likely routes round the

restricted farmland, one sensed the special animation which only comes, one finds, from a sporting fraternity which takes pride in ancient traditions, and whose own spirit is essentially right.

The Essex heritage goes back at least as far as any of those famous grassland hunts Tom Watchorn served in the 1930s and forties. For the county's forests, Epping, Hainault and Waltham, were early Royal hunting-grounds; the lore and love of hunting have been handed on in Essex families at least since the time of the Conqueror; and, when foxhunting caught on in the eighteenth century, this was the zone, west Essex, upon which the big East Anglian sportsmen centred. Men like Coke of Norfolk, the agriculturist and 1st Earl of Leicester, who, with kennels at Harlow Bush, hunted over Col. Montague Burgoyne's estates; Sir William Rowley, of Suffolk, John Archer, and the less sophisticated, if quite as colourful, Rounding brothers, who kept hounds at the Horse and Groom, in Woodford.

It was from Harding Newman's Essex Subscription Foxhounds, of the 1790s, that the hunt we know today emerged. These were bought, in 1805, by young Henry John Conyers, who in turn had sold his commission in the Coldstream Guards for a sum, as he put it, 'large enough to buy dog biscuit with'. When he was obliged to sell up, three seasons later, one of the very great exponents of the 'Noble Science', Major John Cook, having made a considerable name for himself with the Thurlow and the Hambledon, took over. Cook obviously loved the Essex country, and he made this interesting comment on the fox of its most celebrated tract, the Rodings: 'He is stub-bred and stouter than any I have met . . . if you do not get away close to him at the very best pace, he never will be caught. . . .'

As Tom Watchorn vouches, the Rodings, notwithstanding the good sport they offer, are too 'cut-and-dried', too 'civilised' to produce super-foxes today. But that drainpipe customer, near Torrell's, was a flier; and when Tom got them away, what a lovely lightning ribbon his Whaddon-bred hounds made, careering over the flat, via Windmill Farm and Bushy Hayes, with our horses obliged to spread themselves wide to span the gaping ditches which divide those ploughs.

The Essex ditches were just as characteristic in 1812, when Cook went off to the Atherstone and to make such a big name for himself with the Quorn) hunting hounds. In 1857, a 'squarson', the Rev. Joseph Arkwright (grandson of the inventor of the spinning frame) went to the helm, at the age of 70, and established the present kennels. His fourth son, Loftus, who succeeded him, fell foul of one of those yawning ditches in the 1867–8 season, his horse throwing him and planting its hoofs on his chest. Although he could never walk, let alone ride, again, he hunted on wheels for the next 11 seasons, a mail phaeton being fitted with an 'ingenious arrangement' to hold his invalid chair. One who often saw him thus was Anthony Trollope, middle-aged and very heavy, hunting regularly from Waltham Cross, and 'averaging 20 miles to meets without using a covert hack'.

When Arkwright gave up in 1879, and lent his hounds to the country, the popular politician, Sir Henry Selwin Ibbetson, afterwards Lord Rockwood, was persuaded to take the Mastership, and it was in his time (1882) that the present Essex Hunt Club was founded, whose members wear the striking white bird's-eye motif on a dark-blue field, the men on their waistcoats, the ladies on their collars. One who wore it then was that beautiful horsewoman, the Countess of Warwick, and one who stayed to hunt with her was her friend the Prince of Wales. James Bailey, who carried the horn for Selwin Ibbetson and at 29 was the youngest huntsman of his day, became known as 'the Tom Firr of the Ploughs'. He remained with the Essex for 41 years, serving Mr Charles Green (1884–93), Messrs Salvin Bowlby and Loftus Arkwright Jr (1893–9), a committee, with Charles Green as field Master (1900–6); then Mr John Swire (1906–10) and Col. S.F. Gosling, until 1920. Two years later the Essex secured the talent of Jack Boore, son of Lord Willoughby de Broke's huntsman.

Mr Swire joined Col. Gosling during the period 1922–6; Major E.C. Watson – whose daughter, Mrs Gold, is still senior joint-secretary – went in with him from 1926 to 1928, and they were succeeded by Mr Joe Pickersgill, who had been with the Limerick. Mr Dudley Ward, who came into a three-cornered Mastership in 1938, was Master or joint-Master (except during the war years, when Mr A. Douglas Pennant stood in) until 1966, when Mr Paul Carden took over. Mr Ward then joined Mrs Gold as joint-secretary. Four seasons ago Mr Richard Howard, a farmer with much influence on the Essex agricultural scene, and Mr William Bullman began their dual command.

Most of the headlands here have been ploughed

33 Stephen Dobson, huntsman to the Essex, 1867–79.

John Archer Houblon took the Essex, with Lord Maynard bringing in the impecunious Conyers as 'Master-in-the-field' or 'Manager'. On the death of his father in the year of Waterloo, Conyers inherited Copt Hall, near Epping, and was in the money again, so he took over the whole establishment, which he then commanded alone for 38 seasons. From the time he was advised by a sergeant-major, on first joining the Coldstream, to '. . . swear at your men, Mr Conyers, sir, or they will not think anything of you!' he never looked back, and his invective was so rich that he had some trouble in keeping hunt servants. But his 25-inch hounds – mostly of Lord Lonsdale's and Sir Tatton Sykes's brood – were famous all over England.

When Conyers died in 1853, Henley Greaves, a former Master of the Cottesmore and South Wold, took over the Essex, with John Treadwell (who was up now and, with 80 per cent more winter wheat, you have to pick your way gingerly, so Messrs Howard and Bullman took us on a tightly disciplined course when their drainpipe fox described a circle by Rowes Farm. As hounds checked on the plough, just south of it, a *view holloa* rang out from Mr James Radbourne, the hunt chairman, who spotted the fox leaving Rowes Wood. Hounds were soon gaining on him when we heard a number of *holloas* from the road, and saw car followers pointing excitedly towards Skreens. Piloting them round Skreens Park, he headed north by Tye Hall and found his favourite form of bolt-hole, a drain, at the back of the old Skreens drive, where he was given best. Despite Tom's further 40 minutes' drawing, they could not find another, and we hacked back to the boxes in a blinding snowstorm.

I have always thought that Dean Wostenholme conjured the essence and ambience of foxhunting as well as any artist with his splendid set of aquatints of the Essex Hunt, painted in Conyers' time. With these in my mind's eye on 24 January, I was left with the impression that the Essex have maintained their style in high degree and unbroken thread during their two centuries.

(24 January 1976)

Mr Howard since resigned; Mr J.P. Bullman joined Mr Bullman in the Mastership in 1980. D. Catfield succeeded B. Godfrey as whipper-in, in 1976. Tom Watchorn retired in 1980, being succeeded by G. Sutton.

34 Tom Watchhorn, Essex huntsman 1951–80.

The Fitzwilliam

ILLUSTRIOUS MILTON

The kennels at Milton, where Lord Fitzwilliam's hounds met when I joined them on 6 March, are said to be the oldest still in service in the world. In 1760 much of the building was destroyed by fire, and with it the hunt records, so little is known of the Fitzwilliam's early history, or when the building was first used as kennels. But Milton has been in the family without a break since 1499, and I suspect that there was always a pack of hounds with the property. Because the kennel walls carry sign-of-the-Cross *motifs* and Gothic arches, there has been speculation that it is of ecclesiastical origin; but, as Lord Fitzwilliam told me, it is more likely to have been a medieval fortified farmhouse. Anyhow, the fire damage was promptly repaired and the kennels greatly improved by the very sporting 4th Earl, and, except for the removal of some ivy, they look today as they did 200 years and more ago.

The family's foxhunting empire was once considerably larger, for the 3rd Earl married Lady Anne Wentworth, daughter of the Marquess of Rockingham, who died in 1782 without a male heir, so the Wentworth estates at Wentworth Woodhouse, in Yorkshire, devolved on the 4th Earl Fitzwilliam, who soon began to take a portion of his pack north each winter. He was certainly the first of his family to breed hounds scientifically. Having repaired the kennels in 1760, he bought the high-quality pack belonging jointly to Lord Foley and Mr Crewe, who had acquired them from Richard Child, the banker; and Milton's two earliest surviving kennel stud books, which I was privileged to see, are in the handwriting of Will Dean, who came to Milton in 1760 as huntsman with that pack. The Fitzwilliams have always been fortunate in their hunt staffs: Will Dean, a genius at breeding hounds, continued until 1821, having reached the record age for a hunt servant at the time, and for 36 years was brilliantly supported by John Clarke as a whipper-in. Tom Sebright followed Dean at Milton in 1822 from the Hambledon, whose Master was the great and forceful George Osbaldeston. Warmly recommending him to Lord Milton (afterwards the 5th Earl) in a letter that still lies among the wealth of Milton hunting records, 'The Squire' wrote: 'I trust you will excuse my observing that whoever the man may be that has a prior claim to Sebright, *I am certain* he will not answer your purpose as well. Butler, who hunts Sir J. Leeds' hounds, offered, I understood, but he is far inferior to my man. He is very conceited and not near so civil as Sebright, and has not *half* the *experience* . . . .' Coming from such a pen it was not an offer to be lightly declined.

Sebright (the son of the Tom Sebright, who was huntsman to Mr Corbet, the Shropshire Master) began his career at 15, as second whipper-in to Mr Jack Chaworth Musters, in Nottinghamshire, and then whipped-in with Sir Mark Sykes, at Sledmere, before joining Osbaldeston. He had carried the Fitzwilliam horn for 39 years by the time he received his testimonial of £800 and a silver cup in a Huntingdon town hall ceremony, in 1860; but he only survived one year to enjoy the benefit of it, suffering a fall from his grey mare the following season, from which he never recovered. 'He died one Sunday morning, just as the church bells ceased ringing, fancying he saw his hounds to the last', one hunt historian lamented. 'He was mourned by all who knew him, not only as a huntsman, but as a friend. . . . George Carter was promoted from first whip to fill the vacant post . . . an excellent huntsman, and no respecter of persons.' Carter stayed on up to 1888, so that, in 120 years, only three huntsmen ruled at the Milton kennels.

After the 5th Earl's death in 1857, the estates were divided, Wentworth going to the elder son – who established another hunt, the Fitzwilliam (Went-worth) in 1860 – and Milton to the second son, the Hon. George Fitzwilliam, who was, among other distinctions, Peterborough's MP, and a Master who carried the horn himself one day a week, and proved one of the finest amateurs of his age.

'During the Hon. George's Mastership,' wrote the hunt's Edwardian chronicler with a sidelight, 'our present gracious King, then Prince of Wales, paid some visits to the Fitzwilliam country. . . . Upon one occasion he participated in a fast thing from Titchmarsh Warren to Lilford, when the fox doubling back, came at a great pace by Thorpe towards Titchmarsh. HRH was galloping towards the railway crossing when the gate-keeper slammed the gate in front of him, replying to the Royal remonstrance in strong language, and stoutly asserting that he would allow no person to pass until the train had gone through. . . .'

George Fitzwilliam died in 1874, and, because Milton then passed to a boy of eight (who was also George, the present Earl's father), the hounds were taken in trust, first by his uncle Charles, then in 1877 by the Marquess of Huntly, another large landowner in the country, and in 1880 by a cousin, the Hon. Thomas Wentworth-Fitzwilliam.

George Fitzwilliam put in one season on coming of age (1887–8), but did not begin his popular 40-year Mastership until 1896 (after resigning from the Household Cavalry), his first deputy Master and huntsman being that outstanding hound expert, Mr C.B.E. Wright, the man who produced a most significant new influence in the kennels, the extensively used Potent '01 (by their Proctor out of Tynesdale Ardent). At various times during his reign, Mr Fitzwilliam was assisted by a number of other very helpful joint-Masters, Lord Essex and Lord Exeter being two of them, and also his cousin, the 7th Earl Fitzwilliam, one of foxhunting's most distinguished personalities who, not content simply with the Wentworth hounds, ran both the Coollatin and the Island in south-east Ireland, and later, on Lord Galway's resignation, the Grove. The huntsman between 1923–5 was that great fox catcher, Frank Freeman's former whipper-in, Tom Agutter, well known to smart Cambridge undergraduates, who, near the end of the day, when the older generation had hacked home, used to be addressed with, 'now I suppose I'll have to show you *College* boys some *sport!*'

Lord Fitzwilliam, one of the towering figures of the contemporary sporting scene, who originally took on the Mastership as Mr T.W. Fitzwilliam in 1935, and succeeded from his cousin, the 9th Earl, in

35 and **36** Mr George Fitzwilliam (by 'Spy'), Master 1887–8 and 1896–1935. His son, the late Earl Fitzwilliam, succeeded to the Mastership in 1935.

1952, has been well supported at the helm, too; he was joined by the 7th Earl (1935–43); the 8th Earl (1943–6); Lord de Ramsey (1946–57); the former *Times* hunting correspondent, Mr Michael Berry (1950–5); Mr Marcus Kimball MP, now Chairman of the BFSS (1951–3); Major Charles Deane (1955–63), and in 1962, by Major Warre, who remains in the joint command. Incidentally, Mr J.J. Astor, the hunt chairman who, like Lord Fitzwilliam no longer rides owing to a back injury, served with both joint-Masters in that well-known wartime unit, Phantom. Lord Fitzwilliam, the owner of the pack, having recently presented the Veluwe draghounds, of Holland, with six couples of bitches, is also an honorary joint-Master of that hunt.

I wondered, as we moved off on 6 March, how often Dean or Sebright or Agutter had suffered the frustration of a spring drought such as that now facing Steve Roberts. Lord Fitzwilliam said that he had never known worse scenting conditions: it was windy, the sun was shining, dust spiralled from the bone-dry ploughs of this flat country, and Roberts drew, and lifted hounds, and drew again for nearly four hours before they could get on terms with a fox. That was when the temperature changed to a three o'clock snap and they just succeeded in holding the line of one through Hilly Wood, swinging left with him over the Deeping road and through the southern end of Simon and Oxey, until they lost him, 30 minutes later, by Pellett Hall.

The Fitzwilliam were pure English, mostly Belvoir-bred, until the early 1930s when Lord Fitzwilliam's father used the Curre Tuner; but it was not until 1950 that Sir Peter Farquhar produced a new foundation sire for Milton, the Portman Freeman, by which this hunt 'went modern'. With the advent of Steve Roberts in 1961 came another very influential hound: Cattistock Barnard '58. Now you also see in the breeding columns of the kennel list such names as Heythrop Craftsman '62, Tipperary Growler '64, Meynell Badger '66 and Quorn Valet '66.

As for 6 March, it was a perfectly lovely day to be out, especially on Major Warre's handy ex-polo pony, Novelty, and most stimulating to see such stylish hounds as Lord Fitzwilliam's persevere in abysmal conditions like those.

(6 March 1976)

T. Teanby was put on as huntsman in place of S. Roberts in 1978, while H. Elliott was appointed whipper-in for the start of the 1977–8 season. J. Taylor has since joined the kennel staff.

The West Norfolk

A HUNT OF ROYAL HERITAGE

A publican owning a beer-house of fame,
A good friend of the hunt, whom you all know by name –
They tell me his stables and inn are both full,
For there's no pub in Norfolk to touch Litcham Bull.
He has made some good jumps where there used to be gaps –
And it's jolly good stuff that runs out of his taps.
He's a rare chucker-out when you're under the table –
Every horse looks a treat when in Goodings' stable.

That lilt comes from the long and amusing word-portrait of the West Norfolk, which Brigid Wilson, now Mrs David Carey, wrote for the hunt's 1933 Christmas card, and which was sold in aid of the poultry fund. And it was at that same 'beer house of fame', the traditional centre point of the hunt, still kept, until a few years ago, by the late Eustace Goodings, that the West Norfolk met when I joined them for their last Saturday of the season.

Goodings – 'good friend of the hunt' – assumed personal responsibility for the fox-holding welfare of nearby Litcham Warren, which the West Norfolk bought 30 years ago. And he would surely be delighted to know how well the hunt maintains his sterling work, piling up stick heaps and achieving a good bottom, by cutting and laying the bushes and hazels.

Litcham Warren was our first draw, and for such a late-in-the-season meet there was a very fair turn-out to see whether the old covert would yield a fox. Major Michael Marsham, who first hunted here in the 1920s, and who has been hunt secretary since he and his wife returned from Ireland six seasons ago, counted 65 mounted followers, while the hunt supporters' club contingent was as strong as ever, in spite of their annual 'punch and pie' party having taken place the night before.

They were not disappointed. One fox shot out from beneath a stick pile only a moment after Rodney Ellis, the huntsman, cheered hounds in. It was septuagenarian farmer, Mr Bob Bidewell, who viewed him first, and Mr Timothy Barclay, of Middleton Towers, who was Master and huntsman here between 1958 and 1968, who *holloaed* him away. And watching hounds race, as close as sheep and in marvellous style, through thickets and over ditches and the light plough which constitutes the bulk of the West Norfolk's terrain, I was reminded how full of quality this pack is. In their careful policy, Messrs James Haggas and Roger Lyles, the two farmers who

have been joint-Masters here since 1968, have introduced blood from the Beaufort and the Heythrop. They have been using stallion hounds going back to the Duke's Palmer '59. And the results of their 1973 puppy show were an excellent omen: the winners were by a first-class hound lent them by Capt. Wallace – Neptune (by Heythrop Colonist out of a bitch by the great Heythrop Craftsman '62). So at Corbett's Lodge, the kennels at Necton, the way ahead seems clear and bright.

We galloped after them in the Mileham direction, with a strong wind in our faces, the sun struggling to find chinks, and cloud shadows scudding over acres and acres of this light plough, interspersed with grassy heath that stretches away, flat and open, to a horizon punctuated by lone trees and church steeples, telegraph poles and conifer plantations. Such country may not be the cream of foxhunting Britain; yet the tradition of venery is as old here, and the bond between foxhunters are strong, as anywhere else in Britain.

The roots go very deep, for this was a famous county for deer-hounds from the eleventh century, and the first record of the fox as quarry comes as early as the sixteenth, with Sir Thomas le Strange of Hunstanton, Esquire to Henry VIII and High Sheriff. One hundred and fifty years later, his foxhunting descendant, Sir Nicholas, who is claimed as 'first Master of the Norfolk', inspired Roger Mason, living 30 miles away at Necton, to form a pack and provide sport for his neighbouring squires between 1692 and 1702.

The roll is full of names well known in our national history. From Mason's time up to the mid-eighteenth century, the mantle of 'Norfolk's Master' fell on the shoulders of England's first Premier, Sir Robert Walpole, Earl of Orford, who kept hounds at Houghton. In 1755 the orientation of the hunt divided, William Mason, of Necton, and H.C. Henley, of Sandringham, operating on the King's Lynn side, with Lord Townshend (1756–72) to the east where Thomas Coke, the 1st Earl of Leicester, then kept the thread going until 1810, when Mr Wilson of Didlington ran that side of the country.

The term 'West Norfolk' appears to have been first used in 1823, when Sir Jacob Astley – who became Lord Hastings – united the country roughly within its present boundaries. In the 1830s and

forties the hunt was run by a committee under the chairmanship of Lord Sondes and, in 1856, we are told by the hunt's Edwardian chronicler that 'Lord Suffield, of Gunton, re-established the Norfolk hounds, which he hunted for three seasons . . .', he being followed by Henry Villebois (1859–65) a former master of the vwh (Earl Bathurst's), and Anthony Hammond (1865–83), during whose regime the 17th Lord Hastings hunted the north part of the country, with kennels at Melton Constable.

In 1883 the country was reunited under Algernon Fountaine, who bought Hamond's hounds and enjoyed a most successful tour until resigning in 1895 in favour of that gifted Master and great sportsman, Charles Seymour, of Barwick, whose first tour with the West Norfolk lasted seven seasons. Then came Albert Collison (1902–8), the Earl of Romney (1908–10), Capt. Champion (1910–13), Lt-Col. Charles Seymour again (1913–29), Lt-Col. Oliver Birkbeck (1929–37), and Major Robert Hoare (1937–9 and 1945–58) who went to make such a great name for himself with the Cottesmore and the South Notts. It was the redoubtable Arthur Johnson who, having originally been put on as huntsman during the First World War, kept things going in the Second – with the help of Jack Howlett, the man who relieved him as kennel-huntsman for the second Mastership of Major Hoare. It was Major Hoare's successor – Mr Barclay – who *halloaed* our fox away from Litcham Wood.

Horses were showing the effects of that spanking pipe-opener when they reached Mileham Horse Wood, the property of Mr Eric Gricks and his son Dennis, nearly three miles on, and we looked through veils of steam to see which way hounds would turn. Then there was a *holloa* telling us the hunted one had set his mask for Bilney, so Rodney Ellis cantered on with about six couples. Unheard for the moment, the older hounds were still on the line in Mileham Horse Wood; but, by the time Ellis returned, they lost him. Then, having drawn the earthworks by Mileham Castle blank, they tried the site of an old Saxon village – Grenstein Wood. The one they found there tried to jump the wire in vain. It was a heavy vixen, so Ellis lifted them to Eastfield.

Despite patient draws there and at Tittleshall, they could not find another. The Friday night had been stormy, and it was suspected that foxes were stopped up in their earths. Nor are there enough of

37 and 38 Royal followers of the West Norfolk. The future King Edward VII and Queen Alexandra as Prince and Princess of Wales, and HM the Queen as Princess Elizabeth.

39 Mr F.J. Haggas, joint-Master since 1968, and huntsman since 1976.

them in Norfolk, for as foxhunters are all too well aware, this is a shooting stronghold, and no foxhunting county in Britain has suffered quite so badly from the post-war growth of shooting syndicates as the West Norfolk, though they tell me that Lord Townshend, at Raynham, Mrs Don, of Elmham, Mrs Michael Keith, of Hoe Hall, Capt. Birkbeck, of Westacre, Mr Cook, of Sennowe, Maj-Gen. Broke and Mr Foster, all of whom own valuable shooting, are among the many who are generous enough to allow hounds on their land at any time in the season. The hunt has killed 17 brace this season, with never a blank day – a good score in the circumstances.

Associating Sandringham with shooting, one is inclined to forget hunting's unique Royal heritage in Norfolk. Henry VIII, Queen Elizabeth I and James I kept hunting lodges in the county, and some of the Hanoverians stayed with their ministers and generals to hunt there. It was at the express wish of George V, I believe, that Col. Seymour returned as Master in 1918. Edward VII and Queen Alexandra, as Prince and Princess of Wales, hunted regularly with the West Norfolk; so did the Duke of Windsor with his brothers and his sister, the Princess Royal (many of Norfolk's older generation today remember hunting in their company and entertaining them to tea at the end of the day). And so, when they were young, did Her Majesty The Queen and Princess Margaret.

Foxes or no foxes, riding in that company over the lonely farmland around Litcham and Mileham last month, I could well understand why those Royal followers had so much fun with this hunt. For the West Norfolk possess an air of close and happy county fraternity, which comes perhaps from being so conveniently isolated from rubbing shoulders with any other hunt.

(16 March 1974)

G.B. Needham took over as kennel-huntsman and whipper-in in 1976, and was succeeded by T. Bowden in 1979.

The Puckeridge and Thurlow

FOXHOUNDS IN A PLOUGH COUNTRY

Hunting with the Puckeridge and Thurlow from their opening meet at the Thurlow end of the country on the Monday of last week really impressed on me what a happy and fortuitous alliance this has proved. On the Puckeridge side an increasing shortage of money meant some radical measure had to be taken, while the growth of racing studs at the Newmarket and Thurlow end meant a significant loss of country. The increase in pheasant shooting in both territories also resulted in loss of country.

I soon saw what a splendid government the merger has thrown up, for no one could have joined forces more harmoniously than Mr Edmund Vestey, a most effective field Master, at once forceful and gentle, and Capt. Charles Barclay, whose popular 25-season reign (23 with the Puckeridge, two with the present hunt) brings the Barclay family's regime to a total of 76 consecutive years. Mrs Barclay and Mrs Vestey in every way complete the team.

The amalgamation draws together about 500 square miles, and Col. Douglas Kaye, a former Master of the Newmarket and Thurlow who is now honorary secretary and treasurer, delegates to no fewer than three assistant secretaries. It combines also two essentially heavy-going ditch-and-bank countries, in both of which the fox has been hunted since the eighteenth century.

The Puckeridge, with Buntingford in Hertfordshire at its centre, had the older tradition, their foxes being regularly hunted by the Calverts of Albury Hall from the middle of the eighteenth century. In 1794 the name was changed from 'Mr Calvert's' to 'the Hertfordshire', and in 1799 the management of the pack passed to the founder of the Hertfordshire Hunt Club, Mr Sampson Hanbury of Poles, whose kennels were at the hamlet of Puckeridge. In 1819 the Hunt Club acquired Lady Salisbury's pack and territory when she gave up at Hatfield. In 1826 the hunt was renamed 'the Puckeridge'.

Hanbury's Mastership ended in 1832 and was followed by two sad reigns. Firstly that of Lord Petre, who came along from the Essex Union – he had been hunting this privately and clearly possessed no sense of the spirit of a subscription pack – with a bad huntsman, Sam Hort, of whom 'The Druid' wrote in his diary: 'Lord Petre's huntsman is the worst I ever saw attempt to hunt a pack, hurrying and lifting when the hounds should

hunt, and craning and losing no end of time when they should be lifted'. Petre and Hort moved on in 1835, giving place to a tactless young Scot called John Dayell. He was hated by the farmers, whose macabre insult was to hang dead foxes from the trees of his favourite coverts, and there was a sigh of relief and a vow of 'no more experiments with strangers' when the arrogant Dayell returned to Fifeshire in 1838.

He was succeeded by Mr Nicholas Parry, a quiet and charming man and a first-class houndsman who saw four successive huntsmen – everyone of them a gem – out of office before retiring in 1875. The latter-day hunt historian, M.F. Berry, sums up Parry's reign like this: 'for the previous 37 years he had devoted practically the whole of his time to the tasks of breeding a fine pack of hounds and of interesting the Puckeridge country in the science of foxhunting. . . .' However, a dismal period followed. Robert Gosling, of Hassobury, Bishop's Stortford, bought Parry's pack for 2000 guineas. But due to an agricultural marketing crisis, the hunt was going broke. The committee was obliged to halve Gosling's £1500 guarantee. He cut down to two days a week, and from his kennels at Manuden, in Essex, could scarcely reach the Saturday country. In 1885 he resigned.

Nobody suitable came forward for the whole country, and when the Saturday subscribers proposed a bookmaker's son with the unpromising name of Swindell, the 'Goslingites' said no. They dubbed their mid-week country 'the Herts and Essex', so the 'Swindellites' contented themselves with the Saturday country, where (said the 'Goslingites') they played tricks with their foxes and such games as driving three dozen donkeys into Gosling's lawn meets. This civil war lasted until 1894, when both Masters resigned and 'the Herts and Essex pack . . . with all their fine foundation lines, so carefully built by Mr Parry, were sold by auction on May 11, 1894, and dispersed all over the country'. But, happily, a well-liked man in his twenties, the Hon. Lancelot Bathurst, bought Swindell's hounds and in two bright seasons paved the way for the Barclays whose illustrious dynasty began in 1896 and whose name is synonymous with Puckeridge.

But what about their potential allies, the Newmarket and Thurlow, during the century or more we

40 Three Barclay generations photographed during the 1947/48 season. Mr Edward Barclay between his son Major M.E. Barclay (*left*) and grandson, Capt. C.G.E. Barclay, the present senior joint-Master.

have reviewed? That much smaller country, it appears, was first hunted in the second half of the eighteenth century by an enthusiast known as 'Miser' Elwes, then by a Mr Thomas Panton, who was followed by Col. John Cook, author of the classic *Observations on Hunting*. But Cook soon retired (in 1804), complaining that 'foxes and subscriptions are damnably short'. (Upon which an Edwardian chronicler commented: 'the same condition of affairs has existed ever since!') Indeed the next two sportsmen to show initiative in that country did so in a very sparse manner, until that rich genius of the chase, Squire Osbaldeston, having cracked his leg with the Pytchley, took his hounds to Thurlow Cottage 'up to such time as he recovered strength for the more arduous task of hunting Leicestershire. . . .'

The country's demarcations continued to be vague. Mr George Mure, who hunted the 'Thurlow country' for 18 seasons from 1827 as well as the Suffolk, was imitated by his successors, all of whom took in different slices of East Anglia. England's racing Mecca soon became a favourite centre, and in 1884 the hunt was renamed 'Newmarket and Thurlow', the first Master under that title being a Mr Gardiner. At the time that Mr Edward Barclay began his half-century with the Puckeridge in 1896, Mr Edward Molyneux had the neighbouring country. Then, in 1902, we are told, 'the Mastership of the Rev. Sir William Hyde Parker signalised the commencement of a very successful hound breeding policy . . . a close friend of the Rev. Edgar Milne, then Master of the Cattistock, Sir William used to send his young hounds into Dorset to be entered, where they were said to have seen more foxes during cub-hunting than they saw for the rest of their lives in the Thurlow country. . . .'

But in spite of the strong shooting interests – obvious enough from the profusion of pheasants – we saw no lack of foxes around Great Thurlow on 6 November, and were it not for the warmth of the air and the bone dryness of the plough, they might have enjoyed a dashing day. All the same, hunting around the Stour valley in the area of Trundley, Bardniston, Ganwick and Great Wrattling, they killed two foxes and put three more to ground – two of these being from the gigantic Trundley Wood.

The kennels at Capt. Barclay's Brent Pelham Hall are filled almost entirely with Puckeridge hounds (the exceptions being Newmarket and Thurlow Arklow '65 and Trophy '66). Mr Edward Barclay, one of the greatest Masters of all time – he had his own pack of beagles or harriers for 18 seasons before taking the Puckeridge horn – used only Belvoir and Brocklesby blood, breeding specifically for the plough. His son, Major M.E. Barclay (joint-Master 1910–62), to compete with changing agricultural conditions altered the policy and a month before he died, acquired from the Duke of Beaufort a bitch called Worry, a sister of the Peterborough champion, Woeful. Worry's offspring gave a new infusion of quality and lightness, yet retained the full ribs and stronger backs of the traditional hounds.

During our hunt from Stubbins it was interesting to see Winifred '65 (by Puckeridge Manager '59 out of the Duke of Beaufort's Worry '60 mentioned above) as the only hound holding the line by Wrattling Hall over some especially hard plough. Then, with Winifred leading, this tenacious four-day-a-week pack worked up to their fox in a thick fence and killed him after a patient 30 minutes' run

41 Mr and Mrs E.H. Vestey (*leading*). They entered the Mastership with Capt. Barclay in 1970 on the amalgamation of the two hunts.

that was full of resounding music. The final hunt lasted 95 minutes.

There may be no 'quick things across the pasture' here, but if you want to watch hound work which is clever and patient in very difficult conditions, then go to the Puckeridge and Thurlow.

(6 November 1972)

R. Quarmby was put on as kennel-huntsman and first whipper-in, in 1975, and R. Suter as second whipper-in, in 1979.

The Waveney Harriers

BRITAIN'S EASTERNMOST HUNT

Hares thrive well on the low-lying land astride the valleys of the Waveney and Blyth in north-east Suffolk. At this time of the year they are content to make their forms in the extensive plough, or to lie up in the meadows, sparse willow clumps and marshy fields that here and there break up the plough. They skip over the myriad pattern of drainage ditches which keep their habitat reasonably dry; they make easy landmarks of the few elm and oak trees that punctuate the flat landscape. And there is only one railway, and no busy roads, for them to cross.

In the early eighteenth century when those famous Suffolk sportsmen, the Freestones, founded the Waveney harriers, the flatness owned another face: featureless grass, mostly rather waterlogged and therefore not so congenial for hares, a country where sheep and cattle roamed at will. Wool was still the predominant commodity. But when the Freestone grandsons came on the scene, the imagination of 'Turnip' Townshend held sway, the country was put under the plough, the flocks herded into enclosures and big thorn fences marked out the pastures. Then land got more valuable, hunting more expensive and in the 1860s Mr A.G. Freestone made the Waveney a subscription pack. As for the new hedge-barrier look of the country, that suited Mr C.C. Chaston (who took over as Master in 1872) very well, for he was a famous amateur steeplechase jockey who rode no less than 52 consecutive races without a fall.

It stayed a big jumping country for the Mastership of Sir Savile Crossley, later 1st Lord Somerleyton, who carried the horn from 1881 to 1888, and for much of the 60-year tenure of the 3rd Earl of Stradbroke, great agriculturist and administrator, who followed him and who changed the name of the hunt to Henham, his home; and that name was kept until 1954 when the hunt was reorganised as the Waveney Valley. Then, between the wars, away went the sheep and down came the hedges, for which an army of labourers had been needed to control them, and that left only the water-courses, which have always been there, with their dual-purpose of drainage and enclosure.

So it was mostly plough riding and all ditch jumping we had to expect when we met Sir Savile Crossley's grandson, Lord Somerleyton, and his two joint-Masters, Mrs Alexander Stewart and Mr Desmond Longe, at Fressingfield on 18 December. The sun was up and the ancient village made a fine setting for the meet of this well-matched harrier pack and their green-coated staff. Hounds, which had travelled the 25 miles from Somerleyton Hall, near Lowestoft, way up in the north-east corner of the country, were unboxed at the Fox and Goose, once a medieval guild-house. The eighteenth-century Freestones began many a long day's hunting from this inn now shining sunlit white between its half timbering. Then Jim Chesson, their huntsman since 1965, when he came down from the Grove and Rufford, took the $14\frac{1}{2}$ couples down to the Green, parading them beneath the tall fourteenth-century church of St Peter and St Paul, where 70 mounted followers were waiting.

Lord Stradbroke's pack was put down during the war, and the hounds we saw on 18 December originated with the two and a half couples with which Mr C.N. Smith, deputising for the Master, began the 1945-6 season. Mostly of Cambridgeshire and High Peak breeding, closely coupled, standing very level, about 21 inches at the shoulder, and looking hard and silky, one was not surprised to hear they had accounted for $28\frac{1}{2}$ brace of hares, an average of two or three a day, since mid-October when the leveret season began.

Lord Stradbroke's harriers killed less frequently. No one was more experienced than he: in the whole of his long command, 1888 to 1948, he was only absent from home during the years of the First World War and during his tour as Governor of Victoria (1920-26). And he was famous for his painstaking methods, which must at times have been exasperating for his followers. 'To hunt a hare one certainly must practice great patience if one intends to finish with a kill,' he wrote in the harrier chapter of the *Lonsdale Library* series: 'it is very tempting to lift hounds to cut off a detour, but if this habit is persisted in, the huntsman will soon find that his hounds will not keep their heads down, and though apparently doing so, are in reality flashing over the ground, watching each other or the huntsman and ready to dash off after any holloa. . . . Patience is required not only by the huntsman, but by the field. . . .' But, technically sound as this may be, the modern Waveney subscriber becomes restless at 20-minute draws and checks; he demands quick-

42 Lord Somerleyton. He became chairman of the hunt committee in 1959 and has been senior joint-Master on and off since 1966. He was chairman of the Masters of Harriers and Beagles Association.

moving sport – and is given it.

Riding south from Fressingfield to Caterpole corner – almost to the hunt's southern boundary, where the 30-by-16-mile Waveney country marches with the Easton – and there casting left past Redhouse and finding by Canham Farm, we soon saw how energetically Jim Chesson, assisted by two farmer whippers-in, Messrs Fred Hemmant and Ivor Constance, adheres to the Waveney policy of keeping hounds on the move. They lost her near the B1116, but quickly found another, and away they went with their splendid chorus across the ley and the young wheat shoots to the west of Ufford Hall, finally bowling her over in a ditch. The huntsman then lost no time in drawing the ploughland from Pear Tree House to beyond Swan Green, and it was real entertainment to witness the gallop with which these little hounds, making their compact tan, black and white group, traversed the heavy-laden ridges of

plough. Hunting the next hare via Whitehouse Farm
and Lonely Farm to Cratfield Red House, then
giving that one best and heading north again,
hunting two more by Silverley's Green, and Little
Whittingham Green, they covered a further six
miles before he blew 'home'. And they looked just as
bright as they had looked earlier on at the meet at
Fressingfield.

Even in the best tracts of the Shires, it is nearly
always possible to keep up with hounds without
jumping. But you cannot say the same of the
Waveney country. There you have to jump deep
ditches or be left behind. Visitors from the Midlands, with horses only accustomed to timber and
solid brush, often find the Waveney dykes alarming,
sometimes impossible. It is said that if you can get a
young horse across this very sporting plough-and-
ditch country, you can take him anywhere.

The fox is not hunted in this part of East Anglia,
except when the Waveney come upon one by chance.
But the farmers are all for the hunting of hares. It is
essentially hare country; hares are too destructive to
be allowed to proliferate over a valuable arable land
such as this. So the old Waveney tradition continues,
strong as ever; and, in its way, this easternmost of
Britain's hunts might be said to offer the best sport
of them all.

(18 December 1971)

*Mrs A.D. Stewart and Major J.S. Crisp have been in
the Mastership since 1976 and 1978 respectively. Mrs
Crisp joined them in 1980.*

The South-East

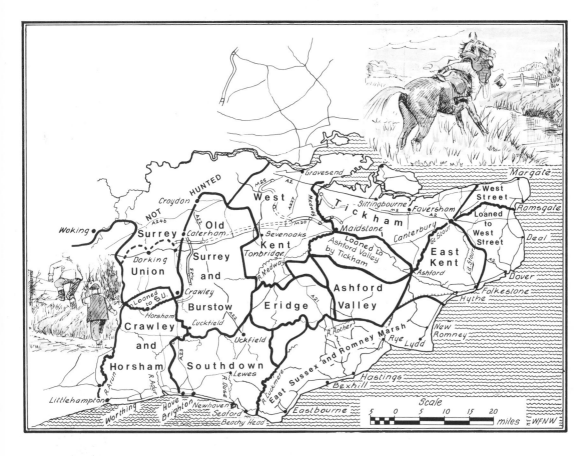

The Crawley and Horsham

HOUND QUALITY OVER WEALDEN CLAY

Foxhunters from remote Elysian regions who imagine Sussex to be a close tarmac mesh, enclosing a hideous pattern of housing estates and an agricultural mosaic rendered impassable by barbed wire and smartly locked gates, should take a look at the Crawley and Horsham in their oak-strewn Weald country, as I did on 23 February.

Although the morning warmed up quickly, following an early frost, Mr David Sandeman, the Master, told me that, as the land had dried out to just the right degree after heavy floods, one could afford to be optimistic about scent. How right he was. Leaving the meet, which was attended by over 80 followers, at the Countryman, near Shipley, Jack Clarke, the huntsman, first tried Benton's and Great Northern wood without success. But when he cheered hounds into Wickwood, one of a brace led them away with as forceful a drive as you could hope to see foxhounds gallop, through Tory Copse, over the sound pasture which Mr Phil Edwards rents from Sir Walter Burrell – with its hunt tiger-traps always apparently in the right place to let you over – past New Barn, Woodman's and Perrylands, until, after 15 minutes' race, they were seconds behind his brush at an earth on Hooklands.

As they turned north to draw Loder's gorse, I was told that no fewer than 22 point-to-point horses have been qualified here this season, which reminded me how this has always been remarked upon as a particularly sporting community. The term 'Horsham and Crawley', a new political constituency, was bandied about pretty freely last month, and must have jarred somewhat on their ears. For, as this hunt has been known as the 'Crawley and Horsham' for 124 years, it seemed odd to hear the names in reverse. Not that they relish having Crawley, its new town or the adjacent Gatwick airport, on their boundaries any more than certain others do. But the original orientation of this hunt was from the unspoilt Crawley of a century and a half ago.

It stemmed from Col. Joliffe with the Merstham hunt, who, although he kennelled in the north of the present Old Surrey and Burstow country, also kept 'sporting quarters' at the Sun Inn, Crawley, to hunt his 'Horsham country'. And when Joliffe's hunt was absorbed in the Old Surrey in the 1830s, Henry Lee Steeres, of Ockley, who had a pack of harriers, took over that country and began to hunt fox there.

Charles Bethune, of Crabbet, bought Lee Steeres' hounds and kennelled them at that same Sun Inn, while Edward Stamford who succeeded to this pack in 1847 kept them at Warninglid. When Stamford threatened to give up, 20 years later, because of 'lack of foxes and support', he was promptly given a guaranteed annuity of £1000. Nevertheless he resigned in 1867.

That year marks the start of better times in the history of the hunt because, at a time of much discontent, an influential landowner, Mr (later Sir Robert) Loder, agreed to help out. Although he himself was not an avid foxhunter, Loder saw that if mid-Sussex sportsmen were to be satisfied, it was no use leaving the establishment to one enthusiast, without proper backing. So he accepted the joint-Mastership for two seasons, in harness with a most dedicated hunting man, Capt. A.M. Calvert, who went on in sole command, also carrying the horn, from 1868 to 1887. During that period the Crawley and Horsham really developed its present shape and character. In 1876 Col. Calvert, as he became, took Lord Leconfield's Old Findon country, from Dial Post to the sea, which he had been hunting for a few seasons by arrangement with his friend, the Rev. John Goring, of Wiston.

Today Mr John Goring, of Wiston, is one of several large landowners on whose hospitality the hunt depends: others include the Duke of Norfolk, on the Downs; Mrs P.A. Tritton, at Parham; Sir Walter Burrell, of Knepp Castle; Lord Glendyne and the Lock estate; Col. John Hornung, of Ivories; Mr Peter Kirch, at West Grinstead Park; Miss Godman, north of Cowfold; and her nephew, Mr Patrick Colvin, next door. In 1877 the present kennels were built at West Grinstead, on land now belonging to a syndicate of the Burrell family – about three miles east of our meet on 23 February.

The fox that led hounds from Loder's copse (named after Sir Robert) and past Brookhouse on my day, was headed, and they lost him near Benton's. The third was signalled by a *holloa* behind, and away they sped with a really lovely chorus over the road above Blonk's, across a sea of plough to Faulkner's bushes and on to Ingram's furze, where the pack divided, some aiming for Mr McPhail's South Goringlee. But two and a half couples of veterans pointed to Major Martin-Bird's well-reputed Cool-

43 Mrs Molly Gregson, Master, or joint-Master, 1939–61.

until 1916, his last three years being with Lt-Col. McKergow. Excepting the years of a wartime committee, McKergow continued single-handed, until the Hon. Guy Cubitt joined him in 1928. Cubitt, a grandson of Calvert, carried on alone, hunting the bitches, while Charles Denton who had come in from the Warwickshire also in 1928, to take over from Bert Peaker, hunted the dog-hounds.

When Col. Cubitt went abroad with his regiment, Mrs H.G. Gregson donned the Master's cap, and because Cubitt was too severely wounded in action to resume the office after demobilisation, she wore it until 1961. Lt-Col. (now Brig.) Henry Green, joined her for the years 1948–51, and Sir Walter Burrell, who has remained chairman ever since those days, was her field Master. In 1961 a triumvirate, consisting of Messrs R.D. Crossman, D.P. Sandeman and R.E. Whittaker was formed. But for the past decade, with Mr Mark Burrell and Mrs Richard Greenwood, Sir Walter's son and daughter, and Brig. Henry Green, acting as his field Masters, Mr Sandeman has been in full command. Mrs Gregson, a much respected expert on the subject since the 1930s, continues to advise on hound-breeding.

Indeed this hunt has a tradition, unbroken since Calvert's day, of the most successful hound-breeding policies. Calvert used Fitzhardinge and Bramham blood – 30 out of the 49 couples he handed over in 1887 were by the great Bramham Moor Chieftan '77. Godman, similarly determined to breed a hound tailor-made for both the Downs and the Weald, persevered with the Chieftan line, fortifying it with Warwickshire and more Fitzhardinge blood. During the Great War, the Crawley and Horsham were lucky enough to have the expert services of W.A. Calvert, Col. Calvert's son, who, in spite of drastic reductions at the kennels, managed to keep the lines strong.

Then Col. McKergow, having boosted the post-war entries with drafts from the Fitzhardinge and Blankney kennels, went on, with excellent and enduring effect, to use outcrosses from the best of Lord Leconfield's and – due to his huntsman being the brother of Alf Peaker of the Brocklesby – Lord Yarborough's, too. Guarding these same lines very closely, Col. Cubitt, another hound perfectionist, also went to the South and West Wilts, Ikey Bell's famous Godfrey '28 being the one he used most.

And no one has taken greater pains than Mrs Gregson to maintain the quality at West Grinstead. The lovely pack one sees today is the legacy of Pytchley strains which, in the 1940s, she introduced to the lines established by Col. McKergow and Col.

ham Gorse, so Jack Clarke lifted the remainder to join them. The one they hunted from there was headed on Smither's Hill. Returning towards Coolham Gorse, hounds marked him to ground on one of the old airfield drains, and the Master, looking very happy with their performance, led us north of Shipley to see what Green Street plantation had in store. . . .

From Calvert's time onwards, the hunt has been blessed with a thread of long and happy Masterships. Lt-Col. Godman, a former Master of the Chiddingfold, who succeeded Calvert, remained in office

44 Hounds at the Countryman, Shipley, Sussex on 23 February 1974. Immediately behind them is Jack Clarke, the huntsman, whose career began as second horseman to the Heythrop in 1928, and who whipped in, successively to seven other packs before he was put on as huntsman to the Crawley and Horsham in 1953. He retired in 1979 after 50 years in hunt service.

Cubitt, and subsequently Heythrop and Beaufort blood. Wiseman '68 from the Chipping Norton kennels, the Duke's prodigious Palmer '59 and the Crawley and Horsham Farley '70, another very handsome hound of Beaufort breeding, all having been influential in recent years.

On the last hunt, from Green Street plantation, we had more fine views of these hounds as they swung westwards, close and hard along the Adur valley, over Mr Eric Covell's Southdown stud paddocks, crossing the hazardous A272 and up to Hoe's, turning right-handed below Dragon's Green, and back through Green Street plantation, finally running this one to ground in Jockey Copse at 3.45. And

there Jack Clarke blew 'home'.

Owing to the line-hunting perseverance of these hounds, we had been constantly on the move for four hours and, thanks to the immense trouble taken by the Master and his helpers to keep this country open, we were up with them from start to finish.

(23 February 1974)

In 1977 a new joint-Mastership was formed, consisting of Mr D.F. Cooke (who continues as secretary), Mr R.N. Ewing, Mr Hardy Gillingham, and Sir Walter Burrell's daughter, Mrs Richard Greenwood.

D. Evans was appointed whipper-in to Jack Clarke in 1977. Jack retired in 1979 after 50 years in hunt service, 26 of these being in the role of huntsman to the C. and H. Dick Chapman was appointed to succeed him at the start of the 1979–80 season, having been kennel-huntsman to the Holderness since 1972.

From the 1981–2 season, the Masters will be Mr Mark Burrell, Mr Michael Richardson and Mr Leslie Weller.

The West Kent

A STRONG WOODLAND CHALLENGE

The West Kent hounds looked just right with Hever Castle as the backdrop for their 1973 finale, because this – as one would expect of such steady rosette winners and the holders of the Peterborough bitch championship – is one of the handsomest packs in the south of England. Bred since the last war by two clever and devoted houndsmen, Mr Auriol Gaselee and the present Master, Mr Richard Thorpe, the chief outside influences in the kennels have been the Old Berks Valiant '46; the Duke of Beaufort's Landrail '46, and Palmer '59, and Palmer's Peterborough champion grandsons, Beadle and Warden; the Eridge Playfair '57, Pilgrim '64, Accurate '64 and Painter '66; and the Old Berks Playfair '60 and Maltster '65. There is much black-and-tan in the pack which comes, Mr Thorpe tells me, from that fine stud hound, the Old Berks Tewkesbury '61. But the West Kent are as level as peas in a pod.

And it is right and proper they should be superior, for this is the hunt whose basic tradition stems from John Warde, 'The Father of Foxhunting', the first Master ever to stage hound and puppy shows, which he did at his home, Squerryes Court, Westerham, until the end of his life in 1838. He was the breeder of a pack which, if not as influential as Hugo Meynell's, was said to be just as effective and highly admired. I say 'basic' tradition, because although the earliest modern record of hunting in West Kent is that of Squire Evelyn, of St Clere, in the 1730s, he hunted anything that got up, mainly hare, whereas Warde, who went on to be Master of the South Berks, the Bicester, Pytchley and the New Forest, entered his Squerryes pack in the 1770s to fox and fox alone. He was, indeed, the first man in the south of England to do that.

Warde's fashion was perpetuated in the county by the Hart Dyke family from 1793 to 1836, their hunt being first known as the 'Lullingstone', where they lived, and then as the 'West Kent'. The kennels and orientation of the hunt then changed six times; Mr Forrest, who took over from the Hart Dykes, moved hounds to Greenhythe, near Dartford. When Mr Colyer, who had the colourful Tom Hills as huntsman, succeeded him in 1845, they were installed at Paddock Hall, Gravesend. Under Messrs Armstrong and Wingfield Stratford, they were kennelled at Wrotham Heath. There they stayed until 1881 during the Hon. Ralph Nevill's 30-year Mas-

tership, when he moved hounds to Otford. This was their home until 1937 when, owing to urban encroachment, new housing was found for them at Puttenden Manor, on the Fairlawne estate, the late Major Peter Cazalet's home. They were transferred to Mr Gaselee's property, Hamptons, Tonbridge, in 1946, and in 1967 they were removed to their present kennels, Home Farm, Southborough, Tunbridge Wells, home of Mr Thorpe, the Master.

The outline of the West Kent country has undergone many changes since Warde's day, too. A southern sector, which splintered away as the West Kent Woodland, emerged as the Eridge in 1879, while another area, to the south-east, went first to the Mid-Kent Staghounds, and then, in 1922, to the newly formed Ashford Valley. One Saturday a fortnight, in his four-day hunting week, Ralph Nevill took in the Hundred of Hoo – the Isle of Grain – which lies north of Rochester and west of Sheppey. And, privately and briefly, during Edwardian times, Mr Arkell hunted this good Thameside farming tract with its large enclosures and convenient coverts. But the Hundred of Hoo was then left alone again until Mr Gaselee opened it up in the 1950s. Mr Thorpe still goes there once a month, though urbanisation has rendered unhuntable the bulk of the hunt's northern sector, which is roughly bounded by Rochester, Dartford and Strood.

With its densely wooded, steep-sided valleys and myriad of rivulets, shaded by oak and ash and hazel, interspersed with pasture, many claim the West Kent calls for a special brand of huntsman. George Bollen, who was taken on by Nevill – and carried the horn during the Masterships of John Warde's descendent, Col. Charles Warde, MP (1891–2), Stewart Saville (1892–5) and Lord George Nevill (1895–1900) – was described by a contemporary as 'one of the best of woodland huntsmen and possessed of a beautiful voice'. During this century nine Masters have also worn the huntsman's cap: W. Gore Lambarde (1904–8), Guy Everard (1908–10), 'Barny' Kidd (1910–13), A. Havelock Allen (1913–14), William Brydone (1915–23), George Davidson (1926–33, whose field Master for a time was Sir Walter Monckton), John Garle (1933–9) and Mr Auriol Gaselee (1952–67). The period of 1923–6 was filled by the hunt's only lady Master, Miss Kathleen Styles, who was afterwards hunt secretary.

45 Stan Luckhurst, huntsman since 1967.

46 The West Kent Payment '72. Winner of the Peterborough bitch championship in 1973, she is by the Eridge Painter '66 out of Chantress '66.

That post has now been held by Mrs E.J. Day for 18 seasons. In 1946 Bob Champion junior was put on as huntsman for the joint-Mastership of Messrs Rodger and Hollamby.

Stanley Luckhurst, who came to the West Kent as second whipper-in in 1955, after leaving the King's Troop, Royal Horse Artillery, and has now carried the horn for six seasons, enjoys a great reputation as a forest huntsman and is often compared with George Bollen. When they drew and found in rambling Park Wood on 29 December, his voice came forth clear and round to the echo, matching his hounds' lovely cry, and he kept things on the move in such a way that he seemed to sense his foxes' every turn and twist. This first fox led the field of 90 on through Trangle Wood, where he was headed and turned; but they found him again in Moor Wood before losing him in the Wilderness. The second pilot started from the plough by Truggers Farm covert, zigzagging us up and down hill past Rock Inn and through Stonewall Park; but, just before reaching South Park, he turned back into Stonewall and

was lost at Lew Cross.

A fresh fox, which was found at Keyesden, ran fast from Stridewood to Bassetts Mill and Frienden Wood, and, after a last fine sprint in the twilight, was given best at a badgers' sett on Hobbs Hill. Riding through all that old woodland and pasture around Hever was a most invigorating experience, and watching the behaviour of the followers was an unusually impressive one; for they are the best disciplined field I have ever seen, keeping tight against headlands, single-filing down the edge of rides, shutting gates with meticulous care, straightening dented fences and yielding to uncivil motorists with charming smiles, as though trained by a drill sergeant. The West Kent are indeed a credit to the ghost of 'The Father of Foxhunting'.

(29 December 1973)

Mr P. Williams entered the Mastership in 1976 and Mr Tim Lyle in 1978. Mr and Mrs D. Donegan and Mr H. Howe joined Mr Lyle in 1980. Mr W. Meakin became a joint-secretary in 1972.

The Southdown

IN SASSOON'S RINGWELL COUNTRY

'Ringwell cubbing days are among my happiest memories. . . . Out by the loose-boxes under the rustling trees, with quiet stars overhead and hardly a hint of morning. . . . In the kennels the two packs were baying at one another from the separate yards, and as soon as Denis had got his horse from the gruff white-coated head-groom, a gate released the hounds – 25 or 30 couple of them, and all very much on their toes. Out they streamed like a flood of water, throwing their tongues and spreading away in all directions with waving sterns, as though they had never been out in the world before. Even then I used to feel the strangeness of the scene with its sharp exuberance of unkennelled energy. Will's hearty voice and the crack of his whip stood out above the clamour and commotion, which surged around Denis and his horse. . . .'

That, of course, is Siegfried Sassoon (alias George Sherston) in the company of Norman Loder (immortalised as Denis Milden), the dedicated young Master and huntsman of the Southdown (the

Ringwell), with the scene at Ringmer in 1912, the season before the ambitious Milden set off for the Packlestone (Atherstone). Today that old Victorian kennel and stable complex, flagstoned beneath solid red brick and brick-red-painted ironwork, stands very much as it stood in their day; and, nursed by Tom Winney, the Southdown's stud groom, the loose-boxes are full of the kind of quality that was officially prescribed, in 1908, for '. . . a country where pace is required; carrying as a rule a good scent, its vale country takes a lot of doing; big fences and banks, and in places very deep going, try the staying powers of the horses; whilst breasting the Downs in the open, unless both horses and hounds are of the best, and bred both for pace and stamina, they have little chance of being in at the finish. . . .'

The kennels hark back, too, to another period when the fox was hunted on the downs and Weald, east and north of Brighton, for they are built on the site of a seventeenth-century barracks, where – a few years after Waterloo, when foxhunters still sported

47 The bitches at Ringmer in 1908. In 1911 Mr Norman Loder (immortalised by Sassoon as Denis Milden) 'asserted his independence by getting rid of the bitch pack'.

a black cravat over a white, winged collar, and Horse Gunners wore the plumed shako, Major Cater, of the Royal Horse Artillery, and his officers kept a pack, calling themselves the 'East Sussex'. But after a few seasons the Board of Ordnance huffily drummed the hounds out. They were moved first to neighbouring Broyle Park and thence to Rushey Green, Ringmer, where Lord Gage built – from the materials of the old barracks, most of which had been pulled down a year or two before – new kennels and stables on the space we know today. Mr J.C. Craven of Kemp Town, Brighton, then assumed Cater's mantle, with John Press as huntsman.

Now Press had been huntsman to another sporting pioneer in this vicinity, Mr King-Sampson, who, from 1815 onwards, kennelled a pack at Hailsham, to hunt both fox and hare; and the question of which of the two hunts – the Horse Gunners' or King-Sampson's – is the forerunner of the Southdown, remains a moot point. Anyhow, the hunt's Edwardian chronicler tells us that 'for some time no hunt at all existed in these parts, but at last [in 1843] Mr Freeman Thomas, of Ratton, Eastbourne, resuscitated the pack, which became known thenceforth as "The Southdown".' To centralise Freeman Thomas's organisation, hounds were soon moved from Ratton to the Ringmer site, and Freeman Thomas also hunted a good slice of what is now the East Sussex and Romney Marsh country, until the

East Sussex was founded in 1853.

Alexander Donovan, who took over the reins from Thomas in 1855, appears to be the one who first made Southdown sport famous. His brilliant huntsman, George Champion, carried the horn for the next two Masters, W.L. Christie (1863–7) and R.J. Streatfield (1871–81), and into the start of the Hon. Charles Brand's 22-year innings. Brand kept a ladies-only kennels, based on Brocklesby and Warwickshire blood – up to his last two seasons, when he entered a few dog-hounds. But his successor, R.W. McKergow, who later became Master of the Crawley and Horsham, bred a mixed pack, beginning with 38 couples, and handed over $47\frac{1}{2}$ to Mr V.P. Misa in 1908. The next move is described in *Memoirs of a Foxhunting Man* like this: 'As soon as he [Milden/Loder] took over the country, he asserted his independence by getting rid of the Ringwell dog-pack, on which the members had always prided themselves so much. To the prudent protestations of the Committee, he replied bluntly that, although the dog-hounds were all right to listen to in the woods, they were too slow for words on the unenclosed downs, and too big and cloddy for the cramped and strongly fenced vale country. . . .'

Following the Masterships of Messrs. C.B. Kidd, F. Moffat Smith (who steered the hunt through the First World War) and R.M. Cardwell, and of Brig-Gen. E.S. Hoare-Nairne, in 1929 another young amateur, with very strong opinions about hounds, appeared on the Southdown scene: this was Mr Arthur Dalgety who, at 30, had already been Master

48 Roy Goddard, the huntsman, in the same setting at the time of the author's visit in January 1975.

of the Dunston Harriers, and for four seasons of the Vine, in whose country he had also kept a private pack of staghounds. And while he was with the Southdown, in addition to hunting 'the Committee's coloured pack' in the vale, he took his own white hounds (largely founded on Sir Edward Curre's blood) on to the Downs twice a week. So Dalgety carried the horn four days a week in Sussex but, not content with that programme, in 1936 he took on the joint-Mastership of New Forest Buckhounds with Sir John Buchanan-Jardine (who, incidentally, persuaded him to introduce Drumfriesshire blood into the Ringmer kennels). Dalgety was never a man to be much curtailed: throughout the Second World War he managed to keep the Southdown country freely open with 20 well-fed couples.

Since the last war the hunt has been blessed with many benefactors: Mr Gerald Askew, for example, who came in as Master with Major C.T. James in 1952; his brother Ian, who succeeded Major James in 1956, and later bought the kennels and stables from the hunt trustees and substantially improved them; Major B.M.H. Shand, who joined the Askew brothers in 1956, and has now devoted 19 seasons to guiding the hunt's destinies; and the Southdown hunt followers, who have made many contributions to the kennels, such as a Dutch barn, extra heating apparatus and a refrigerated flesh-storage house.

Between 1960–72 that well-known Peterborough figure, Major R.E. Field-Marsham, assisted in the breeding of the Southdown, using Beaufort and Eridge sires. Now half the pack are from Badminton, which is explained by the fact that in 1972 Mr P.N. Whitley succeeded Mr Askew to join Major Shand in the Mastership: Mr Whitley's wife, Lady Mary (a joint-Master of the Brighton and Storrington Beagles), is a niece of the Duchess of Beaufort, whose

49 Major Bruce Shand with his daughter, Mrs Andrew Parker-Bowles, out with the Duke of Beaufort's. Major Shand was a joint-Master of the Southdown from 1956 to 1972.

husband, following two dismal Southdown breeding seasons (1971 and 1972), generously gave the hunt 12½ couple.

How much lighter are the Southdown now than 'Denis Milden's' bitches? Doubtless he would consider the modern foxhound rather harrier-like; but not if he was shown how difficult it is for it to wriggle through the present-day obstacles; and if he were to witness how – in such conditions and out only two days a week – they still catch an average of 35 brace a season under Roy Goddard who, in this his 14th season, recently accounted for his 1000th.

On alternate Wednesdays they hunt their rolling western country – between the river Adur and the London-Brighton road; other Wednesdays find them north-east of Lewes, and Saturdays in the vale between Haywards Heath and Hailsham. The Downs, which since Sassoon's time have lost much gorse and gained much plough, and an electric railway to boot, are for the autumn and the spring, or for soaking occasions, such as 25 January, when I should have hunted. That day the meet was changed from Ringmer to Firle, but, sadly, when it dawned, the Downs were too windy and fogbound to risk hunting.

They are still composed of more pasture than arable, and looking up towards them under the afternoon's clearing sky, with cloud shadow scudding over the grass, it was not difficult to empathise with the foxhunting poet, recalling October: '. . . The mornings I remember most zestfully were those which took us up to the chalk downs. To watch the day breaking from purple to dazzling gold while we trotted up a deep-rutted lane; to inhale the early freshness when we were on the sheep-cropped uplands; to stare back at the low country with its cock-crowing farms and mist-coiled waterways; thus to be riding out with a sense of spacious discovery – was it not something stolen from the lie-a-bed world? . . . I would be dragged out of my daydream by Denis when he shouted to me to wake up and get round to the far side of the covert; for on such hill days he often went straight to one of the big gorses without any formality of a meet. There were beech woods, too, in the folds of the Downs, and lovely they looked in the mellow sunshine, with summer's foliage falling in ever deepening rifts among their gnarled and mossy roots. . . .'

(January 1975)

Major Shand and Mr Whitley have since resigned from the Mastership, and their places have been taken by Mr H.J. Hecks (from 1975) and Capt. J. Harding (from 1977). Mrs C.A. Lee joined them in 1979.

The Surrey and North Sussex Beagles

BEAGLE EMIGRANTS FROM LONDON

During the second half of the eighteenth century and the first half of the nineteenth, the ancient pursuit of hunting hares with 'foothounds', a pursuit which had once provided the greatest in the land with their sport, was out of fashion. This was owing to the new enthusiasm for foxhunting, to the increased regard for the hare as a game animal; and, perhaps, to the attitudes of the likes of that stalwart of Surrey hunting, Mr Jorrocks ('Beagles! Quite little things in fact I doesn't know what to say about beagles. Be rather *infra dig*, wouldn't it?') Due to all these factors, the beagle declined as a hound type, he became diminutive and slow.

Then, during the middle of the nineteenth century, sportsmen such as Col. Thornton and the Rev. Philip Honywood, deploring this loss to the sporting world, bred something like the foxhound type of beagle we know today, and for those who did not insist on hunting by horse, their hounds showed magnificent sport. The centre of beagling's revival appears to have been north Surrey. One Victorian writer reckoned the number of beagle packs in England in 1862 did not exceed ten. And certainly at that time there were at least five hunting between Guildford in west Surrey and Bromley in north-west Kent.

Were there not photographs to support the fact, it would be rather difficult to imagine the pony traps and hacks converging for meets at Croydon and Kingston, alongside the walkers who had come by train from Redhill and Sutton, Victoria and Charing Cross; the men in their tight Norfolk jackets and leggings, the women in nicely tailored tweed coats, voluminous hats, multi-buttoned boots and layers of ankle-length skirts, tripping across the deep plough by Surbiton. Only the hunt staff, in green jackets and white breeches, bore much resemblance to the Surrey beaglers we know today. But the atmosphere of those photographs is just the same: the gaiety and high spirit of townspeople enjoying the salubrious freedom of their nearest countryside.

Up to the First World War, there were plenty of hares in what is now the southern half of Greater London. To the east, the Morden harriers, which were first recorded in 1834, used to meet at Tooting junction and the village of Streatham; sometimes their Master, Squire Heathcote, even made excursions north of the Thames; while the Epsom and Ewell beagles, who shared the Morden country, hunted with little restriction around Sutton and north Croydon. As late as the 1940s an Epsom resident could remember Squire Blake of the Worcester Park, which took over the Morden country, cheering his beagles after a long run, as they killed a hare under the walls of Wandsworth prison. W.G. Grace, the cricket giant, was a faithful follower of the Worcester Park and, with him as captain, the hunt entertained the farmers to an annual match against London County at the Crystal Palace. How 'W.G.' would mourn, if he came alive today, to see his beloved hunting country turned into a brick and concrete jungle.

The Buckland, the next pack of beagles on the east Surrey scene, were formed by Major F.W. Beaumont of Buckland Court, Reigate – a former Master of both the Eton and the New College – when he returned from the Boer War. It would not be easy now ever to envisage a repetition of Beaumont's famous seven-mile point as far afield as from Reigate to Holmwood, south of Dorking. By the early 1920s all these hunts lost so much country due to building that they became one hunt: the Worcester Park and Buckland.

A similar fate was in store for the beaglers of west Surrey. The Surbiton was founded by a most stubborn and irascible personality, Mr Rhodes Cobb, in order to keep members of his rowing club fit in winter, and it enjoyed long runs by Kingston and Wimbledon. It became the West Surrey in 1909. It is equally remarkable to remember that 60 years ago the Guildford and Shere dragged up to their hare across the wide open spaces between Byfleet and Leatherhead. The name of the Chertsey beagles, which became 'Mr Bailey's Foot Beagles' as early as 1896, was ominously changed again to 'the Horsell

Foot Beagles' when their kennels had to be moved down to Horsell. From all these hunts emerged 'the West Surrey and Horsell'.

Between the wars, by remorseless degrees, Surrey's three surviving hare-hunts, the Worcester Park and Buckland, the West Surrey and Horsell, and the Guildford and Shere, sought new country in south Surrey and north Sussex, areas once exclusive to mounted hunts. The Guildford and Shere had to be disbanded in 1939. Since the war, such death-traps have materialised as the roaring dual carriageways between London and Brighton, Worthing, Newhaven and Guildford, and the electrification of the main railways. The two remaining hunts not only had to contend with the sprawl of Greater London and agricultural intensification, but also with the growth of industrial estates, and the emergence of Gatwick airport and Crawley and Edenbridge new towns, and the thickening of shooting syndicates in this country of prosperous guns.

The outlook is unpromising: the country now faces the looming of the M23, the east-west M25, which will prevent every meet north of the present A25 which slices the northern territory between Guildford and Westerham; and, worst of all, the electrification of the Oxted-East Grinstead, Oxted-Tunbridge Wells and Redhill-Tonbridge lines.

Yet these were not the main considerations when the Worcester Park and Buckland and West Surrey and Horsell contracted two seasons ago to form Surrey's only surviving hare-hunt: the Surrey and North Sussex, with main centres at Reigate, Oxted, Guildford, Horsham and Haywards Heath. Illogically, this was prompted by an upsurge from the natural world: the proliferation of roe deer. These have colonised so thickly, particularly in the woodlands between Horsham and Guildford, as to deny huge tracts of land to the West Surrey. Anyone who has hunted hounds where deer roam prolifically, especially roe, know it is not worth the candle. The Surrey and North Sussex can scent roe most of the day from their kennels at Ifield Wood, near Crawley. And among the 30 to 40 hare pads nailed to a wall of those kennels is a roe foot: they pulled him down last season.

Theirs is a cold-scenting country. This applies as much to their southernmost territory as anywhere. When I saw them out at Staplefield, a few miles north-west of Haywards Heath, on 12 February, the ground was sopping wet from the previous night's storm and all agreed conditions should have been right for brisk hunting. The first two hours proved

50 Mr Rodney Cooper, the huntsman (*middle*) lifting hounds to a *holloa* when the author was following on 12 February 1972.

them mistaken: those very conditions induced the hares of Tyes Place, their first draw, to seek shelter in thick coverts nearby, not the sort of places that hares could be readily pushed through, and where their scent was disguised by the rabbits. At last one was put up by Sidnye Farm and hunted, via Toll Shaw, as far as Bigge's Farm. But here they threw up, and in spite of patient casting by the huntsman, Mr Rodney Cooper, they failed to rediscover the line, scent being thwarted, apparently, by the westerly wind.

The second hare, which was viewed along the north-east of Toll Shaw, was again lost in the wind. So Mr Cooper lifted them back to the plough at Sidnye. As they drew, a hare was spotted running in the next field. The wind had dropped now and so had the temperature, and when hounds were laid on, they fairly flew, not checking before they were foiled by sheep on the heavy ploughs south of Upper Sparks. It was a beautiful sight to watch them cast themselves after this check.

Mr Trevor Lloyd, a previous Master, who has had a lot to do with their breeding, made much use of that great hunter, Aldershot Farrier '55. Many others are out of a very useful dam, Shropshire Pleasure '63. And when they turned short of the Cuckfield-Warninglid road, then ran close and hard

with a fine chorus across Upper Sparks, one saw what obvious nose and drive such lines have given them. Their hare was now exhausted by the heavy plough and it was most exciting to come up to the crest at the end of this 43-minute run and see her bowled over next to the drive at Mizbrooks Farm.

This was a nice reward for the skill and patience of Mr Cooper, an amateur, who whipped in to the Worcester Park from 1963 and now carries the Surrey and North Sussex horn on Saturdays. The way these hounds go can be counted as a triumph, too, for Gordon Laing, the kennel-huntsman. His career has been mostly with foxhounds. It began in the stables and kennels of the Duke of Buccleuch's in 1949 and continued with the Berwickshire, the HH and the Thanet and Herne. He transferred to harehounds when he came to the Worcester Park in 1968.

What splendid recreation the joint-Masters, Gordon Laing, Mr Cooper and the three amateur whippers-in provide; beagling is, after all, largely a townspeople's sport, and for those of Surrey and North Sussex there can be few better ways of enjoying the countryside than a day out with their hunt.

(12 February 1972)

Mr R.S. Cooper and Mr B.E. Wilson joined the Mastership in 1978 and Messrs T.W. Merrick, M.F. Swinden, R.W.D. Hemingway and C. Barclay have been turning hounds to Mr Rodney Cooper since the article was written.

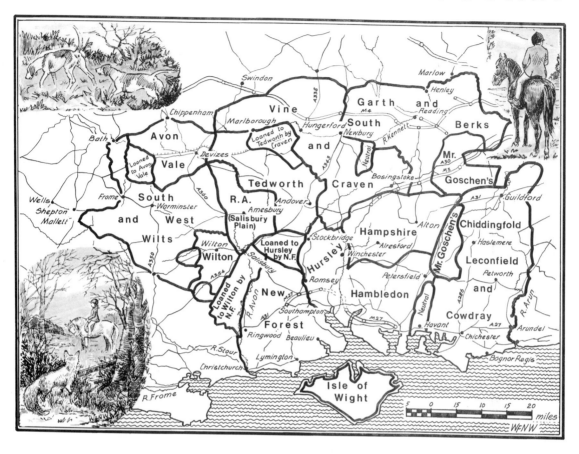

Swindon
Chippenham
Marlborough
Bath
Avon
Devizes
Loaned to Avon Vale
Vale
Wells
Shepton Mallett
Frome
Warminster
South
and
West
Wilts
A350
A360
R.A.
(Salisbury Plain)
Amesbury
Andover
Tedworth
Loaned to Tedworth by Craven
Vine
Garth and
Reading
Marlow
Henley
South
Hungerford
Newbury
and
Craven
R.Kennett
Neutral
A343
Basingstoke
Berks
Mr.
A30
M3
Goschen's
A31
Guildford
Chiddingfold
Haslemere
Alton
Alresford
Hampshire
Stockbridge
Winchester
Mr. Goschen's
Leconfield
Petworth
and
Wilton
Salisbury
Loaned to Hursley by N.F.
Hursley
Romsey
Petersfield
A286
R.Arun
Wilton
A354
Loaned to Wilton by N.F.
A31
R.Avon
New
M27
Southampton
M27
Hambledon
Neutral
Cowdray
A27
Arundel
Forest
Ringwood
Beaulieu
Havant
Chichester
R.Stour
Lymington
Bognor Regis
Christchurch
R.Frome
Isle of Wight
5   0   5   10   15   20
miles
W&NW

The Royal Artillery

GUNNERS TO HOUNDS

'Foxhunting is a kind of warfare' wrote Beckford 250 years ago, 'its uncertainties, its fatigues, its difficulties and its danger, rendering it interesting above all other diversions.' Eighty years later we have it from the pen of that cynical critic of the regular soldier, Surtees, through the mouth of Jorrocks, that ''unting is the sport of kings, the himage of war without its guilt and only five-and-twenty per cent of its danger.' Indeed warfare was always concomitant with the chase. And, following the Royal Artillery's hounds across Salisbury Plain on 8 April, one recalled how close the soldier's heart has always been to the hunting-field. The roots are very ancient. Ever since those days when human livelihood depended upon success in the chase, young leaders were selected from among the able hunters. For venery, it was held, brought out all the qualities of the fighting man: stamina and agility, cunning and personal initiative, courage and pride, the cultivation of an eye for country and the will to win.

When, two centuries ago, Hugo Meynell's development of the foxhound's drive to match his nose, coupled with the fresh impact of land enclosure, rendered the hunting-field England's most exciting arena, it became the sporting officer's chief peace-time domain. And not only in peace. To name only a few examples, Wellington's army of the Peninsula kept a three-day-a-week pack (hunted by the legendary Tom Crane who, sticking to his motto, 'where my foxes go, so do I', smartly ended up a prisoner of the French to the embarrassment of the 'Iron Duke'). These hounds were later presented to the garrison of Gibraltar and provided the basis of the Army-run Royal Calpe hunt. Over the years several regimental packs in India hunted jackal; in the Boer War the bobbery pack at Pretoria provided the prime source of officers' recreation; during the First World War every day officers in Flanders rallied their men by hunting horn, while in Salonika, Col. Railton hunted his pie-dog pack within a stone's throw of the enemy lines. In 1939 Major Selby-Lowndes took a pack of beagles with the BEF, while Lt. F.B. Edmeades, afterwards Master of the Royal Artillery Hunt, included harriers in his baggage (and was gaoled by the French civil authorities for hunting them). And no sooner did Hitler's war end than drafts of hounds found their way to three different kennels in Germany for the amusement and recreation of the British Army on the Rhine.

Field-Marshal Sir Evelyn Wood insisted that 'the British have one incalcuable advantage which no other nation possesses, in that our officers are able to hunt and than which, combined with study, there is, during peace, no better practice for acquiring the gift which Kellerman naturally possessed.' In *Pink and Scarlet*, published just before the First World War, General Alderson bids his reader to 'enquire how the young gunner learnt to tell at a glance that yonder hill should be a good position for his guns, and that there is most likely a cart track to it by those stacks. Say to him, "did the Shop or Shoeburyness teach you this?" In nine cases out of ten the young officer's answer is, "it comes naturally after having hunted a bit". . . .' The General then indulges in this splendid indignation: 'Some Commanding Officers are bad about hunting leave and will not be good about providing soldier grooms. This, I consider, proves them absolutely unfitted to command, for presumably they do not even know. what are the essential characteristics of a fighting officer.' Nor is this so very remote. Well after the last war, the author of this book, then a subaltern commanding a wing of a cavalry training regiment, who, besides being Master and huntsman of the regimental beagles, having a gun in a nearby syndicate and keeping one horse for three days' foxhunting a fortnight and another in training for point-to-points, was still asked by his sporting colonel, with all sincerity and incredulity, why he did not more regularly follow the local fell hounds. And, rightly, hunting leave and encouragement to hunt are still (when possible in these busy times) the order of the day in such horsed units as remain and in regiments of the armoured cavalry.

In the case of the Gunners, this spirit is fostered by an inheritance of unique value, one that is denied to the Cavalry of the Line: a mounted unit. The King's Troop, RHA (in fact, of battery strength), stationed at St John's Wood, London, not only enshrines all the old Horse Gunner tradition, symbolised in the prestige of 'the Jacket', but bestows on the Royal Artillery immense opportunities in the whole world of equitation and mounted sport. They have the King's Troop, and they have another asset – the only regimental pack of fox-

51 The hunt moving onto Salisbury Plain on 8 April 1972, the author's day out with them.

hounds left in the Army.

The hunt's history begins in 1907 when Capt. A.E. Hussey, MFH, handed over his sector of Salisbury Plain to the Royal Artillery garrison at Larkhill, and his officers promptly organised a pack of harriers to hunt it. These were put down on the outbreak of war, but in 1919 Mrs Hobart lent them the Isle of Wight harriers for one season. In 1920, with the help of the regimental sports fund, they bought in the Instow pack of West Country harriers and hunted hare very happily up to 1939 when all hounds were destroyed except seven couple. On wartime Salisbury Plain, the hunt casually diverted from hare to fox when the cavalry at Tidworth adopted the reduced pack and added five couple of foxhounds for good measure. In 1942 a battalion of the Parachute Regiment took this motley kennelful on strength, having two season's fun before handing them over to their rightful heirs in 1944.

But Major H.C.R. Gillman, RA, who became Master in 1950, was not at all happy with the amateurish breeding policy. He sought the advice of Sir Peter Farquhar, of the Portman, and of Major John Morrison (afterwards Lord Margadale) of the South and West Wilts, who presented him with six couple of high-quality bitches. And the first litter of the new Royal Artillery pack, which was by South Shropshire Prompter '47 out of the well-known South and West Wilts Dangle '45 (by Poacher '42 out of Middleton Villager '35), produced the 1954 Peterborough reserve champion, RA Daystar '52. They were then off to an excellent fresh start. And the year of that litter's entry saw the hunt officially registered by the MFHA. The Gunners had the good fortune not only to find a generous benefactor in Morrison and a capable pack architect in Gillman, but another gifted houndsman to take on the horn, one who contrived to remain in this station from 1954 till 1957 and again from 1961 to 1970: none other than Major F.B. Edmeades, the officer who in 1939 got locked up by the Gendarmerie for hunting French hares. He led the RA hunt to 60 kills in his first season and, on Gillman's foundations, maintained a pack that would be admired anywhere. He is also responsible for taking on the invaluable Taffy Austin, who is now completing his 12th season as kennel-huntsman.

For Mr Philip Holloway's meet at West Lavington Manor on windy 8 April, Col. Edmeades (now retired from the Army and about to assume joint-Mastership of Cornwall's Four Burrow) acted as Field Master to Lt-Col. P.R. Heaton-Ellis, a three-day event rider and former King's Troop commander, who took over the Mastership and the horn at the start of the present season. Such was the gale blowing that day that – although under the north lee

of the plateau of Salisbury Plain, we enjoyed three sharp runs in the morning, hounds marking the ground at Stibb Hill covert, Ram's Cliff and New Copse Down – conditions up on the Plain itself were nigh impossible. At 1.00 p.m. they picked up a fox on the edge of Candown gorse and raced him close and fast over Ball Down, but could make no more of him on Urchfont.

The long white-dried grasses of the chalky Plain made for good scenting, but on 8 April the 60 m.p.h. wind blew it to the heavens. Even in the thickest gorse coverts they could not wind him. To add to this confusion the almost completely open landscape was alive with hares. There were roe deer, too. And without this pack's carefully nurtured South and West Wilts breeding, instead of trying without pause as they did, they might well have rioted or jibbed at the conditions.

People are apt to think of Salisbury Plain as one big battlefield, torn and ugly; but although you must pick your way between shell-holes and avoid expended mortar bombs, and although the naked rolling landscape is a little marred by rusty gun and tank targets and red flags that warn you of angry artillery on the nextdoor ranges, nature heals abrasions inflicted on her surfaces very quickly, and the starkness and wildness of this sole large tract of uninhabited land in the south of England is still uniquely refreshing. How fitting it should remain a field of recreation for what is, perhaps, the Army's oldest traditional sport.

(8 April 1972)

Major C.D.B. Thatcher, RA, succeeded Col. Heaton-Ellis as Master and huntsman in 1978.

The Eton College Beagles

ACADEMY FOR FOXHUNTERS

It must have been a year or so after Pearl Harbor that two American corporals, one fat and bland, the other small and clerical, holding tourist guides as they wandered across Eton's football grounds and dreaming perhaps of military glory, approached us with: 'Say, can you guys show us just *where* the battle of Waterloo was won?' We were Lower Boys running to a meet of the school beagles; and instead of

treating the GIs to a sparse and prosaic history lesson, we might well have posed a truer, if less relevant claim than that attributed by the Iron Duke: that in shire and province alike, more feuds against fox and hare have been won on the *hunting* fields of Eton than anywhere else in the world.

For it has always been this belief in the school beagles as a training ground for foxhunters, prompting the exuberant *floreant canes Etonenses* spirit that has kept the institution vigorous for a century or more, in spite of great financial, territorial and prejudicial difficulties, and increasing competition in other fields of school sport. In 1917 the headmaster was bombarded with letters of protest after the hunt was disbanded on the advice of the local wartime food officer. 'Sir, now that hostilities have ceased,' ran one letter to the College *Chronicle* in 1918, 'ought not the Eton Beagles to be got together and start hunting again? . . . Very few boys have had much chance to learn anything about the sport of kings during the war, and the Eton Beagles have always been a nursery of a large number of Masters of hounds in this country. Yours truly, three ex-Masters and two ex-whips of the ECH.' The hunt was duly revived in 1919 and has not missed a season since.

It all began in the late 1850s when there were three private packs in the school, none of which were recognised by the Masters, all of which met secretly. The principal of these belonged to Edward Charrington, who, said a contemporary, 'loved a horse and who loved a hound, fond of music and fond of dancing, who spent every moment of daylight in cultivating the instincts of a clean country-bred Englishman.' R.E. Moore, an influential sixth-former, who took over Charrington's hounds in 1860, boldly applied for the headmaster's blessing, and thereafter beagling was an official sport at Eton. Meanwhile, a rival pack run by the Collegers or King's Scholars, which had started in 1857, was still not recognised, and when a terrified whipper-in was literally buttonholed in the College cloisters by E.C. Hawtrey, the Provost, and asked what 'ECH' on his buttons meant, the boy replied, 'your initials, sir!' And Hawtrey, an awesome figure, but susceptible to flattery, strode away beaming. But, disdainful of the authorities, the Collegers had a perfectly amicable agreement with the Oppidans (originally those who lived in the town and paid for their education, as opposed to the Collegers, who did not): the King's Scholars took the country east of the Slough road, the Oppidans the west. Then, in 1866, the hunts amalgamated.

But how they contrived to put in the long and successful runs recorded in the Journal Book is difficult to imagine. They had between morning school and lunch, afternoon school and evening chapel, and chapel and 'lock-up', never more than two hours at a stretch, including changing and long doubles to and from meets. A.J. Pound, the last Master of the College pack, hunted regularly after 7.30 school, breakfasting on 'beer and biscuits' at the Dolphin in Slough.

The Oppidans' kennels on Dorney Common were 'a miserable and ramshackle construction, and a bagged fox resided within earshot of the musical harmony of his relentless pursuers. Joby Minor, the most artful poacher in Eton, was kennel-huntsman. . . .' The College kennels situated at the playing fields and run by 'a rogue called Ward', who was to serve the amalgamated hunt, were only a slight improvement. It was Rowland Hunt, the brilliant crosscountry runner and Master in 1876, who persuaded the headmaster to have the hounds moved to a hut at the rear of the Turkish bath in Eton High Street. Here the proprietor, William Lock, who was 'short and fat and pig-headed, and rarely wore anything but a pair of scarlet bathing drawers', agreed to look after them as kennel-huntsman for £53 a year. This compromise lasted for 22 years – until the advent on the hunt staff of two very powerful personalities: the Grenfell twins, Francis and Riversdale.

Through personal appeals to Masters of Foxhounds and others, the Grenfells raised £1000, had the kennels at Datchet built and replaced Lock with the famous George Champion, great-uncle of Jack (Old Surrey) and Nimrod (Ledbury), and who himself came from the Zetland. The twins (who were to be pen-portrayed by John Buchan) also persuaded the school bursar, Mr R.S. de Havilland, to be treasurer. 'Having disposed of all last year's pack,' wrote Francis proudly in a letter to the *Chronicle*, 'I have bought an entirely new pack of hounds, $15\frac{1}{2}$ inches and very level.' Richard Howard-Vyse (son of the Master and owner of the Stoke Park beagles), who was Master in the 1901–2 season and had whipped-in to Francis, said of the brothers: 'they were the keenest fellows I have ever met; devoted really, but out beagling they cursed one another into heaps. . . .' Both were killed in the First World War, Francis winning the VC, Riversdale trying to equal the score.

From the Leadenhall market customers of the 1850s and 1860s onwards, Eton beaglers prized a fox above all. S.G. Menzies, who was Master in 1907–8, killed three and put two to ground. In one long hunt his quarry 'went into the Lower Master's garden, where he got under some logs; however, hounds pushed him out into Jordan and over the Field, eventually killing a full-grown cub in the fives courts after a very fast hunt of 30 minutes. Truly a triumph for beagles. Point of $2\frac{1}{2}$ miles.' Capt. Wallace, now chairman of the MFHA, as though foreshadowing his

52 The Eton College Hunt in 1877. Rowland Hunt (*middle*) moved the hounds into new kennels behind the Turkish bath in Eton High Street, where they remained until 1899. Hunt was afterwards Master of the Trinity Foot and then the Wheatland.

future career, killed 60 brace of hares and a fox in his first season (1936–7) and 75 brace and three foxes in his second. In 1967 M.R. Milburn took hounds to his Northumberland home where $21\frac{1}{2}$ brace of hares and six foxes were accounted for in 25 days.

But what a luxury Northumberland is, compared with the Windsor district. Soon after the First World War, with the spread of the Slough trading estate and the electrification of the Southern railway, all the land west of the kennels was rendered un-huntable, and the construction of the M4 meant the loss of a great deal more. Now the only local meets are at Boveney and the nearby Sanatorium, and the

best centres are as far afield as Winkfield, Ascot, Wokingham and Beaconsfield. But the ECH have many friends willing to organise areas outside their official country. Among these are the Flemings of Merrimoles, between Nettlebed and Henley-on-Thames, where hounds met on 3 March.

Crossing the Nettlebed-Reading road and proceeding over High Moor that afternoon they came up to Howberrywood Farm, and there their kennel-huntsman, Archie Jones – who follows in an unbroken tradition of long-serving and valuable kennel-huntsmen, since the Grenfells got in George Champion – *holloaed* away their hare. At first scent was excellent and hounds made the most stimulating music as we watched them streak north-west over the plough and bear right-handed through a larch plantation by English Farm; and with 30 boys who had come by bus, all with much the same message of

53 Approaching Howberry Farm, Oxfordshire when the author joined them on 3 March 1973. Wearing the hunt's brown velvet coats are (*left to right*) Archie Jones, kennel-huntsman; O. Williams, field Master; A.J. Sparrow, Master and huntsman; J.H.R. Manners, second whipper-in and T.H. Birch-Reynardson, third whipper-in. The first whipper-in was then W.D. Floyd.

speculation ('they're sure to catch her now!'), following the pack's circle on their tighter ring. These were the hounds of Eton Miner '36 stock and of the celebrated line of Woodman '45, and with their tenacity they certainly showed it. Their hare was headed away from the Henley road and scent was fainter now as she returned along the side of Joyce Grove and Swan's Wood to Howberrywood, stopped a moment, then jumped up in front of hounds by the farm.

On they ran through Nott Wood, steeply uphill to the larch plantation, twice round that and on to English Farm, where they lost her among fresh hares. But there was anything but a waning of enthusiasm on the part of the field, indeed there was a strongly noticeable reluctance to retrace steps for the bus. Although the hare is still just the quarry for training potential foxhunters, alas, at Eton, with a

bus to catch, she no longer provides an excuse for getting back late for lock-up.

(3 March 1973)

Among the names of those who were Masters, huntsmen and whippers-in and have since become famous as Masters of Foxhounds are: the Earl of Halifax (joint-Master, 1930–31); The Duke of Northumberland (Master, 1931–2); Capt. R.E. Wallace (Master, 1936–8); Sir Hugh Arbuthnot (Master, 1939–40); the Duke of Beaufort (whipper-in, 1917); Major G.A. Gundry (joint-Master, 1930–31); Capt. C.G.E. Barclay (whipper-in, 1937–8); and Capt. S.T. Clarke (Master, 1953–4).

The Hon. J.H.R. Manners and T.H. Birch-Reynardson were Masters during the season of my visit. The following have since worn the cap: Mr J.A. Gold (1975–6); Mr C.W. Smyth-Osbourne and Mr M.P. St Aubyn (1976–7); Mr R.C. Soames, Mr H.T. Holland-Hibbert, Mr E.A. Tarlton and Mr G.N.J. Willoughby (1977–8); and Mr T.R.G. Vestey (1978–80). Mr J. Vestey and Mr R. St Aubyn (1979–80); and Mr J.R.B. Moore and Mr J.H.R. Warburton-Lee (1980–81).

B. Maiden succeeded A. Jones as Huntsman in 1979.

The Garth and South Berks

ADJACENT HUNTS REUNITED

Nimrod took a jaundiced, not to say desperate view of the Garth country: 'It partakes of a sort of Cimmerian darkness,' he warned; 'the follower must beware of its sands and clays, bogs and heath, its immense fuel hedges, deep blind ditches, and bad foxes. . . .' and Mr T.C. Garth himself, who was Master for half a century (1852–1902), complained: 'it is these awful plaguey holes in the heath which throw a horse down'. But whatever the hazards of the Berkshire going, Garth supporters have always been particularly proud of their territory, so that the Victorian subscriber who enthused with 'these hounds hunt an historic country and awake the woodland echoes once roused by many a Plantagenet knight or Norman king', seems to be a more typical observer. Indeed, nostalgia flows through much of what has been written of this hunt. Charles Kingsley injected some of his sentiments as a Garth follower into the *Lay to the Brave North-Easter*:

Chime ye dappled darlings through the sleet and snow
Who can over-ride you? Let the horses go.
Chime ye dappled darlings down the roaring blast
Ye shall see a fox die, ere an hour be past. . . .

The Garth are proud, too, of their century and a half tradition, which began with the Rev. Henry Ellis St John, who purchased the Duke of Bridgewater's hounds to hunt the country in 1810. Seven years later this sporting vicar of Finchampstead sold his hounds to Sir John Cope, of Bramshill. Then, in 1843, Sir John (who enjoyed 33 years' Mastership) relinquished a portion of his country to Mortimer George Thoyts, of Sulhamstead, who thus founded the South Berks. But that was only a temporary splinter. In 1850 Cope gave his hounds to the country, Mr Wheble taking over the South Berks area.

The year 1852, which marked the start of Garth's great career, saw the official division of the country and also, apparently, a good deal of that emotional fever that so often occurs when anything unpopular happens to hunt boundaries. 'It was not without some trouble and heart-burnings that the country was divided', runs a diary entry of the Rev. P.H. Ditchfield, 'and even a challenge to a duel was sent by an irascible member of Mr Garth's hunt to a brother sportsman in the south, the challenger being forced to cool his heels on the Continent till the excitement passed. But the quarrel was settled by arbitration and the said irascible gentleman was obliged to make an apology.'

There may have been some disagreement over the manner in which Sir John Cope's hounds were distributed; or, perhaps, jealousy on the part of the South Berks, who claimed more ancient lineage. For, like the Craven, they are descended from the celebrated Yattendon Hunt Club, and Mr G. Thoyts had succeeded to their Mastership from Mr Poyntz, of Newbury who, as a Yattendon member, had taken over the South Berks sector as far back as 1780.

Edward VII was a faithful subscriber and attendant at Garth meets, and his brother-in-law, Prince Christian of Schleswig-Holstein, the Warden of Windsor Park, was said to be 'one of the hardest going riders we have'. Such grandeur and *élan* attracted large fields and, as one Edwardian remarked: 'Reading is a well-to-do and popular centre, many residents keeping hunters there, and gentlemen who live in London are enabled, by the Great Western train service, to appear at the best meets without the objection of early rising on dark and bleak winter mornings.'

At the time the South Berks was flourishing under the Mastership of C.E. Palmer and Cecil Aldin, the artist, the Garth had the good fortune to follow Mr R.H. Gosling (1902–19), a widely acknowledged hound expert who went largely to the Beaufort and the Puckeridge for his breeding, laying a much respected foundation at the kennels at Bracknell. It was the combination of this pack and the skill of Wyndham Daniels, their huntsman for 28 years, that gave the Garth such a high reputation between the wars. And yet, when the two hunts reunited in 1962, it was the South Berks, whose breeding prospered so well under Col. Rodney Palmer, that provided 90 per cent of the pack, when the new kennels were built at Mortimer.

Such a merger had seemed quite natural to many people (not least the Palmer family, whose influence was strong in both camps) a long time before. Miss Effie Barker, a Garth Master for 28 seasons (who remembers being 'blooded' by Wyndham Daniels as far back as 1922), recalls her father discussing a possible amalgamation under the name 'Bramshill hunt', with Mr Guy Hargreaves of the South Berks

in the 1920s. Eventually it was the growth of the new town of Bracknell after the last war, coupled with road development, that clinched the alliance. Now the joint area comprises a fair balance of arable and grass, 30 miles by 20, the bulk of which is divided between the Stratfield Saye and Englefield estates, the hunt being duly grateful to the generous support given by Lord Douro and Mr William Benyon, the respective landowners.

Last Saturday, 9 January, over 100 followers – delighted to be out again after the fortnight's frost – met Dennis Boyles, the huntsman, with the bitches at Stratfield Saye. The field included Miss Effie Barker, the Hon. Mrs Nicholas Villiers, who shares responsibilities with Major David Black, the Master, and Capt. Robert Campbell who is due to take over as joint-Master and huntsman next season. At 11.30 a.m. Boyles led his $19\frac{1}{2}$ couples of bitches to Misselbury Copse, and, the ground being extremely soft, Major Black spoke firmly to the field at the first covertside about the vulnerability of the farmland.

At 11.45, one of the brace of foxes found at Misselbury was closely pursued across the grassy Devil's Highway, but was headed by a car at the Little Brick Kiln. Hunting more slowly, hounds now ran him left-handed through Smith's Copse, over Perrin's Farm and into a drain on Mr Froom's Little Park Farm. A strong breeze was up, scent got worse after midday and little could be made either of the second brace that were found in Hasker's, by Butler's Land, or of the next fox that was hunted up from Tubb's Galley to Southend Farm.

It was the last fox of the day that gave the real sport, although only 15 followers stayed to honour him. Scent picked up again, and at 2.45 p.m., after finding in a patch of kale by the church in Stratfield Saye Park, hounds ran with great zest through the park, down the Pheasantry and across the Devil's Highway, checking at Perrin's Farm. Now – significantly led by Daylight (out of their Dabchick '59 by Playmate '61, both Peterborough award winners), and Pleasant (a wonderfully sharp bitch of Old Berks breeding) – they coursed very swiftly and close huddled below Beech Hill village, pushing him several times around the neighbouring copses, but eventually losing him among the houses, where he had to be given best. This was a hunt of some two hours, and six miles as hounds ran, and only half a dozen followers riding well-spent horses were left to hear Dennis Boyles sound 'home'.

54 Mr T.C. Garth. He took over 'Mr Garth's country' from Mr Wheble in 1852.

55 At a children's meet of the Garth at Newlands, Arborfield Cross in January 1938. Mrs Simonds advises.

Sir John Cope of Bramshill, in Victorian Berkshire, would have approved of the way hounds ran across his old country last Saturday. He would indeed approve, too, of the happy reunification of these two hunts.

(9 January 1971)

Capt. R.A. Campbell joined Major Black in the Mastership that summer. Capt. Campbell, carrying the horn, continued to act as Master on the committee's behalf from 1973 (when Major Black retired) until 1976. Major Black then formed a new joint-Mastership with Mr G.J.G. Luck. Messrs N.D. Best and G.W. Freeman then made up a Quaternity for the 1978–9 season, after which Major Black and Mr Luck retired, but stayed on as Chairman and Vice-Chairman, respectively. The new joint-Mastership, first appointed in 1978, consists of Messrs G.W. Freeman, N.D. Best and J.W.M. Maunder.

Ian Langrishe, who took over the kennels from Dennis Boyles in 1971, has hunted hounds since 1976.

56 Capt. Robert Campbell. He was acting joint-Master, or Master, and huntsman from 1973 to 1976.

The Hambledon

THE BEST COUNTRY SOUTH OF LONDON?

Preparing this account of the Hambledon just a week after my Atherstone visit, I wondered for a moment why, a century and a half or so ago, some of the great names of Leicestershire kept bobbing up again in this south-east corner of Hampshire: John Cook, Squire Osbaldeston, Bellingham Graham and Tom ('all-round-my-hat-cast') Smith. Was it simply because their money ran out? Or does Gêlert give us the answer? 'The Hambledon is considered to be the best country south of London', he wrote for *Fores' Guide*, in 1850; 'round Waltham Chace and Durley there is plenty of grass; the foxes fly, and the sport is undeniable.'

In fact, with its thin layer of soil over chalk, it never was a brilliant scenting country, and much of it is dreadfully built up; but there is still lots of pasture and ample, thick-bottomed coverts. The plough is light, too, and although this is one of the most intensive pheasant-shooting areas of Britain, there are sufficient foxes. Indeed, as I witnessed on Saturday, 22 November, it is a very sporting country, and Gêlert's verdict could be readily repeated today.

About 70 of us met at Ashton Farm, near Bishop's Waltham, home of Mr John Loader, the hunt chairman (who is unfortunately out of action owing to a fall). With a sparkling sun doing wonders on the last autumn leaf, but not so much for the prospects of scent, we followed the senior joint-Master and huntsman, Col. Frank Mitchell, and his hounds south-west towards the celebrated Durley region and the first draw, a jungle of sallow called Wintershill. Here, with the most impressive co-operation between Col. Mitchell and his mercurial kennel-huntsman and first whipper-in, Douglas Hunt, from the brace and a half foxes roused, hounds forced one away, which led them west, behind the Alma Inn, near Upham, then slowly through Moplands to Greenwood.

He circled inside this covert several times, hounds tight on his brush, then left at his point of entry; and giving us lovely views of the pack, and some good timber jumping too, pointed on across the fields to Park Hills, where he tried a main earth, but found it stopped. On he fled, left-handed through Hall Lands, turning short of the Gore, and finally to Fairoak Sandpit, where he was accounted for at 1.30: a great two-hour run, and horses and riders very hot.

That then is the brand of south-east Hampshire sport, which those nineteenth-century flyers of the shires heard so much about. Where did it all begin? A Mr Land appears to have been the pioneer of foxhunting around Hambledon in the 1780s; then, in 1880, Mr T. Butler was engaged to collect a pack of 'not more than 30 couple nor less than 20 couple' (Aesop quotes the minutes in *Sporting Reminiscences of Hampshire*) '. . . no weather should stop the hounds going out to the meet, unless the snow should be one foot deep at the kennel door . . . the hounds to be at the cover at 9 o'clock from the 10th of October to the 5th April. . . . The hunt to dine monthly during the season,' and (to spite Napoleon) 'no French wines are to be called for on the forfeiture of £5.'

John Cook, major of light dragoons, author of *Observations on Foxhunting* and a native of Christchurch, Hampshire, who was to make such a name for himself in the Midlands and East Anglia, now put in his two seasons (1804–6), and really placed the Hambledon on the map. Seven Masterships later – after de Burgh, Powlett Powlett, Delmé Eyles, Richards and Nunez – came grand Bellingham Graham from the Pytchley, commenting, when told that the guarantee was only £700, that 'it will hardly pay for my spur leathers'. Osbaldeston, with his dashing whippers-in, Sebright and Burton, was next to be lured from the Shires. But, according to Brig-Gen. Hope, in *History of Hunting in Hampshire*, 'foxes were scarce, and his hounds were too fast for a plough country, being used to Leicestershire grass.'

After another two short commands – Walker (1822–3) and Shard (1823–4) – came the great Tom Smith, whose career went confusingly parallel to that of Thomas Assheton Smith (of Quorn and Tedworth renown). Although these were early days for 'Gentleman' (or later, 'Craven') Smith, we smile to hear Nimrod's condescension: 'Mr Smith will make a good huntsman with a little more experience . . . I may go so far as to say he has proved himself worthy of the support of the country.' 'Scrutator' (*Recollections of a Foxhunter*), taking a closer look at him, observed: 'I have seen him, when the scent failed, doing the work hounds ought to have done, through his extraordinary knowledge of the running and wily movements of the animals he

57 Lt-Col. Frank Mitchell. He was a joint-Master from 1960 until the hunt's amalgamation with the Hursley in 1978.

was pursuing.'

In 1829 John King – 'King of the West' – began his immensely popular 12-year Mastership and Delmé Radcliffe, author of *The Noble Science* and honorary secretary of the newly resurrected Hambledon Hunt Club, echoed the praise his hounds always won:

. . . Not a fault to be found with so splendid a pack
As the bitches of King, nor for tongue do they lack. . . .

Walter Long, of Preshaw Hall, coming after him, had three Masterships (1841–8, 1856–9 and 1872–4), with Tom Smith's second tour, Capt. Powlett's, Col. Bower's and Capt. Sullivan's in between. Bower, who was blooded in the year of Waterloo and hunted a short-tailed cob to the age of 90, was fondly known as 'The Father of the Hunt'. Walter Long, Jr. took over in 1874, and T.W. Harvey in 1889. Then the Hon. Frederick Baring, upon whose resignation in 1900 it was found more convenient to divide the country into 'East' and 'West', the western half going to Capt. William Standish, who was in turn responsible for the reunification seven years later. He remained at the helm until 1915, when Mr Sam Hardy joined him and they were joint-Masters until 1921.

It was after ten years with the Kildare that Major Talbot-Ponsonby took the Master's cap and the horn, in 1926, hence Hope's comment that 'he found the cold-scenting conditions and big woodlands were very different from small Irish gorses and sound pastures'. Major Jack Blake, who had been 'the most efficient honorary secretary', succeeded Talbot-Ponsonby, with two well-known hunt servants in support: George Tongue and Walter Gupwell (father of Brian, the Duke of Beaufort's huntsman). Hounds were evacuated to the North Cornwall kennels in 1941 and to the HH in 1944; and the man who revived the Hambledon in 1945 was Capt. Paul Vivian, RN, whose apprenticeship had been with a service pack at Havant during the war.

Col. Mitchell's experience goes much deeper than that, for he has hunted in Hampshire since he was a boy, and is a former Master and huntsman of the Vine and field Master of the HH. It was 16 seasons ago that he and his wife took over the Hambledon from Mr and Mrs Muirhead. Mrs Mitchell – a sister of Mr Stewart Tory, of the Portman – stood down in 1971 because of her 'riding back', and Mr Michael Poland, who used to carry the Aldershot beagles' horn, came in as joint-Master the following season. He is responsible for the hound-breeding which, for the past 25 years, has been based on the Portman blood of Sir Peter Farquhar's time, with recent outcrosses from the New Forest Welsh element and the Duke of Beaufort's.

On 22 November I saw these hounds well and truly tested by their afternoon foxes. Owing to the late harvest of rape seed, Mincingfield Wood was not drawn during cubhunting, so the litter put on foot there at 2.00 p.m. did not know the meaning of straight flight.

Just as the selected quarry escaped to an earth by Durley Mill at 2.20, a *holloa* from behind recalled hounds to Mincingfield, so they hunted a second one from that 'green' litter. He described a remarkably devious course, making two or three large circles round Nether Hill, Durley Manor and Durley Sawmill, and, after switching direction many times, climbed the slope from an old flour mill to a big stand of cupressus by Calcot House where at 3.30, to everyone's delight, hounds were duly rewarded for their pertinacity and intelligence. And there Col. Mitchell blew 'home'.

During the unexpectedly exciting day one could not fail to notice the Hambledon's splendid aura of confidence and stability, qualities which are duly valued by the hunt's well-contented host of subscribers. Let us hope that in the field, in the kennels and at the committee table, their present regime continues for many seasons to come.

(22 November 1975)

The Hambledon amalgamated with the Hursley, prior to the 1978–9 season, as the Hursley Hambledon. The Mastership of the new hunt was made up of Messrs L.M. Olden, R.L. Trigg, T.W. Parker and M.D. Poland. Douglas Hunt continued to carry the horn, and, during his first season under the amalgamation, killed 50 brace of foxes.

The whole of the area described in the first hunt of the article was later placed out of bounds to the Hambledon by Marwell Zoo.

The Isle of Wight Foot Beagles

HAREHOUNDS FOR ISLANDERS

Thousands of people ferry the Solent each summer for a day or a weekend simply to walk the Isle of Wight's ancient trails and paths, to gaze from the cliffs to the Channel and back over the Straits to Hampshire, and to view, from the rolling downland, the wooded and grassy combes with their diverse colours thrown up by Wight's luxurious soil. *All this Beauty is of God* goes the Island's motto; and, although you do not see the hikers on the boats between November and February, the winter holds another beauty, and there is another way to enjoy it – by spending an afternoon with the Isle of Wight Foot Beagles, as I did on 4 January.

That Saturday, the foxhounds met at 11.00 a.m.

at eighteenth-century Palladian Gatcombe House, three miles south of the capital, Newport, and at 1.00 p.m. their host, Sir Robert Hobart, was out again to welcome the beaglers, who made more than the customary contrast to their mounted associates. The Islanders are proudly independent; their island is a county in its own right; they have always wished to remain distinct from the mainlanders, or the Overners, as they call them. From the mainland beagles, too: no hard velvet caps or starchy white stocks for them, but green garberdine deerstalkers, with white shirts and British Field Sports Society ties.

Their hounds are also different: not more than 13 inches at the shoulder; their backs scarcely come

58 The Beagles soon after they were re-formed in the 1920s. *Left to right*: Mr (later Lt-Col.) Francis Mew, and Miss Mew (joint-Masters) and Albert Mason (huntsman). Col. Mew is President of the Masters of Harriers and Beagles Association.

level with their huntsman's lower calf. Concise at every point, they remind you of Parson Honywood's miniatures in *The Merry Beaglers*. The senior joint-Master, Lt-Col. Francis Mew, who has bred these midgets, argues, reasonably, that their slower pace allows the followers to witness more sport: 'As one grows older and slower, there is little pleasure in seeing hounds find and then not seeing them again for half an hour. And, if they have thrown up,' he adds, 'how can the huntsman know the critical place when he has been outrun? After all a beagle hunts a hare by scent until it overtakes it.

If hounds are too fast, this cannot happen, and one might as well go on horse-back and take to harriers.' Except for the presence of what Col. Mew calls his 'fluffies' – two couples of IWFB beagles crossed with 12-inch rough-haired Vendéen bassets – this is a level and delightfully well-matched pack. The size of the hounds does not much inhibit their power to overhaul hares.

The IWFB had Col. Mew first at the helm half a century ago when he was 21, and, indirectly, it was his father, Francis Templeman Mew, who began it all. For when, in 1906, F.T. Mew disbanded his private harrier pack, which he had founded in 1888 with the help of Mr Seymour Pittis, of Hale, the Island would have been bereft of hare-hounds, had not Henry Young proposed to fill the gap with beagles. The Youngs, like the Mews, were one of the Island's oldest sporting families. Deputy Master of the Island Foxhounds, Henry was the son of the honorary secretary of that hunt, whom *British Hunts and Huntsmen* described as 'the doyen of hunting in the Island. . . . He commenced with the pack in 1853 and has not missed a single season since'.

Henry Young leaves on record the birth of the IWFB: 'It was in October, 1906, about the time that Mr Frank Mew was giving up his harriers, that I advertised for $14\frac{1}{2}$ inch beagles. Then, one afternoon in November, a landau pulled up at my yard gate, and out got the occupant, followed by $6\frac{1}{2}$ couple of beagles. So, on January 10, 1907, I started off to go to Hale, complete with $9\frac{1}{2}$ couple and kennelman. We soon found hounds packing very well for a 45-minute hunt. . . .'

My Saturday broke with such a heavy dew that even by midday the sun had made little impression on the drenched meadows, which lent a quality of intense sparkle to a landscape that is anyhow celebrated for its soft-bright hues and dramatic contrasts of light and shadow. No fewer than 75 of us were out to relish it. First they drew the plough below Hill Farm; and, from our dominating position on the ridge, we could see the Hampshire coast, the river Medina flowing less than three miles away and into Newport, and, closer still, the walls of Carisbrooke Castle. There had been hares on the Isle of Wight for less than 80 years when Charles I was imprisoned there, before his last sad journey to Whitehall. 'There was not a hare in our Island until Sir Edward Horsey was Captain of the Island in 1574,' wrote Sir John Oglander in 1632; 'at what time Sir Edward procured many from his friends to be brought in alive, and proclaimed that, whosoever should bring in a live hare, would have a lamb for him; by his care the Island was stored. We had infinite of coneys, but not one hare, and I wish his successors may be as careful in preserving them as he was in first storing.'

Nor would Sir John complain on that score now. Starting from Garsten, the first pointed her head to Hill Farm, but, being turned back by some late arrivals, she skirted the little copse behind the foxhound kennels, returned almost to her form, and continued across the valley to Barkham Wood, then on to lofty Dukem Down, where hounds checked, with nearly everyone there to see them do it.

The IWFB has given immense fun over its span of 70 years, to a very varied host, besides the Islanders. To quote one example: soon after Edward VII endowed Osborne on the nation, and it became a

naval school, many cadets came out with Young's beagles as well as with the bassets, lent them by Lord North. When war broke out in 1914, Young disbanded his kennels, but a few were put out to walk, and a cadet battalion, stationed at Parkhurst, then enjoyed fine sport with them. Young tells how, at the end of the war, the cadet battalion moved and left the pack to the garrison battalion, the Munster Fusiliers, and soon how 'their place was most fortunately taken by the Royal Irish Rifles, a very kindly and sporting regiment, who hunted the country without subscription during the four years they were stationed on the Island. . . . When they moved to Germany, in 1922, the Rifles took the hounds with them.'

It was in the following autumn that Col. Mew, then a Cambridge undergraduate, stepped in. He and his sister collected beagles from the Christ Church, Lord Portman's, the Farley Hill and Major Birkbeck's, to form a fresh pack. Col. Mew told me that by the early thirties this had become very level and was hunting well, but that in the spring of 1939 an epidemic of gastro-enteritis devastated the kennels. And so ended another era, for there was then no more harehunting on the island until that famous MFH, the late Mr Arthur Dalgety, brought his beagles with him, when he became Master of the Isle of Wight foxhounds in 1955. He hunted both quarries until he left in 1960, taking his beagles with him. Then, at the request of many residents with happy hunting memories, Col. Mew and Mr Denys Danby, the leading veterinary surgeon, collected hounds from all over England – the Aldershot and the Castleton were the largest contributors – to form the basis of the pack we know today, which has hunted right across the Island ever since. On Mr Danby's death in 1968, Major-General R.A. Pigot joined Col. Mew as joint-Master.

Gen. Pigot said that although the IWFB hounds were lost in 1943 (the famous Gaiety line irrevocably), they were fortunate in being given Royal Rock Frolic, who was tail female descendant of the Isle of Wight Pamela; also Newcastle and District Ranger, who was tail male descendant of Isle of Wight Garnet. So they did get back one of their breeding lines.

After checking on the downs above Barkham, these unique little hounds soon recovered the line and hunted her through Dukem copse and – showing a lovely musical streak of white on the sheep pastures – on as far as Westridge Down, where scent expired, to end a 50-minute run. Returning to Garston Farm, they immediately found again, hunting in view of the field up to Bowcombe and back on

59 Hounds at Gatcombe House, when the author joined them on 4 January 1975. *Left to right*: Lt-Col. P.S. Mitcheson (hon. secretary), Jim Brodie (kennel huntsman and second whipper-in), Sir Robert Hobart Bt, Teddy Kennett (huntsman), Lt-Col. F.J.T. Mew (joint-Master), Major-Gen. (now Sir) R.A. Pigot (joint-Master), Peter Stevens (whipper-in) and Harry Kennett (first whipper-in).

to the heavy plough beyond Barkham, where they gave her best after a further 25 minutes. Nor was that all. Their huntsman, Teddy Kennett, then cheered them into the roots by Froglands to make a double figure-of-eight around Lukely Brook, before blowing 'home' in the twilight at Plaish. 'All England in miniature' – that is what they call the Isle of Wight. To own a largely unspoilt and very varied hunt country of 155 square miles, whose boundary is the sea, plenty of hares and a pack of hounds that can stay with their quarry and yet not lose their field – what more could a close-knit beagling fraternity such as this possibly ask for?

(4 January 1975)

The South-West

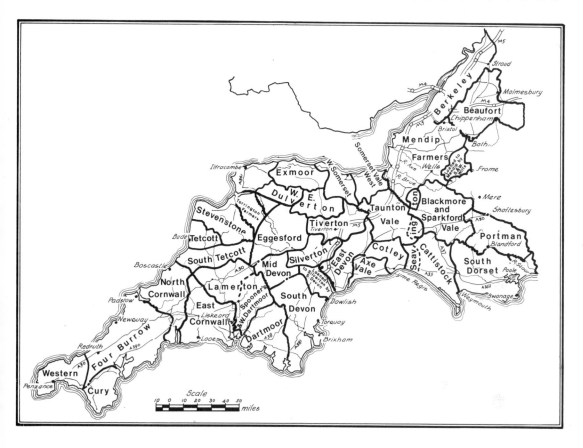

The Cattistock

A TRADITION OF FINE AMATEURS

Hunting with the Cattistock from their Corscombe meet on 26 January, I had hoped for a still, crisp day in this rolling country of sheep and cattle pasture, and a sight of one of Britain's most gifted amateur huntsmen in control: Major Michael MacEwan. But we got neither: driven by a 40 m.p.h. wind, the rain fairly lashed at one's eyes for most of the day, while foxes preferred to stay in covert. As for Major MacEwan, he was suffering from a heavy fall, incurred the previous Wednesday, and could only limp to Corscombe, so David Goring, who is now in his fifth season as kennel-huntsman and first whipper-in, was hunting hounds.

MacEwan's misfortune reminded me that the man who began the Cattistock's remarkably long and consistent record of successful Master-huntsman combinations was killed after his horse rolled on him under a wattle-topped bank in 1885: the 7th Earl of Guilford. But this, of course, was later on in the hunt's history. For the heritage of the Cattistock stems, like that of all the Dorset hunts, from the medieval spirit of the ancient hunting forest of Cranborne Chase; then from Thomas Fownes, of Steepleton, who established around 1730, what an early edition of *The Sporting Magazine* described as 'the first real steady pack of foxhounds in the Western part of England', and who sold his house and kennels to Julines Beckford, Peter's father. While Peter Beckford developed in east Dorset the knowledge that was to make him so famous, the Rev. J. Phelips, of Montacute, established a pack at Cattistock Lodge, calling his hunt 'The True Blue', and was followed in that country by Mr Chaffyn Grove, MP for Weymouth.

Then came Beckford's great protégé, James John Farquharson, who from 1806 to 1856 embraced the whole of Dorset, and corners of Somerset and Wiltshire, in his foxhunting empire, hunting the bulk of that country from his home, Eastbury, with kennels at Cattistock – as Thomas Fownes had done – to serve his western meets.

Farquharson's Dorsetshire hunt finally broke up under impatient pressure from such sporting landowners as Sawbridge Erle Drax, Lord Portman and G.D. Wingfield Digby, while 'the Squire's lower country', as the Cattistock was called – roughly the area of Dorset west of the line Dorchester-Yeovil – was taken over by Lord Poltimore. Pupil and friend of those two great West Country foxhunters, Lord Portsmouth and Jack Russell, Poltimore had assumed the Mastership of Parson Hole's North Devon hounds in 1856. With kennels at Cattistock and John Evans as huntsman, between 1860 and 1872 he gradually hunted more in Dorset and less in Devon, establishing the Cattistock country as it is today. When he resigned, the hunt went subscription, Mr John Codrington being, in 1872, the first Master appointed by a committee.

When Lord Guilford succeeded Codrington, he had already completed nine seasons as Master and huntsman of the East Kent, and because he was at once popular, dashing and experienced, the Cattistock subscribers immediately took to the idea of an amateur and, after the two one-season Masterships that followed, their committee agreed that 19-stone Reginald Chandos-Pole should carry the horn when he took over. Chandos-Pole came from the Meynell, which he had hunted since 1881, and, according to an Edwardian chronicler, 'brought in an era of great prosperity . . . "Candy" Pole bought the Blankney dog-hounds, and made three packs for use in the Cattistock kennels; he did things *en prince*, was an ideal horseman in spite of his welter weight, and rode some of the most beautiful cattle (three *per diem*). . . .' Successful as he was, however, Chandos-Pole took his hounds back to Derbyshire after nine seasons, and John Hargreaves, the next 'gentleman huntsman' on the scene (under whom, incidentally, the present kennels were built in 1897), left for the Blackmore Vale after only three.

For the first 30 years of this century the Cattistock was blessed with its longest and most famous holder of that joint office: the Rev. 'Jack' Milne, a former Master of the Trinity Beagles, who went on in the 1890s to found and hunt the North Bucks Harriers. At the start of his term in Dorset, Milne combined his parish duties with those of a two-day-a-week Master and huntsman quite smoothly, but his hitherto indulgent Bishop got restive when the vicar progressed to a four-day hunting week: 'It has come to the point, Milne, where you must either give up hunting, or give up the Church'. Milne was no ditherer: 'It will be the Church, my Lord!'

Not content even with four days, Parson Milne formed three packs, and his friend, W.F. Fuller, who followed him on from the North Bucks Harriers, and

60 The joint-Masters in 1930: Mr A.H. Higginson and (*right*) Parson Milne, who hunted hounds from 1900, not retiring until 1931.

who, as Col. Fuller, was later to make such a name for himself with the VWH (Cricklade), hunted the Cattistock the other two weekdays. Between 1926 and 1930, Milne made the same arrangement with Major Lord Digby, and Britain's foxhunting farmers may owe these two the special status since accorded to their profession, for the joint-Masters introduced the novelty of allowing 43 especially selected farmers to wear the velvet cap and black hunt button.

Parson Jack, who was said to have accounted for 7882 foxes in 31 seasons, was a great breeder of hounds and the winner of many prizes on the flags at Peterborough and other shows; but as a votary of the conventional 'Belvoir Tan', he was sad when that sporting anglophile, A.H. Higginson, who had just completed 17 years as President of the United States, MFHA, and who took over the joint-Mastership from Lord Digby in 1930, turned out to be a 'Welsh enthusiast'. Up to 1938 Higginson hunted the bitches, with a professional taking the dog-hounds.

Col. H.C. Batten (1938–50), who carried the 'amateur tradition' into the post-war era, was Milne's son-in-law, while Mr Edward Gundry, who succeeded him, was the parson's grandson. They were followed by another well-known huntsman, Major Bobby Peel (1957–61), who brought along a number of his own bitches from the South Dorset, which established Salesman '44 predominance in the Cattistock kennels, and also a fresh infusion of Welsh blood through Carmarthenshire Denton. Lt-Col. J.E. Spencer (1961–3), whose joint-Master was Sir S.G. Hammick, the present field Master, and Lt-Cdr. Oram (1963–5) were next to carry the horn. Major MacEwan's entrée was to hunt the bitches during the first season, while Oram hunted the dog-hounds.

Sole huntsman and breeder of the pack for eight seasons now, he has used Badminton and Heythrop strains, the Duke's Porcelain '63 and Beadle '66 and the Heythrop Carver '63 being the principal influences. Over the past five years the predominant Cattistock sire has been Caesar '68, who has three lines to Heythrop Brigand. The Cattistock kennels have had considerable success at Peterborough, Ardingly and Honiton, 1972 being their most triumphant year. The pack have accounted for an average of above 80 brace of foxes a season.

Although they did not kill on stormy 26 January, we were entertained to bursts of their outstanding cry and drive, particularly when, after finding their first fox in Coombe Bottom, they ran straight for Catsley Lane, north of which, when Goring cast again, they pushed a fresh one down to Milking Barton, where they marked to ground in a bank.

During the middle of the day we rode over Brig. and Mrs Block's fine fields, and the never-failing rhododendrons at their Benville Manor produced one that led the way up to Chelborough Batch, and, albeit the rain-laden gale was now really fierce, one was still able to appreciate this lovely Saturday country, which covers the well-grassed Ryme and Hardington Vale on the Cattistock's north. (They hunt the stone-wall country above the Waddon Vale in the south on Tuesdays and the central downland on Wednesdays.) That Saturday country is strongly fenced, but owing to the traditional goodwill of the farmers and the work of several members under the guidance of Cdr. Eyre, the wire fund secretary, you can cross anywhere with little trouble. The accounts of Mr George Pinney, the hunt secretary, show 50 per cent of the income to come from functions, so that as much as £1000 a year is spent on the country.

61 Mr Charles Stirling. He took over as Master and huntsman in 1977.

In such wind they could make nothing of a reluctant fox in Chelborough Batch and took a long time to get one on the move from Norwood gorse. When they did, Miss Gloria Abbey was still there, representing the joint-Mastership; so was Sir Stephen Hammick, the field Master, and George Pinney, and his brother James who is to make up a quorum next season with Miss Abbey, Lady Theresa Agnew and Major MacEwan. So we bent our heads for Wooden Cabbage Farm and on to Dogwell Farm where Goring called 'home' in the now impossible climate.

(26 January 1974)

Mr N.C. Stirling took over the Mastership in 1977, moving south from the Braes of Derwent which he had hunted from 1974–7. Mr Stirling, a former Master and huntsman to the Eton College Beagles, also carried the Cattistock horn, thus continuing the tradition emphasised in the article.

In 1980 David Goring was relieved as his kennel-huntsman and first whipper-in by R. Herring.

Since 1977 the country has been hunted seven days a fortnight, and the former joint-Master, Major J. Ames Pinney, has taken over as the wire fund secretary, and continues his brother's role of keeping the country open.

Commander Eyre has been hunt secretary since the 1974–5 season. In 1979 Mr F.A. Crowhurst joined Mr Stirling in the Mastership. In 1980, Mr Stirling stepped down, to be replaced by Mr A.L. Austin, who also acts as huntsman.

The Cotley

HARRIERS INTO FOXHOUNDS

Of the few packs of hounds whose pedigrees can be traced through more than a century to their hunt's formation, the Cotley Harriers, who hunt the green and tightly enclosed hills where Devon, Somerset and Dorset converge, probably provide the most revealing single lesson in the evolution of modern hunting.

For when Thomas Deane, of Cotley, formed his pack of hare-hunting 'lemon and badger-pies' in 1797, the harrier was still the squirarchy's favourite hound, and, in much of the West Country, it remained so for the next century and more. But during the Victorian period, at the same time that enclosure programmes intensified, hares became scarcer and foxes more prolific. To adjust to these

circumstances, Thomas Deane's descendants might have decided on one of two alternatives: to continue to hunt hares in increasingly difficult conditions, or to draft their pack and buy foxhounds. But they went instead for a brave compromise, one that has proved an unqualified success: they bred up the weight and speed of their harriers to transform them into foxcatchers. So that today, although we see the Cotley listed in the foxhounds section of *Baily's*, we also find them entered in the *Harrier's Stud Book*. And, in spite of the various introductions of foxhound strains in the kennels at Cotley, the blood of the old West Country harriers remains thickest in their veins. Nor has their character substantially altered since the eighteenth century.

This careful adaptation could never have been evolved without the unrelenting dedication of the family in whose hands the Cotley Harriers remain today – the Eameses. This ancient family of Devon yeomen provide one of the most fascinating sagas in

62 The Cotley hounds in 1894. With them are their Master, Edward Eames (*centre*) flanked by his brother John (*right*) and nephew, Thomas Deane Eames, outside Broadoak, Cotley, Devon, where hounds were kept during Edward Eames's 43 years' Mastership.

63 Lt-Col. Richard Eames, who has been Master since 1939.

the history of hunting. For Thomas Deane's heiress-presumptive married another devoted hunting man, Thomas Palmer Eames, who assumed control of the pack on the death of their founder, in 1855. And here a connection already existed, because Eames's Palmer cousins had hunted the Cotley country for at least a century before Deane's career began.

Thomas Palmer Eames was Master and huntsman for 31 seasons before he handed over the horn, in 1886, to his much younger brother, Edward, who kept it until 1929. Then Edward's nephews, Richard and Deane, took over. In 1939 they were succeeded by Richard's son, the present Master, Lt-Col. R.F.P. Eames, who, in his turn, for more than 30 years has continued to fashion the Cotley harrier to suit the ever-changing character of this corner of the West Country. And to hunt them personally – in spite of a knee injury, incurred on active service with the West Somerset Yeomanry, which keeps his left leg stiff and sore. So the Eames family have, during only four reigns, held the Mastership and the horn for 118 years.

The thread of these hounds' breeding is tenuous at one point only – in 1832, when an outbreak of rabies occurred at Cotley. (You can still see the railings of the original, now ruined, kennels, through which the hounds were shot.) But Deane was not to be defeated by that. He bred extensively from the sole survivors of the tragedy, a bitch called Countess and her whelps, then at walk with the Eames who was to be his son-in-law. And here, too, that splendid band of nineteenth-century sporting clerics, appear in the Cotley saga. For Deane was also lucky enough to secure the pick of the celebrated kennels of the Rev. E.C. Forward, who had died recently, besides presents from – among others – the

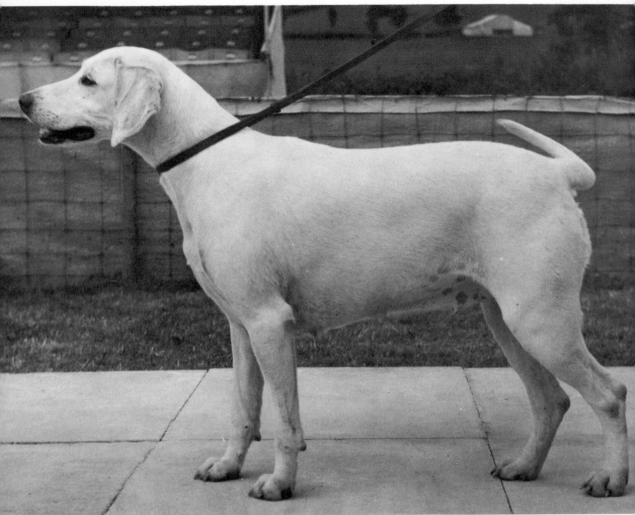

64 Cotley Songstress.

Rev. Harry Farr Yeatman, whose kennels were full of the blood of Parson Froude's famous pack. (Of these the great Jack Russell had said, 'they are light in their colour and sharp as needles – plenty of tongue, but would drive like furies. I have never seen a better or more killing pack in all my life'. Later, after hunting with the Cotley, Parson Jack considered it a great triumph to secure a draft from them.) Anyhow, Thomas Deane soon kennelled a level pack of 20-inch harriers again at Cotley.

Under the Eameses, hunt records showed a steady increase in the ratio of foxes to hares: Thomas Palmer Eames accounted each season for about 130 hares and a few foxes, as chance occurred; but, under Edward, the average changed to the region of 30 foxes and 60 hares, until the hare interest dwindled

to such an extent between the wars that, officially, the last was killed on 4 November 1938. But, apart from the fact that the pattern of big Devon banks, topped with barriers of oak, ash and hazel, was inexorably tightening, for all his nose and tenacity, the West Country harrier obviously lacked the element of speed and stamina necessary to press those tough hill foxes over a distance.

So far the only outcrosses to be used consistently came from the Taunton Vale Harriers. New blood was needed – foxhound blood. Experiment was tentative: Tiverton strains were tried, and, in 1918, they used the top award-winning Silverton Dalesman; then, with an eye to whiteness and Welsh tongue, they went to the Curre. Yet there was virtually no difference in the pack's appearance until a few years after the last war, when Col. Eames went to the College Valley, the stroke which was to earn the Cotley the fame it now owns.

The Cotley, being then practically pure West Country harrier, and the College Valley a blend of Border, fell and Foxhound Kennel Stud Book blood, no affinity existed between the two. So the nick owed little to studies of genetics and line breeding. Col. Eames, who had for long been a close admirer of the genius of Sir Alfred Goodson, decided in 1949 to use College Valley after seeing Sir Alfred's Ruffian with Dr R.N. Craig, the Baronet's brother-in-law, who was then Master of the East Devon.

Col. Eames's instinct said, 'right build, an inch taller than mine, predominantly white, just what I want'. The first Cotley litter, sired by Ruffian, proved his judgement. The dog-hounds grew to 22–23 inches, the bitches to 20–21. To the retained light colour, superior nose, beautiful neck and shoulders and clean hard-wearing feet of the Cotley, was added the strength and pace of the Northumberland sire. (Fortunately, Col. Eames's initial anxiety – that their pace might prove too much for their noses – was quickly dispelled.) Soon another quality was added: a loud bell-like tongue, typical of Lakeland and Border. This asset, Col. Eames told me, came particularly from the College Valley Belford '58, who has sired three litters over the past decade.

A single good day with the Cotley is enough to convince you that only exceptionally gifted line-hunters, who turn tight on their fox, are a match for this country, hounds that will drive on across the pasture, and yet can afford to be slowed up by the maze of tall, thicket-topped banks. There was a fine example of this during the afternoon of the Cotley's opening meet, which took place at Col. Eames's home, with nearly 100 mounted followers, on 3 November. After spending the morning drawing up over the point-to-point course, past Chardstock and over Burridge Common and running a fox to ground by Chardstock House, followed by some rather scrappy local hunting, Col. Eames lifted them to Whitehouse covert. Here they drew for a whole hour before finding at 2.00 p.m.

From the other side of the combe we saw their twisty fox make four or five great circles; we saw three roe deer cross their line and two fresh foxes roused in thick-bottomed Whitehouse, while the hunted fox made several sudden turns. We saw each member of the pack momentarily checked as he or she struggled with the banks; and yet the white hounds of Cotley – with that priceless blood, nurtured by Thomas Deane, in their veins – followed the line in single file, giving the semblance of a string of white beads, or drops of milk flying from a tap, until at last they overhauled him at Brockfield.

This was a classic hound-hunt: from the moment they found, Col. Eames demonstrated the habit of his ancestors, never speaking to the pack, never heeding the *holloas*. But when they killed there was a rousing *who-op!* from the whole ring of green coats: Col. Eames, his son, Vyvyan (joint-Master), Don Davies (kennel-huntsman), David Eames, Bob Burrough, and his son Johnny, and Douglas Legg, and his son Roger (all amateur whippers-in). That, too, was in the true tradition of the Cotley harriers.

(3 November 1973)

The Dulverton

WEST COUNTRY CENTENARY

How many of the Western foxhunting countries took their shapes as a result of the big landowners of the nineteenth century (such as the 2nd Lord Poltimore and J.J. Farquharson) or wide-ranging venerers (like Parsons Russell, Hole and Froude) being obliged to relinquish segments of their sporting empires because they had over-reached themselves, or because they were challenged by rival sportsmen? Like some Ruritanian state, the Dulverton country – that charming tract of hillock and combe, half moorland, half pasture, lying on the south side of Exmoor and the Brendon Hills – is one that came into being in this way.

The country was hunted in the early nineteenth century by Parson Froude; then, through an agreement with the Hon. Mark Rolle, founder of the Stevenstone, by the 5th Earl of Portsmouth, Master of the Eggesford. However, when in 1875 Rolle offered to hand it over completely, Lord Portsmouth declared he was unable to do the country justice, but that he knew of someone who could. This was his friend, John Froude Bellew, of Rhyll Manor, who had just inherited the nucleus of his uncle's (Parson Froude's) famous pack. Accordingly, that autumn, the Dulverton was constituted as a separate country. And Squire Froude Bellew (described by his biographer as 'a typical John Bull . . . and ardently acting the part') became the father of the hunt.

In those far-off, tranquil days, Froude Bellew obviously foresaw his foundation lasting for at least 100 years. But a toast at the centenary dinner, which took place on the evening following the Dulverton East's opening meet – 'to the next 100 years' – was proposed with a trifle less conviction. Even so, hunting that showery day, 1 November, from Churchtown, West Anstey – the home of the senior joint-Master, Mr Ben Burton – I sensed every sign of endurance, because this hunt's exceptionally happy fraternity, more than half of them farmers and their families, seem to belong, part and parcel, to the land. And what a land it is: the white and blue sky was temporarily invaded by vast ink-black clouds that put half the landscape in deep shadow, to make the most dramatic contrasts, where the sun shone through, with vivid pasture enclosed by the hedge-topped 'Devon banks', black heather and bottle-green gorse and golden bracken and beech-and-oak-strewn combes. You could scarcely imagine a more dazzling mosaic, and at times it was bright enough to glimpse, way off in the south-west, the purple outline of Dartmoor, and on the eastern horizon, Dunkery Beacon's 1700 feet.

Walter Perry, who (since 1971, when he handed over the Devon and Somerset horn) has hunted hounds with marked success, led them to a bramble patch on the edge of Churchtown Wood. Here they found their first fox, and staying very close on his brush for a mile – as far as Furze Hill, where they ran him to ground – proved that scent was reasonably good. Returning to Churchtown, he then drew over Gup Hill and the Ridge road and on towards Danesbrook. Finding again by Slade bridge, hounds packed well up as they raced along the stream's north bank; then their fox turned back, to be accounted for at an earth below Shircombe.

Riding Mr Burton's Lupin (just the handy, short-coupled sort for this country) and guided by the hunt secretary, Mr John Pugsley, whose farm they were on, I imagined, as I watched this hunt, the many times that Victorian Squire Froude Bellew and his successors must have followed their hounds along the woody Danesbrook. From 1886 to 1889 came Connock Marshall and, for the next two seasons, L.E. Bligh; then E.C. Dawkins (1891–9) and Jasper Selwyn (1899–1905), both of whom also lived at Rhyll Manor. The country being Masterless from 1905 till 1908, the committee invited the West Somerset, the Tiverton and the Exmoor 'to work the districts bordering on their territories', and the invitation was accepted 'on the understanding that the Dulverton committee pay for poultry damage and tips to keepers'. At last, for the 1908–9 season, Sir Gilbert Wills stepped in, but he and his assistant Master, Mr Ernest Hancock (who inherited Rhyll Manor) had to leave everything to the committee and huntsman for most of the war. 'I hope it will still be possible,' Sir Gilbert wrote (in a letter still pasted in the hunt minutes book) from the Royal North Devon Hussars camp in 1915, 'to keep the little pack going in the absence of Hancock and myself until we are through with this troublesome and wearying war.'

But Sir Gilbert withdrew from the Mastership on his return, and the split into East and West came about like this. Lord Poltimore (grandson of the Lord Poltimore of Cattistock fame), was elected joint-Master with Mr Hancock in 1919. But, five years later, finding they could not hunt the whole country regularly on a two-day a week basis, they decided to divide the responsibility, Poltimore operating in the west, from his home, Court Hall, North Molton, and Hancock in the east, from Rhyll. In 1940 Lord Poltimore put in his resignation but, according to the minutes, was persuaded to stay on, 'provided the country be divided into two portions, to be known for the time being as the Dulverton (East) and Dulverton (West)'. Even so, the central committee flourished up to the mid-1960s.

On the West side, Mrs F.W.B. Smith (very well known in the show ring) became hunt secretary in 1939, and in 1952 joined Lord Poltimore's son-in-law, Sir Dennis Stucley, in a new Mastership. Tragically, a few months ago, Mrs Smyth died. Her husband now wears the Master's cap.

Ernest Hancock's widow took the East side in 1932, putting on her son, Tommy, as huntsman, and a very successful amateur he proved for three seasons before his ten-year innings with the Devon and Somerset Staghounds began. Mrs Hancock was joined, in 1940, by Mr Wallis Whitmore, one of the hunt's great benefactors, who came to Devon from the Old Surrey and Burstow country, and remained as Master for 31 seasons – three of them with Major Frank Rothwell, the present chairman (and a former hunt secretary). Then, in 1968, Mr Burton, who used to be joint-Master of the Hertfordshire, took

65 Lady Caroline Gosling, who joined the Mastership in 1973. She is a daughter of the Earl of Halifax, the Middleton's senior joint-Master.

the reins. Two seasons ago he invited Lady Caroline Gosling to come in with him.

A daughter of that most talented huntsman and breeder of hounds, Lord Halifax, of the Middleton and Middleton East, Lady Caroline lends considerable knowledge and influence to the kennels at Smallcombe, East Anstey. Through her, they acquired from Lord Halifax, the good stallion hound Middleton Grasper '68, sired by the Tipperary Growler. Three more splendid presents to the joint-Masters were from the Duke of Beaufort; an outstanding dog-hound called Tartar and two lovely bitches, Fancy and Brittle. Tartar and Brittle also go back to the Tipperary Growler.

With Lady Caroline leading the field on 1 November, I had ample opportunity to witness the working qualities of the Dulverton East. After that second fox went to ground near Shircombe, Walter Perry – a fine houndsman – drew over Anstey common towards Brimblecombe, where they found at about 1.30; and, with their heads well down all the way, dashed across the heather to kill in the open, right in front of us, on Molland Common. Another Brimblecombe fox pointed his mask down the extent of a thick mile and a half long valley called Combe Wood, which set their music fairly echoing, without a break, until he was headed at the end of it. The Anstey common bracken yielded the fifth, a fast one that nearly shook them off with his twisty course. Scent began to fade after 4.00 p.m., and they ran right past him, secreted in a gorse thicket near Molland Moor gate, but, turning back 150 yards, they quickly chopped him in his hiding place. That was the third fox accounted for, and the 48th since cubhunting began. And because there is said to be higher density of sheep here than anywhere else in the world, the local farmers are as well satisfied with the score as Walter Perry is.

After a day like that, I felt confident enough that if John Froude Bellew returned to a Dulverton meet today, he would be so delighted with the hunt spirit and the sport still shown where the Yeo, the Barle and Danesbrook flow, that he might even forgive them for dividing his beautiful old country into 'East' and 'West'.

(1 November 1975)

Mr R.A. Pearce joined Mr Burton and Lady Caroline Gosling in the Mastership in 1976, Mr R.A. Day, from the Cambridgeshire, in 1978 and Mr J.E. Pugsley in 1980.

Keith Pinnell was put on as huntsman in 1978, with Ralph Glibb as whipper-in.

The Four Burrow

FAMOUS HOUNDS OF THE FAR WEST

If not many people in the hunting world today fully appreciate the great mark made by the Four Burrow kennels on British foxhound breeding, they have probably at least heard of one Four Burrow key-name in the kennel stud book: Whipcord '05. Of this celebrated dog-hound, Ikey Bell wrote: 'he was first-rate in every requisite of the chase, remarkable for his muscular back and loins, buttocks and second thighs; a long low sort on the best wearing legs and feet. He had good shoulders, neck and ribs, and he was as hard as steel, as are his descendants. . . .' Whipcord was probably the most influential stallion hound of the first half of the twentieth century. The Badminton, Curre and Tiverton kennels, in particular, have been full of his blood. Consequently in Edwardian times the Four Burrow kennels were among the three or four preponderant in England (being used extensively of all in the Duke of Beaufort's kennels).

This Edwardian tradition continued. One of Whipcord's descendants was the famous Four Burrow Pleader '38, whose ancestry can be traced directly and accurately (mostly through Fitzwilliam records), on his tail female to Mr Darley's Damsel, which was entered in 1738, and on tail male (through Whipcord) to the Brocklesby Bumper, 1748. Pleader had 13 grandchildren shown at Peterborough in 1949. They collected several prizes, including that of champion bitch. During the last war no kennels saved any but top-rate blood. And, of the Duke of Beaufort's $12\frac{1}{2}$ couples entered in 1944, no less than $10\frac{1}{2}$ were by Pleader '38. Of the $14\frac{1}{2}$ couples of dog-hounds in the Four Burrow kennels in 1947, four

and a half were used as stallion hounds by as many as 14 other packs. The names Pleader '38, Filbert '39 and Lifeguard '39 resounded through foxhunting Britain. Their vein is strong today.

All this success is due to the Williams family, whose name is synonymous with Four Burrow. Indeed in any kennels that can boast a more or less continuous breeding influence, resulting in a really good level kennel, one so often finds the principal interest resides with a single family: Beaufort and Williams-Wynn, Berkeley, Percy and Fitzwilliam, Barclays of Puckeridge, Pelhams of Brocklesby, Eameses of Cotley . . . Williamses of Four Burrow.

Cornwall's leading tin miners since the middle of the eighteenth century, the Williamses were first represented at the head of the Four Burrow by Sir William Williams in 1854. By that time the hunt had already been in existence for 86 years. For it was on New Year's Day 1780, that the county landowners, led by the Vivian brothers and Sir John Rogers, founded the hare and foxhunting Four Burrow Hunt Club, so called because the Four Burrows (Stone Age burial grounds) lay as a prominent landmark at the centre of their terrain, which contained all Cornwall between Bodmin and the Lizard. It was a club and a country that showed consistently good sport, killing, for instance, $85\frac{1}{2}$ brace of hares in 1794, 102 brace in 1795 and 95 brace in 1796. Some time during the Napoleonic wars this buoyant fraternity appointed Mr Turner, MP for Truro, as Master. And the club continued to hunt mainly hares, until Mr Charles Danbury's Mastership, which began in 1839, a time when English sports-

66 and 67 Mr George Williams, Master, 1857–78; and Mr John Williams ('Scorrier John'), Master, 1878–1907.

men everywhere were fostering Reynard's population with much greater care. So the Four Burrow were then entered to fox only, and we read in *Fore's Guide to the Hounds of England*, 1849, that 'the country is as wild as the winds, includes a fine range of grassy moors and is, above all, well stocked with foxes.'

During Enys Vivian's reign (1840–49) the hounds that hunted them still contained more old West Country harrier blood than anything else, but Mr Daubuz, who followed him, changed the policy, bringing in, we are told, 'annual unentered drafts from Lord Fitzhardinge's and the Oakley'.

In 1854 Sir William Williams, as chief personality in the capital province of the world of tin and copper, saw that to command the Four Burrow was to head the sporting world of Cornwall, and although he himself possessed little instinct for foxhounds, he was a big enough character to launch the tremendous family influence that thrives today. In 1857, after Fred Williams had been Master for a season, George Williams of Scorrier, a most skilful houndbreeder, began 21 years of Mastership. He bred consistently to Lord Portsmouth's Eggesford kennels, which were full of Belvoir, Bramham Moor and Puckeridge blood. And very successful his experiments proved. So that when his son John Williams – the great 'Scorrier John' – took over in 1878 at the age of 18, a fine pack was waiting for him. But searching for still better strains, John Williams decided to go mainly to the Berkeley. Indeed Whipcord '05 was by Berkeley

68 Mr John Williams, Master, 1955–77

Vanguard '99, himself a famous hound. And with 'Scorrier John' hunting hounds throughout the Mastership, the hunt's Edwardian correspondent does not surprise you when he writes that 'no better sport can be found outside the Shires than in this part of Cornwall'.

When John Williams gave up the Four Burrow, Lord Waterford bought 25 couples of his bitches to form the foundation of his famous Irish pack, while Mr S.H. Christy, the Williams relation who then took over the Four Burrow, kept the remainder. Three seasons later, Mr A. Wallis-Wright came in with his own pack of Irish black-and-tans, hunting the Four Burrow country till 1913, when he took

them on to the Woodland Pytchley. That year the country was divided into Four Burrow and Four Burrow East, the latter then being hunted by Mr Cardell's St Columb Harriers.

It was not until 1922 that 'Scorrier John's second son, Mr Percival Williams, in spite of very nasty war wounds, returned to Scorrier, revived the Four Burrow hounds and took up the thread of the Williams story. He built his pack by collecting unentered as well as entered drafts from the Stevenstone, Western, South Dorset, Berkeley, Dartmoor, Quorn and Tiverton, regaining all the Whipcord blood he could, particularly through Berkeley Weathergauge, North Warwickshire Tarquin and Tiverton Actor and his son, Artist. As a 1930s' reporter put it: 'under Mr Williams' Mastership, the fortunes of the Four Burrow have now returned to all their former glory. This is a beautifully-bred working pack, whose blood has become much sought after by other hound-breeders'. In 1955, Mr John Williams resigned from the Blues to join his father in the Mastership, and has been in sole charge since 1964. He was lucky enough to inherit, too, the services of Mr Magin Hancock, who took over as secretary in 1932; and, as kennel-huntsman, Sidney Butler, who began his career with the Four Burrow in 1929.

Crowan Feast day, the hunt's most famous meet, was cancelled due to hard weather, so it was on the following day, 2 February, after the astonishingly swift thaw, that I was privileged to see the Four Burrow at Crowan. Then, with a warm ground and a humid atmosphere from the start, there was little question of a decent scent. Yet how well this level, well-conformed pack tried. They kept closely with one fox from a find in Long Croft to a drain in Praze reservoir, while we enjoyed some refreshing grass riding, regularly and closely interrupted everywhere by Cornwall's granite banks, grass-faced and sharp on the top, where your horse pauses for just a moment before descending.

Very steadily they traced another from Crowan Cross over the Releath road to Polcrebo Downs, then via the village, towards Long Croft and right-handed under Rocky Hill, where they could make no more of him. But here, on the gorse-thick brakes, I saw how well they could live up to their reputation for 'close-cover penetration'. These brakes have thickened considerably since the advent of myxomatosis and Mr Williams, knowing that a smaller hound is better at negotiating them, keeps more bitches than dogs in the kennels; a quite different emphasis from his father's.

Then one of a number of foxes in Black Rock raced to Buscaverran, circling to ground by Crowan beacon. Bolted, he was pressed in this faintest of scents by Rocky Hill, being marked to ground in a Buscaverran hedge. Finally, at 3.30, still attended by a dozen farmers and their families, caked freely with the black mud that lies wet over the country's non-porous granite, Mr Williams tried Wimbleton's brake. The air was crisper now but this usually fine foxholding covert proved blank. He sounded 'home'.

The Four Burrow are a splendid pack to be out with, in a glorious country to go, and their Master has indeed been successful these last 17 years in maintaining the Williams tradition.

(2 February 1972)

Mr Roy Tatlow succeeded Mr Williams in the Mastership in 1977, and he was followed in 1980 by Messrs. B. Warren and T. Burley.

The Portman

WHERE THE HOUNDS OF THE BECKFORD RAN

Seeing Geoffrey Harrison, huntsman to the Portman since 1969, bring hounds to Mr Richard Miller's Mount Pleasant Farm, near Okeford Fitzpaine, last Wednesday, soon had one imagining what that part of the Dorset countryside was like 200 years ago. For it must have been in the early 1770s that this end of the startlingly vivid vale of Blackmore first echoed to Peter Beckford's horn. And smack in the middle of the present Portman country you can still see the kennels and stables at Steepleton, the property that had always carried rights of hunting in the ancient game forest of Cranborne Chase, and which Peter's father, Julines Beckford, bought from Thomas Fownes.

Fownes was the country's first foxhunter (from 1730 to 1745), but Beckford may be counted as the richest fount of the Portman tradition. Not only has his treatise on 'the noble science' remained a classic to this day but he taught 'the Meynell of the West' all the secrets of the huntsman's art. So perhaps the most important copy of the classic *Thoughts upon Hunting* is that one inscribed *For James John Farquharson Esqr from the author.*

Son of a self-made Scottish business man who settled at Langton House, Blandford, in 1775, Farquharson set the seal of modern foxhunting on Dorset. For in 1806, when he was 23, he bought a nucleus of high-quality bitches from a Mr Wynd-

69, 70 and 71 Masters of the Portman who were celebrated breeders of hounds: The 2nd Viscount Portman (Master, 1858–1919); Major W.W.B. Scott (Master, 1930–31 and joint-Master, 1928–30, 1931–2 and 1949–52); and Lt-Col. Sir Peter Farquhar (joint-Master, 1947–59).

ham of Dinton, built his kennels at Eastbury and Cattistock up to 75 couples, maintained a stableful of 50 horses and for the next half-century hunted the whole of what is now the Blackmore Vale, Cattistock, Portman and South Dorset countries. Being neither a particularly talented huntsman nor a great breeder of hounds, 'the Meynell of the West' was a misnomer. 'The Squire' was the more apt nickname, for Farquharson ranked among the really great landlords and agriculturists of the West Country. As a hunting man he combined personal authority and organising ability with immense charm and utter devotion to the chase; and having the benefit of the best hunting tutor in the world he knew precisely how to provide scintillating sport. The records of his two very gifted huntsmen, Ben Jennings (from 1807) and James Treadwell (from 1837), are full of monumental hunts in every corner of the country from Shaftesbury to Bridport and from Yeovil to Poole.

All good Masters are jealous of their country but Farquharson was too jealous. Towards the end of his reign, rivals were on the march. J.S.W. Erle Drax – in breach of an agreement, apparently between his father and Farquharson – established the Charborough country, while the 1st Lord Portman was hunting from Bryanston over his estates round Blandford. They needed more country. Farquharson would not give an inch, until G.D. Wingfield Digby who had a pack at Sherborne led the crescendo of protest, and 'the Squire', rather than relinquish any of his vast country, resigned and sold his hounds at Eastbury in 1857. Two seasons later new hunt boundaries were decided and the north-eastern portions – Cranborne Chase and the end of the vale of Blackmore, sandwiched between the Stour below and the Nadder on top – went to Lord Portman. With Steepleton at the centre of his country, give or take a few coverts, he got Beckford's domain. He called it the East Dorset.

But Portman died after a single season and was succeeded by his son, William, who was to enjoy the Portman's halcyon era, no fewer than 61 glorious seasons – the last dozen of them aided by his son-in-law, A.W. Heber-Percy – and ending with his death, aged 91, in 1919, when the pack went subscription. The 2nd Lord Portman bred up one of the most beautiful of the pre-Great War kennels – Belvoir, Brocklesby, Fitzwilliam, Oakley and Warwickshire were the principal influences – and according to his contemporary, Cuthbert Bradley in *The Foxhound of the 20th Century*, 'they are a hard-driving quick pack with a great cry, for Lord Portman has always been

72 Mrs John Woodhouse who looks after the hunt horses, receiving a stirrup-cup from a former point-to-point champion jockey, Mr Richard Miller, who was host at Mount Pleasant Woolland, on the author's day out on 15 November 1972.

most particular about a hound throwing his tongue and never keeps a mute one, however good-looking he may be'.

That is what Lt-Col. D.H.C. Worrall – formerly joint–Master and huntsman to the South Dorset (1957–62) and now the Portman's joint-Master, with particular responsibility for hound breeding – impressed on me last week: 'The fact is, in our undulating hill country, they need more music than most, otherwise the field soon lose them'. Tongue was always considered of prime importance in the Portman, not least by Capt. William Browne, who filled another long Mastership – 1919–45 – a period which was broken only around the late twenties and early thirties when Major W.W.B. Scott and Commander Monro stood in for him and in the first two years of the last war.

From all accounts there was little to choose between Browne's high skill as a huntsman and that of Lt-Col. Sir Peter Farquhar, who began his 11 seasons with the Portman in 1947. But Sir Peter ranks with Ikey Bell, the Duke of Beaufort and Capt. Ronnie Wallace as one of the great influences on the development of the modern foxhound, and the Portman could not have enjoyed the services of a team with a better eye for a hound than his and that of Major Scott who shared a triumvirate with Capt. E.F. Beckett between 1949 and 1952. In the 1960s the Torys – Dorset sheep farmers and foxhunters for many generations – with Stewart and his son Percy as joint-Masters and huntsmen, held sway. And now it is another family of equal fame – the Woodhouses.

There were six Woodhouses enjoying the delectable Wednesday country after the sharp night frost on 14 November: John, who has been honorary secretary for 20 years and has combined that office with the joint-Mastership since 1969; Richard, another joint-Master, who farms, race-rides (he trained and rode the winners of the Cheltenham Foxhunters Chase in 1967 and 1970, and rode in the 1971 National) and also organises the Saturday country with huge panache; their elder brother Edward, who runs the family business; and all three wives. Mrs John Woodhouse is in charge of the hunt stables. And at Mr Richard Miller's meet (another race-rider incidentally – he is 1972 champion point-to-point jockey) at Mount Pleasant Farm, and throughout the day, I felt the Woodhouses' warm and jocular influence on the hunt's brotherhood.

From the moment hounds found their first fox by Lockett's Farm, which gave us a 35-minute burst, finishing at Woolland House, it was perfectly clear that these Portman foxhunters – with their grass country par excellence liberally broken up by good thorn fences – are not satisfied unless they are 'having a go'. Hounds pressed on the heels of five foxes that day. Unkennelling their second on Mr Frank Kent's Stoke Wake, they led us over Bulbarrow, into the Blackmore Vale country and right up to Mappowder. But here he took the road and his scent went dead. That was four miles as hounds ran, over beautiful turf; but turf that is unlikely to remain as sound much longer, for the Portman's vale country is usually an ocean of mud by mid-November.

That is why they were losing foxes last Wednesday: too dry. A consistent problem is that of roe deer, and there were a lot about, but hounds never raised their heads at them, let alone rioted. Here Col. Worrall's most effective restraint is to keep an extra high proportion of third, fourth and fifth season hounds in the pack. But this, of course, makes it especially important to breed for quality.

The principal lines of the Portman still go back mainly to South Dorset Salesman '44, North Cotswold Landlord '44, and Meynell Pageant '44. The standard is very high, and quality hounds and quality horses are the hall marks of the Portman. All this is in a country that is devoid of railways and dual carriageways and one which – apart from the obvious innovations and the fact that hedges are slowly, but relentlessly, being rooted up – has changed remarkably little since Beckford's day.

(15 November 1972)

When the Hursley and Hambledon amalgamated in 1978, Mr Hugh Dalgety, who had been Master and huntsman of the Hursley, transferred to the Portman, joining Mr Richard Woodhouse in the Mastership. Mrs Dalgety and Mr R.N. Miller formed a quaternity with them in 1980. Mr John Woodhouse continues as honorary secretary and Geoffrey Harrison as kennel-huntsman and first whipper-in.

The Stevenstone

IN THE SPIRIT OF PARSON JACK

Fine scenting conditions in north Devon on 23 February gave the Stevenstone one of their best galloping days of the season: with a field of 40 we enjoyed two good runs over the rich bank-and-ditch-chequered hillocks of the Torridge Valley, and were able, in such free-going country, to keep up nearly all the time. Nor were there many moments of the day when pasture, plough and dell did not ring to the music of Mr Frank Sumner's smart and level bitch pack, whose predominantly Heythrop and South and West Wilts blood give them a drive and tongue and air of light-boned quality that is the envy of many other West Country hunts.

Following away down the typically steep-banked

73 Parson Jack Russell.

Suddenly a pack of hounds careered across the road, followed by a large number of sportsmen in black coats. The bishop leaned to his chaplain with a solemn whisper: 'Dear me, this neighbourhood must have been visited by some fearful epidemic. I never saw so many men in mourning before'. The chaplain, identifying the mourners as brethren of his own cloth and personal friends, shook his head: 'My lord, the only bereavement these black-coated gentlemen suffer is not being able to wear pink'. Flabbergasted, the bishop watched them pass, one after the other: the Rev. John Froude, of whom a biographer said that 'he was well known in the western countries for his utter disregard of episcopal and indeed of all human authority, less so even than for the celebrity of his hounds'; the Rev. W.H. Karslake of Dolton, a passionately keen Master of harriers; the Rev. Harry Farr Yeatman; the Rev. Peter Glubb, who 'hunted a very killing pack near Little Torrington'; and, of course, the Rev. Jack Russell, ardent venerer of stag, fox, otter and hare, who bred the celebrated terrier and miniature foxhound. Such men were adored by their parishioners, lampooned by the wits:

This parson little loveth prayer
and Pater night and morn, Sir!
For bell and book hath little care,
But dearly loves the horn, Sir!

It was not long before Bishop Philpotts, 'diabolically astute and well informed', discovered the full extent of his clergy's sporting interests. And considerable embarrassment they caused him. An enemy of Russell's later told him that Parson Jack had hunted one day when he should have been burying a child. But Jack Russell was immensely popular and the mother gave evidence in his favour. The bishop was 'much disappointed at the result of his inquiry' and having dismissed the mother, rounded on Russell again: 'But the fact remains you keep hounds and your curate hunts with you. Will you give up your hounds?' Russell declined, adding, 'there are many other clergymen in your diocese who keep hounds, my lord, why am I singled out among so many?' Upon which, the witness tells us, the bishop 'groaned in despair'.

There is no doubt it was Russell and his colleagues, more than any before them, who infused these parts of the West Country with the spirit of the chase. For although, between 1803 and 1830, the country between Barnstaple, Bude and Hatherleigh was hunted with a pack of foxhounds under the joint-Mastership of Lord Rolle of Stevenstone, Mr Stevens, of Cross, and Russell's friend, the Rev.

road from the Old Vicarage, Abbots Bickington, some 12 miles south-west of Bideford, I conjured a picture of this undulating country as it must have been in the great Parson Jack Russell's day, a century and more ago. Then, of course, there was very little enclosure, much less grazing and no forestry plantation at all; but many more of those wild tracts of gorse and marsh grass and rush, over common and bog that punctuate the Devonshire farmland we know today.

That is how it would have looked when Henry Philpotts, Bishop of Exeter, was travelling through this sector of the Torridge Valley on a visitation tour soon after his appointment to the diocese in 1831.

74 Farmers over a bank close to Chollaton, Devon, when the author followed hounds on 23 February 1972.

Peter Glubb, vicar of Little Torrington, an early nineteenth-century observer says that 'here the sport of legitimate fox hunting, being utterly ignored by the majority of the natives, it is their practice to kill a fox whenever and however they could catch him. Foxes are tracked to ground, the church bells ring and the village turns out with picks and shovels . . .' But when Russell took over this country, in conjunction with the large area he was already hunting, he proceeded to educate them. He once threatened to horsewhip a party of foxshooters, afterwards claiming 'from that day forward I secured for myself and my successors not only the goodwill and co-operation, but the friendship of some of the best fox preservers that the country of Devon, or any other county, has ever seen.'

When, in 1853, Russell relinquished his hunting rights in the Torrington area to Mr John Moore-Stevens, it was fairly said to have been 'steeped in the tradition of the sporting parsons'. And, backed by this spirit, the new Master, who called his hunt the North Devon, held sway for six years. But in 1859 came a sharp contrast in the character of the local hunt. That year the Hon. Mark Rolle of Stevenstone, the richest man in Devon, who had recently inherited an estate of 55,600 acres, bought Moore-Stevens's hounds, delineated the Stevenstone boundaries more or less as we know them today (the principal exception being that the country to the east of Torridge is now on permanent loan to the Torrington Farmers), and began his long career as Master. During Rolle's first Mastership, which lasted until 1883, the year Russell died, Stevenstone sport reached its zenith and was regularly enjoyed by the ageing Parson Jack. Sir William Williams took over as Master from 1883 till 1892, but Rolle then reassumed command until 1895, and enjoyed a third reign between 1900 and 1907, when he died. His great-great-nephew, Lord Clinton, is now president of the hunt committee.

Riding well up front on our swift-moving 23 February was a retired farmer who can connect the bulk of this hunt's history: Mr Joe Bond whose first

75 The senior supporter at that time, Mr Joe Bond. He first rode with the Stevenstone in 1898, aged eight.

season with the Stevenstone, aged eight, was in 1898–9, remembers Mark Rolle quite vividly. With still greater clarity he recalls the leadership of Mr David Horndon, who was Rolle's assistant Master from 1902–7, was on his own as Master from 1907 to 1914 and from 1930 to 1936, and who had such a great success as a hound breeder.

Another veteran follower was 77-year-old Mr George Heywood, the hunt's father-figure, who was Master from 1949 till 1955. He has seen many changes in the Stevenstone country: they include the disintegration of the big estates, the reclamation of great stretches of common and marshland, and the huge claims of the Forestry Commission, as well as the bulldozing of miles of banks to make easier work for the farm tractors.

Yet there is comparatively little wire, the conifer plantations have by no means monopolised the scenery, while the tall-banked motor lanes are still reasonably quiet. And from the moment of our first find on Bulkworthy's old rifle range by the Torridge, very rarely were we obliged to follow through gates or gaps.

Cantering over Mr Lewis Bellew's farm to Five Lanes and Chollaton, fording the swift-flowing Torridge, climbing the bracken slopes to Haton and on to Hankford, we were up and over a host of oak-and-beech-fringed banks, dividing four miles or so of good firm sheep grazing, before scent ran out on the plough at Thorne. The second fox piloted these light and smartly matched bitches from Bulkworthy to Doves moor and back again, until his scent, too, dried up at Thorne, giving us a six-mile run to end a magnificent day.

The whole country is behind Stevenstone; when Mr Sumner came here from the West Warwickshire in 1966, and asked the farmers where he could go, the unanimous reply was 'anywhere you like, any day of the week, but have a care of our bank tops.' And many of those farmers are out on Stevenstone days – Mondays, Wednesdays and Saturdays – punishing those banks a little themselves.

It is just as well there is no M-way to Bideford and these fine hills, or the Stevenstone would attract visitors. More visitors, probably, than they could cope with.

(23 February 1972)

Mr D.R. Isaac took over the Mastership from Mr Sumner in 1979. Mr Isaac carries the horn alternately with A. Garrigan, who was appointed huntsman in 1980.

The Tiverton

FINE STRAINS OF A DEVON PACK

Arriving in east Devon to hunt with the Tiverton 12 days ago, and looking across the bright pasture of the Exe Valley, with its little silver re-entrants (or goyles) and steep, softly rounded hillocks, intersected by a close chequer of stout banks, I thought this would be a fairly free horseman's country. And, up to 20 years ago – given an active 'Devonian' to ride – indeed it was. But since the mechanical trimmer replaced the manual cut-and-lay, as a closer inspection showed, the hedges topping those banks – being two or three feet high and thick as gauze – are no longer negotiable, so the foxhunter makes for the gaps and gateways and finds it quite a challenge to stay with hounds, although on the forward slopes, he is often afforded long and lovely views of their work.

It never was the Midland sportsman's conception of Mecca. 'Devonshire is certainly the worst country I was ever in', Nimrod wrote in the 1820s. But he went on to report with some amazement that 'nearly half the resident gentlemen and the greater part of the yeomanry keep what they call "a cry of dogs"', and added that at Huntsham, near Tiverton, the Rev. Doctor Troyte 'keeps a pack of foxhounds as his brother and father have done before him for the last 50 years'. Parson Troyte's family (who presumably gave two hoots neither for Nimrod's spit-and-polish manner nor his shires) emerge again in the Tiverton story, but, in the 1830s, it was a Mr Worth who provided the sport and, in 1841, a Mr Cockburn. Then, in 1843, Sir Walter Palk Carew, on retiring from the South Devon, lent both his hounds and the services of his gifted huntsman, John Beal, to his first cousin, Thomas Carew, of Collipriest, Tiverton, who was to be described by his obituarist as 'an unusually good specimen of the old-fashioned benevolent sportsman – his hand ever in his pocket, and a heart large enough to keep an entire countryside going'. At the end of 14 seasons, however, Carew disposed of his pack, and, after an interim season (Mr Cooke, 1857–8), the ubiquitous Lord Poltimore moved in to hunt the country.

A foxhunting protégé of Lord Portsmouth and Parson Russell, Poltimore, who had taken over the North Devon hounds from Parson Hole in 1856, now extended his empire into east Devon and Dorset too. For the meets around Tiverton, he brought hounds in a van-and-four from Poltimore Park, Exeter, and hunted the area for two or three weeks at a stretch. Apparently his final Tiverton visit was for cubbing in 1865, after which he hunted progressively less in Devon and more in Dorset, where he established the Cattistock country approximately as it is today.

That winter a hunt committee composed of Sir Thomas and Mr Walter Carew, Messrs Besley, John Heathcoat Amory (later Sir John), William Rayer, and the Rev. George Owen, of Calverleigh, appointed an acting Master and huntsman – Mr William Collier, who had previously hunted a pack of harriers. This experience is said to have 'made him rather slow when pressing a straight-necked fox across country. . . . Mr Collier was at his best' (the critic continued) 'when drawing cover, and had an unusually fine note on the horn, an accomplishment which he was somewhat overfond of displaying. . . .' Anyhow, that arrangement jogged along quite happily until 1873, when Sir Thomas Carew's grandson, William Carew Rayer, of Holcombe Court, took over the hounds, and ran the show for 19 seasons at his own expense, calling it 'Mr Rayer's'. His huntsman was Richard Holmden, formerly of the Lanarkshire and Renfrewshire, and his whipper-in was George Potter who went on to serve the Tiverton through the similarly long Masterships of Mr W.C.L. Unwin (1892–1910) and Sir John Heathcoat Amory's heir, Ian (1910–31), who moved the hounds to their present site at Hensleigh.

By the 1890s the Tiverton was getting quite fashionable and famous: 'Those who remember what a *rara avis*, indeed was a visitor 50 years ago', commented their Edwardian chronicler, 'would rub their eyes in astonishment at the number of orthodox pink coats and bevy of fair ladies . . .' while the new Master, who had bought the hounds from Mrs Rayer and then bred up a first-class pack, using Atherstone, Belvoir and Grafton sires, was also celebrated for his tenacity ('Mr Unwin does not spare himself . . . he has been known to dig out a fox by candlelight at 8.00 p.m. in November'). George Potter's third successive Master, Sir Ian Heathcoat Amory, won a still greater claim to fame, for it was he who bred – among many other paragons – the Tiverton Actor '22.

Sir Ian's 1917 entry consisted of just three couples, all sired by Berkeley Whipcord '12 – a son of the Berkeley-bred Four Burrow Whipcord '05,

76 The committee and others at a meet at the Castle, Tiverton, Devon, on 22 February 1869. *Left to right*: Mr Chichester Nagle, Mr Thomas Carew, Capt. Walter Carew, 'Squire' Besley, Mr William Rayer, Mr W.P. Collier (acting Master and huntsman), Mr Thomas Beedle, Mr Thomas Clarke, Mr John Heathcoat Amory, the Rev. G.W. Owen and Mr Frank Cockburn.

whose impeccable ancestry could be traced to the Brocklesby Drunkard 1745 – and out of Lonely '12, who shared with Berkeley Whipcord the illustrious name of Warwickshire Pedlar '01 in her pedigree. One of the whelps, Lictor, was selected to be crossed with a bitch called Bertha, whose ancestor was Warwickshire Traveller (another of Lord Fitzhardinge's beauties); and among the progeny, whelped in 1921, was the great Actor, who was to become the prototype of the modern foxhound. Initially, I am told, it was on Lord Knutsford's recommendation that Actor was used so extensively at Badminton, with the Cattistock and elsewhere. A generally far-sighted breeder, Sir Ian used pure Welsh blood (from the Ystad) as early as 1911, and afterwards the Brecon Tetrarch.

77 Mr Martin Scott (joint-Master and huntsman, 1969–77) with hounds near Rose Ash, Devon, on 22 February 1975. A son of Major Bill Scott, of Portman and North Cotswold fame, Mr Scott went to hunt the VWH in 1977.

When Sir Ian died, as the result of a fall in 1931, his two older sons, Sir John and Derick assumed the Mastership; during the war they were joined by Brig-Gen. The Hon. Lesley Butler, who, when the brothers stood down in 1946, shared the command with Lt-Col. Sir G.J. Acland Troyte, a descendant of Nimrod's friend. Thereafter Masterships were short; Sir G.J. Acland Troyte with Mrs Channer (1948–9) and, until 1950, with the Earl of Eldon, who then continued alone till 1952, when Mr R.L. Pugsley (1952–3) and, secondly, Lt-Col. William Heathcoat Amory (1953–4) acted as Master for the committee. Mr G.P. Roffe Silvester (1954–8) was followed by Mrs W. Heathcoat Amory, with Mr R.L. Pugsley (1958–62) and Mr A.E. Sturgess (1962–4); Mr Sturgess and Major and Mrs How (1962–9); and Mrs W. Heathcoat Amory and the present senior joint-Master, Mr Martin Scott, who also hunts hounds (1969–71). Mr Scott was joined in 1971 by Mrs F.C.B. Fleetwood-Hesketh, and, at the start of this season, by a former hunt secretary, Mr R.J. Pearcey. Col. Heathcoat Amory, who is now hunt chairman, is Sir Ian's third son, and the elder brother of Brig. Roderick, joint-Master of the Sinnington.

Mr Scott, whose appointment with the Tiverton followed a season's apprenticeship as amateur whipper-in with Capt. Wallace, tells me that he has used several Heythrop outcrosses and bred from a number of their bitches, too (using the Old Berkshire Grammar '61, which was bred by his father, the celebrated houndsman, Major W.W.B. Scott), thus adding, in the Hensleigh pedigrees, many additional lines to Actor. He also has a litter from a Heythrop-College Valley cross and has made use (extensively) of the Meynell Badger '66, given him by Mr Dermot Kelly, and (once) of the South Dorset Bridgeman '70.

He brought hounds to Rose Ash, a hamlet in the north-west of his country, near the Eggesford and East Dulverton borders, when I rode with them on 22 February, a sunny, hazy day with spring on the hills and the hedge-tipped banks, and 35 followers there to relish it. As they drew along the streambed of the Crooked Oak, a fox was viewed away opposite Nutshill; so Mr Scott lifted them in a flash to the line (in the style of the Heythrop's Master), and with a scarcely serving scent, they ran down the East Quince to the Crooked Oak, where despite steady perseverance, they lost him at 12.15.

They found another in Big Brook, and, notwithstanding a considerable movement of foxes between this point and Yard Wood, they held him to Rose Ash. Checking for a moment on the green where the meet was, they feathered north around the village and soon hit off the line again, running with a great chorus through Pearchey. Only three minutes or so in front of them now, their quarry turned right-handed short of the Quince cross-roads and northwards over the Crooked Oak, crossing into the East Dulverton country, where, momentarily, scent ran out north of Avercombe. But, with a long cast on the north side of the Bishop's Nympton – Ash Mill Road, they traced him to ground by Avercombe, where their Master blew for home in the golden light of 4.00 p.m.

By this hunt's standards it was a moderate day, but it produced quite enough to show why the pundits rate the Tiverton as among the top-quality packs of Britain; and I was very far from agreeing with Nimrod's stricture, for even if the day had been blank, riding for five hours round those delightful hills and quiet lanes was something to remember for a long time.

(22 February 1975)

Mr F.A. Pugsley succeeded Mr Scott in the joint-Mastership in 1977, Mr R.J. Pearcey remaining. R. Street was put on as huntsman for the 1977–8 season with A. Allibone as whipper-in.

The West Midlands

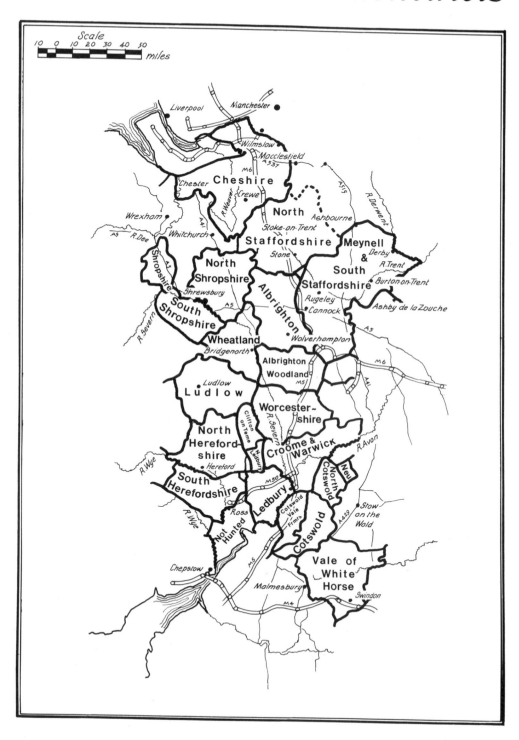

The Cheshire

IN TRADITION WITH BLUECAP

This obelisk, reader is a monument rais'd
To a shade, though a hound, that deserves to be praised;
For if Life's but a stage whereon each acts a part,
And true greatness a term that's derived from the heart;
If fame, honour and glory depend on the deed;
Then, O! Blue Cap, rare Blue Cap, will we boast of thy
breed . . .

The obelisk upon which this rousing dedication is inscribed, now standing by the Cheshire's kennels at Sandiway, is a splendid symbol of the high premium which this hunt has placed upon hound excellence, proved in competition, from the very beginning. For not only was Blue Cap a superlative foxhound, he also won the most celebrated hound-race in the history of the sport. The date of the race was 30 September 1763, and it was in the previous winter that John Smith-Barry, the enterprising and high-spirited son of the 4th Earl of Barrymore, had founded the Cheshire Hunt. So dazzling did the reputation of his pack become, that the great Hugo Meynell, Master of the Quorn, and originator of true hound-breeding, with obvious misgivings, challenged Smith-Barry to a hound race over a hot drag-line on the Beacon course at Newmarket, a distance of four miles. The account of this marathon is wonderfully evocative of the devil-may-care competitive spirit of early foxhunting England. Hugo Meynell had a reputation that must be confirmed or lost; boasts ran high and the Cheshire bloods, flushed with excitement as they sang their warlike ditty, determined to follow to a man:

They talk of Hugh Meynell and what he can do;
But we'll ride 'em or fight 'em this Leicestershire crew.
And we'll teach 'em, eh ho!
How the Cheshire will go.

Each Master ran two couples with a 500 guineas side-bet, while the odds were 6–4 on the Meynell. The Cheshire's four-year-old Blue Cap, a big piebald (who, on hunting days, had a weight tied round his neck to prevent him outstripping the rest of the pack) was accompanied by his powerful daughter, Wanton, and both sides' entries went into six weeks' training on a diet of sheep's feet, oatmeal and milk. 'The pace was so terrible', said a witness, 'that in three miles, half the horses were beaten. As the hounds swept over the heath to within the last mile, all but 12 followers came to a standstill and the

horse ridden by Cooper [huntsman to the Hon. John Smith-Barry], who led the field, was blinded for life. At the finish Cheshire's Blue Cap came away from the Leicestershire entry and won by 100 yards. . . .' Smith-Barry won a small fortune. His Blue Cap's blood lasted at least half a century in the Cheshire kennels.

But the Cheshire Hunt sprang from a firmer foundation than the initiative of a single young nobleman and the prowess of his hounds. For the hunting tradition of Cheshire can be traced in an unbroken thread at least to the document of 1285 whereby the Abbot of Chester granted the right to chase both fox and deer in his forests. Half a millennium later, in 1762, came the smart and youthful Tarporley Hunt Club, whose harehunting members brought out their private packs of harriers by roster and whose first president was the formidable 29-year-old Prebendary of Lichfield, the Rev. Obadiah Lane. It was as a prominent Tarporley member that Smith-Barry began to hunt his pack of foxhounds and from the club's base that he established the Cheshire. He had been Master for 21 seasons when he died in 1784.

John Smith-Barry was succeeded by his tactless nephew, James, who was warned off most of the neighbouring estates and had to be replaced by Sir Richard Brooke and Mr Egerton, of Tatton Park, sponsor of the new kennels at Sandiway. Maintaining the Smith-Barry tradition of hound quality, the Rev. George Heron, who succeeded to the Mastership in 1801, collected regular drafts from the Meynell. This ageing cleric had been assisted by Sir Henry Mainwaring, who took over in 1818, extended the country very considerably, built three independent kennels – at Wrenbury, Peover and in the Forest of Delamere – and hunted four days a week on a guarantee of £2000 a year. Mainwaring's continuous pedigree quest included an annual tour of the best kennels in England.

Nineteenth-century sportsmen regarded the Cheshire as one of the most dashing hunts in the country. Leicestershire could scarcely rival the Cheshire bucks. 'In the 1820s and 1830s', relates an early historian, 'some extraordinary runs took place, in which many of the hardest riders in England participated: Tom Cholmondeley, Lord Delamere *[the pride of all Cheshire, the bold Delamere]*, Bromley

78 The Hon. John Smith-Barry (Master 1763–84).

Davenport, Tom Trafford, Rowland Egerton-Warburton [the hunting poet] and Capt. John White'. Of Cheshire's Jack White, such a familiar figure on his big Merry Lad, who went on to be Master from 1841–55, Nimrod wrote: 'Taken in the double capacity of a rider of races and rider to hounds, Capt. White is decidedly the very best.'

Mainwaring's first huntsman was David Jones who, after campaigning as groom to a Peninsular War general and becoming in turn jockey, trainer and huntsman, went blind in a Chelsea workhouse. From Mainwaring and bluff and charming Squire Geoffrey Shakerley to Jack White, the gallant huntsman Joe Maiden (1832–44) served no less than five Masters. None could complain of his lack of tenacity. In 1829, on paying a quick visit to the kennels before driving to Lichfield races, Maiden mounted the copper when a feed was on the boil, lost his balance and slipped into it and was hideously scalded from toe to hip. He twice broke his left leg, and had ten pieces of bone removed; but he continued to hunt six days a week with one stirrup-leather nearly half the length of the other. Joe's one-eyed whip was Tom Rance who saw out seven Masters and six huntsmen and who vowed that 'he would rather break stones on a road than be a huntsman'.

As 'The Druid' pointed out: 'There was no finer characteristic of Tom than his genial tone and polite manner when steering his hounds at the end of his drooping whip-lash through a crowd of horsemen in a narrow lane: *jest stand o' one side, gemmen, if you please; beg yer pardon; a little mossel to let the hounds pass: thank ye sir; now gemmen, be so good; thank ye, sir. . . .'* We may well envisage such a scene at Egerton-Warburton's *Day wi' the Cheshur Fox-dugs* and round Farmer Dobbin reminiscing:

I seed Squior Geffrey Shakerley, the best 'un o' that breed,
His smoiling feace told plainly how the sport wi' him
  agreed;
I seed the 'Arl ov Grosvenor, a loikly lad to ride,
I seed a sight worth all the rest, his farencly young
  broid. . . .

The *'Arl ov Grosvenor* (afterwards 1st Duke of Westminster) of these verses was followed in the Mastership by Reginald Corbet, who held the record tenure of 35 seasons (1866–1901). But the last four of these were with the South Cheshire, for, in 1877, when Corbet inherited Adderley Hall, well down in this very big country, he proposed a division, and Capt. Park-Yates, a former Grand Military Gold Cup winner, retired from the Third Dragoons to

take the North. He was followed in 1896 by the Earl of Enniskillen, while in 1901 young Reginald Corbet took over from his father. In 1907 the 2nd Duke of Westminster offered to take on the whole Cheshire country in its original boundaries, single-handed, and this he did lavishly and with great verve for four years. During the First World War this hunt prized a great leader in old Col. Hall-Walker, afterwards Lord Wavertree, MP for Widnes, a leading owner of the Edwardian era and Founder of the National Stud. Walter Midwood, who won the Grand National with Shaun Goilin, had the Cheshire from 1923 until 1931, in which year the country was again divided into North and South, until the last war when the hunts were finally reunited.

Col. Ben Heaton kept the country open during the war and was joined in the Mastership in 1946 by Mr John Paterson, who died in the hunting-field in 1955, at the age of 74. Mr Philip Hunter (who has just celebrated 25 years as Master of the Cheshire Forest) took on the second responsibility of the Cheshire for four years from 1954, being then joined by the Earl of Rocksavage (now Marquess of Cholmondeley) in 1956, who continued in office with Col. Gerald Grosvenor (afterwards 4th Duke of Westminster) and Viscount Leverhulme until 1959. With the expert Jim Stanley as huntsman, Col. Grosvenor was senior Master to Lord and Lady Leverhulme until 1962 and, as Duke of Westminster, with Lord Leverhulme and Mr C.R. Tomkinson during the 1962–3 season. Mr Tomkinson, the great-great-grandson of Major Tomkinson of Egerton-Warburton's oft-quoted song – *Were my life to depend on the wager, I know not which brother to back, the Vicar, the Squire, or the Major, the purple, the pink or the black* – was then in sole command until joined in the 1970–71 season by Mrs J.E.K. Rae, and now by his wife.

As for the Cheshire kennels, there the Blue Cap tradition set a seal upon top standards. In the eighteenth century, hound races were the test, in the nineteenth came Peterborough. Smith-Barry, Heron, Mainwaring, Shakerley, White, all were passionate hound men; and so on through the Victorian period. The Cheshire have since been consistent Peterborough winners. Lord Rocksavage and the 4th Duke of Westminster were both well-known hound perfectionists of the old school. Then, with the advent of Johnny O'Shea (the present huntsman, a native of Queen's County and former whipper-in to the Laois, who came from the Meynell in 1966) the Cheshire began to breed on lighter lines, going mainly to the Meynell, Heythrop and Beau-

79 Johnny O'Shea with hounds. He has been huntsman since 1966.

80 Mr J. Heler, Master of the Cheshire since 1976.

fort, so that most of the pack are of Portman ancestry. Thus they have returned to the strong Meynell liaison with which their story began. This has paid off in no mean style: at Peterborough last July, for example, litter-brothers Luther and Lurcher '70, by Heythrop Luther '67 out of their Careful '68 by Meynell Camper '65, won the section for the best unentered dog-hounds. And Johnny O'Shea has a good dozen more of the Luther-Lurcher stamp to show you at Sandiway. In the 1963–4 season the Cheshire killed 69 brace of foxes; in 1966–7 the tally went up to 103, in 1968–9 to 110 brace and last season to 120 brace. Does this ancient and illustrious hunt thus hold the record?

(A non-hunting visit: 4 August 1971)

Mrs Rae was joined by Major D.P.G. Moseley in 1972, and they shared the command until 1974. Major Moseley then stood down and Mrs Rae was joined for the 1974–5 season by Mr M.E.S. Higgin. Mr Tomkinson re-assumed the Mastership in 1975 and Mr J. Heler has held it since 1976. Col. P.B. Sayce took over as secretary in 1974. At the time of writing (spring 1981) Johnny O'Shea is in his fifteenth season as huntsman.

While maintaining their fox catching record the Cheshire have also done very well on the flags. In 1979 they enjoyed a brilliant summer at the shows. At Harrogate they won the bitch championship and also found the reserve champion dog-hound, besides several other first-prize rosettes. At Peterborough they won the class for the best two couples of dog-hounds.

The Ludlow

SEEN THROUGH A CLEE HILLS MIST

Standing on the hills a few miles north of Ludlow, Downton Hall is one of those homes that exudes foxhunting in every corridor and room – if not so famously as Scarteen, Milton, Mount Juliet or Badminton, then at least as strongly. The house, with its 5000-acre estate, belongs to Miss Mary Rouse Boughton whose father, Sir Edward, a former Master of the Mendip and the Wheatland, founded the North Ludlow in 1932 and hunted that country with his own hounds until 1939, when he was obliged to disband it. From the end of the war Miss Rouse Boughton and her mother devoted much of their lives to the Ludlow, and they were joint-Masters from 1952 till 1973. Of Lady Rouse Boughton, who died at the age of 80 on the night of this season's opening meet, Capt. Wallace, the Chairman of the MFHA and himself a former Master of the hunt, wrote in *Horse and Hound* that under her, 'no stone was left unturned to see that the hunt occupied its proper position in the countryside, and whether in the interest of the farmers, the Pony Club, or the hounds, Daisy never spared herself, even when incapacitated by falls. She kept, and expected, the highest standards, and was a true character of her countryside. . . .'

That countryside is, by no comparison, an easy

one in which either to wear the Master's cap, to carry the horn, or simply to follow hounds. Lying in Shropshire, Herefordshire and Worcestershire, the Ludlow country extends all of 20 miles east to west and 20 north to south. For the most part it is privately owned, with – taking the largest shares – Lord Boyne (Burwarton estate) and Miss Rouse Boughton to the north, Capt. Lumsden to the south-east, Mr Lennox to the west and Mr Salwey, the hunt chairman, on the south side of the town. The Forestry Commission is also a large landowner, but the area is mostly valuable stock farming and especially sensitive to large numbers of horses; its general character is wild and hilly, and its heights, varying from 300 to 1700 feet, are divided by steep-sided dingles, with wire on either side; its diverse enclosure is tricky to negotiate; there are large expanses of forest, and numerous places, such as felled trees, covered with bramble, which are as secure for foxes as castles. As in all hill countries, the Ludlow weather is moody, and meets are particularly susceptible to interference by snow and mist.

After an encouraging thaw earlier in the week, followed by drenching rain, fog was the hazard on the day of my visit, 7 February, when hounds met at

Downton, where Miss Rouse Boughton, resplendent in scarlet, had three table-loads of refreshments spread on her lower terrace to receive 30 mounted followers and as many on foot. Waiting on the field just below the gardens, we kept glancing hopefully upwards at the sun's forlorn efforts to break the white vapour. And when, at one moment, it cleared enough to see the house, the Master, Brig. John Stephenson, handed over his horse and drove to the valley in the hope that it might have lifted there; but he soon returned with a headshake: no, it would not be safe to hunt. So we all rode back to the boxes, and that was that.

Next day proved the clearest contrast you could imagine, with cloud shadow scudding over the luminous, steeply rolling pasture, a kind of landscape beloved of Lionel Edwards. Brig. Stephenson, who came to live here when he retired from the Army in 1971, showed me some of the landmarks: the Titterstone, in the Clee Hills, for example, all the way down which, about 200 years ago, William Childe, of Kinlet, galloped, to the marvel of his friends, on a loose rein.

It was he who established the first pack of foxhounds in this country before joining Hugo Meynell, in 1780, in Leicestershire, where he became famous as 'The Flying Childe', being one of the first foxhunters to follow directly on the line of the hounds, no matter what the obstacles. Nimrod relates that Childe used to have the Titterstone Clee ringed with bonfires to turn the foxes from their point.

We passed the ancient Royal stronghold of Ludlow Castle, tall and splendid with the sun slanting through its ruins. Each year more than 1000 people turn out there for the Boxing Day meet. They have indeed gathered under those walls to see the hounds ever since William Adams, a Ludlow solicitor, founded his pack in about 1800, moving from harriers to foxhounds, which he brought from Major Bland, the founder of the Worcestershire, and hunted them with the help of a whipper-in called John Deyas, who rode a mule with which he reached every sort of rocky hilltop and cranny impossible for horses.

Messrs Forester, Dansey and Pardoe were three more early nineteenth-century squires to keep foxes on the move around Ludlow; but the one who really carried on the Adams tradition was Frederick Stubbs, of Wetmoor, assisted by his son Orlando, a brilliant young man across country, and breeder of hounds and horses. Three long and happy Masterships followed Stubbs. Mr Willoughby Hurt-

Sitwell (1854–64), who took over at 26, carrying the horn himself, was the first; then, after Major W. Murray's short interregnum (1864–6) which was terminated by ill-health, came Mr Charlie Wicksted (1866–86), an exceptionally popular Master, who bred up one of the most influential packs in Britain; then Sir William Curtis, who put in a total of 21 seasons. It was a year or two after he had the honour, at the age of seven, of being blooded to the Berkeley by the celebrated Harry Ayris that Sir William's family moved from Bristol to Caynham Court, near Ludlow, where in 1891 he built the kennels that serve the hunt today. The kennel-huntsman throughout this steady reign was Clarence Johnson who, as soon as Curtis resigned, transferred to the Albrighton Woodland. He was later with the West Norfolk.

Skimming through Curtis's diaries on the Sunday afternoon, I came across an entry that worked vividly on the imagination; it was bordered above and below by bands of black ink and dated 22 January 1901: 'Scent fair. Bitches $16\frac{1}{2}$. Horses, Carol and Common, Cork and Toby. . . . This evening Her Majesty the Queen died at 6.30. Hounds did not hunt again till after the funeral. . . . There was some frost and snow during the interval. God save the King.' Of Curtis's tenure one of the hunt chroniclers, Sir Richard Green-Price, wrote: 'This was the heyday of prosperity of the Ludlow country. No pack so free from bickerings and grumblings; indeed it has always been reckoned the tightest and most gentlemanly hunt in this side of England.'

If Ludlow lacked quite the same ideal harmony during the next 30 years or so, it was due to short Masterships. Mr Frederick Milbank, of the Bedale family, held office alone until 1909, being then joined by Mr Herbert Allcroft, a lawyer who had been hunting in the country since 1885. The names Meredith, Charlton, Coldwell and Kennedy then largely recur in the list until the war when a committee took over – and the country was still kept open.

The Ludlow was Capt. Wallace's first country as a MFH, and those who remember him vouch he showed outstanding sport, not only with the foxhounds, but with his otterhounds and beagles, too. He was followed by Sir Hugh Arbuthnot, who in turn went behind Capt. Wallace to the Cotswold in 1952, the year in which Lady Rouse Boughton and her daughter began their long innings.

There was no one immediately available to follow when the Rouse Boughtons wished to hand over in

81 Miss Rouse-Boughton holding the Ludlow entry that came second in the class for two couples of entered dog-hounds at Peterborough in 1968.

1973, so it was a saving grace when Brig. Stephenson stepped in. He agrees that the light, active close-coupled type is the hound for this country; and, while carefully guarding the excellent lines already established, he has recently gone to the Portman, the Eglinton, and the Puckeridge for outcrosses. On 7 February I was immediately impressed by this pack's lovely look of quality and it was rather frustrating, to say the least, to see them led from the meet round the back of Downton Hall and straight into their box, all on account of that capricious fog that so nearly budged.

(7 February 1976)

To the great regret of the whole hunt, Brig. Stephenson was killed in a motor accident in 1977, and his place as Master and amateur huntsman was taken by Mr Kenneth Beeston, who hunted the Atherstone country for 11 seasons. He was succeeded, in 1979, by Miss G.M. Harrison, who was joined, in 1980, by Mr E.P. Lycett-Green, who carries the horn.

K. Nixon-Heron was taken on as kennel-huntsman in 1978, but was later relieved by D. Furmage.

The Royal Rock Beagles

THE WORLD'S OLDEST BEAGLE HUNT

Tinley Barton, a young farmer and land agent living in the Wirral Peninsula of Cheshire in the early 1840s made it plainly known that he would not always be content to ride along behind a huntsman, be it in pursuit of fox or hare. He wanted a pack of his own. And like so many people who harbour their wish genuinely and tenaciously, he fulfilled it with apparent ease. For, at the end of 1844, someone made him a present of three couple of 13-inch hounds, 'rabbit beagles' as they were called, and with his friend, John Okell, he proceeded to hunt hares over his own and the neighbouring farms. There was only one organised pack in the Wirral at this time: the foxhounds kept by Sir William Massey Stanley, of Hooton Hall. And in agreeing to share his country, Sir William made just one stipulation – that Barton should *ride*, so that he could whip hounds off if they ran towards any of the fox coverts.

The two friends invited their neighbours to the meets, and the sport became so popular by the early spring of 1845 that, with Barton as Master, they decided to 'form a club, for the purpose of hunting hares in The Hundred of Wirral'. And since most of the members lived in the vicinity of Rock Ferry – a 'Royal ferry' ever since William IV had used it when Duke of Clarence – and because the principal meeting-place was the hotel of that name, it was decided to call the hunt 'the Royal Rock'. Some were in favour of harriers, but it was thought unlikely the farmers would tolerate a second mounted pack in the country, and for the equally good reason that the subscribers were young men engaged in business in Liverpool, 'not desirous', as they put it, 'of plunging into the expensive sport of hunting on horseback', the final decision was overwhelmingly in favour of foot beagles. And thus the first subscription beagle hunt of all time was born.

But what beagles? Barton's gift-hounds were really not large enough to make their way through the strong, close fences of this flat cattle country, nor had they been deliberately bred to hunt. Just at that time, however, Capt. Anstruther Thomson was disposing of his pedigree pack, purchased mainly from the great enthusiast who had resurrected this hound type from the 12-inch 'lap-beagle', to which it had degenerated at the end of the eighteenth century, into a useful 14-inch harehunter – Parson Honywood, of *Merry Beaglers* fame. And the man

who bought 12 couple of them for the Royal Rock, at the price of £25 2s 6d was Christopher Rawson, who was to succeed Barton as Master.

Next summer the Royal Rock's pioneer huntsman, Thomas Kay, described as 'a rough Lancashire man, whose dialect was unintelligible, even to the hounds', was commissioned to 'beat up all England for further supplies'. And not only from England, for that past winter having seen the cruellest phase of the potato famine, they secured several drafts – with only their passage to be paid for – from Irish beagle-owners, who had to economise after remitting their tenants' rents.

Kay, who had been engaged for '£1 a week, a house and a uniform of scarlet coat, green waistcoat and white breeches and leggings', resigned in 1846, for 'family reasons' (he had a wife and nine children to support) – but he died that summer when, taking his hounds to bathe from the end of Rock Ferry pier, he fell into the river. 'When he sank,' related Christopher Rawson, 'the dogs landed on the pier, and hunted his back trail full cry all the way to the kennels, to the surprise of his poor wife at hearing the hounds hunting in sorrow. . . .'

The members raised £75 for her, and, to fill her husband's place, found a paragon called Humphrey Jones, 'a speedy and tireless runner', said a biographer, 'and a most agile leaper, usually carrying, in addition to his whip, a pole with which he was able to clear hedges and gates, flying them in his stride'. But Jones overdid it and died at 38, being succeeded in 1854 by his fellow-Welshman, John Davies. Two more Welshmen followed Davies: John Vaughan (1854–63) and Charles Williams (1863–86), who came from a Montgomeryshire harrier pack.

The year Humphrey Jones died saw the birth of the Chester (now Cheshire) Beagles and the beginning of the RRB's territorial problems. The new neighbours were at once made welcome, for up to this time there was plenty of country in the Wirral's north, and there seemed to be no reason why they should require land further south. But the Birkenhead-Hoylake-Wallasey conurbations were expanding fast, and from an early date the Royal Rock hunted in parts of north Wales. Now, in the 1970s, that tradition is more important than ever: with the help and generosity of the Vale of Clwyd Beagling Association and the Flint and Denbigh

82 Followers catching up at the turn of the century.

Hunt, they take hounds about one day a fortnight to either the Mostyn or the Northop estates. And for over 20 years now the Cheshire Beagles have loaned the RRB part of their country south of the Ellesmere Port-Chester canal – outside Wirral.

Everything was perfectly amicable between hunting men in north-west Cheshire, until the Wirral harriers came on the scene, when several of the Wirral foxhunters, having had their suggestion that the RRB 'go mounted' snubbed, formed their own pack.

And the most towering figure in the Royal Rock's history, Lt-Col. Vincent Ashfield King, an original member, who had by then been Master for 15 years, wrote to the somewhat arrogant and 'beagle contemptuous' Master of the harriers, J.R. Court, that it was 'perfectly clear that in the lower end of the Hundred there is neither sufficient land nor sufficient hares for two packs of hounds'. But, although an acrimonious correspondence ensued, the two hunts then co-existed happily up to 1939, when the Wirral harriers were disbanded.

An equally dramatic hunt crisis was narrowly averted in 1882, when Col. King died. According to the RRB's nineteenth-century historian, Nathaniel Caine: 'the hunt had become identified with King,

and to some of the older members it appeared impossible and undesirable to carry on any longer'. Although he was irascible, jealous and autocratic, the self-styled 'Ould King', whose world revolved around the beagles and his battalion of Cheshire Volunteers, was a much loved man. However, the young followers' vote for the RRB to continue prevailed, and Louis Rudd Stevenson, a former civil engineer and cavalry officer, 'filled the honourable post for seven seasons to the satisfaction of all'.

Sixty years later another Stephenson was Master, another of those lovable men that the world of beagling turns up so readily. Huntsman from 1947 (when he was 58) to 1954, and joint-Master between 1948 and 1954, it was written of Phil Stephenson by his obituarist, Mr W. Victor Smith (himself a former Master, and the present chairman), that, 'when, in 1967, he resigned the chairmanship, his fellow-members held him in such affection and admiration that they created for him the special office of President, an office unique in the Royal Rock's history.'

Visiting them on 9 March, I had the feeling that the Royal Rock would never be short of leaders of King's and Stephenson's stamp. There were nearly 100 followers at Mr and Mrs Wetherell's meet that afternoon at Thornton Hough (the village built by the 1st Lord Leverhulme, 70 years ago, in much

83 Mr T.D. Harvey *left* (joint-Master since 1967) with his
daughter, Mary, and Mr Jock Radcliffe.

earlier Wirral styles). And only the halt and elderly
kept to the four great elm drives radiating from Lord
Leverhulme's Thornton Manor.

There were 60 or more near the heels of huntsman
Mr Terence Harvey, who was joint-Master (first
with Mr Beazley, then Mr Smith) and huntsman
from 1958, and has been in sole command since
1968. And, with hounds continuously on the move,
it was no mean feat for all those nine-to-fivers and
their wives and the seven-to-seventeen-year-old
'Leverets' section (the hunt's answer to the Pony
Club) to stay with Mr Harvey, a solicitor, but a well-
known athlete, too, who has run no less than 20
times in the six-and-three-quarter-mile Cheshire
Beagles' point-to-point, and has secured the best
time more often than any other runner.

Despite the north-east wind; the flat horizon's
ominous blue haze; a lack of rain on this light,

sandstone-based and quick-draining soil; manure spread on nearly every field of grass we ran across; and that host of sportsmen unavoidably crossing and re-crossing the line, there was a reasonable scent. And, considering there were far too many hares about, it made a happy lesson to watch the RRB's fast and level pack stay so faithfully with each quarry, so that, apparently, they hunted only three hares throughout the afternoon and each of these for a minimum of 45 minutes. These beagles were so close when the last clapped just short of a rhododendron thicket, I thought they must have her. But when she jumped into the bushes ahead of their noses and the one they followed away was obviously fresh, Mr Harvey blew 'home'. And after three hours on the trot, we were glad enough to return to Thornton Hough and Mrs Wetherell's sumptuous tea.

(9 March 1974)

Mr R.B. Symonds, who joined Mr Harvey in the Mastership in 1977, has since carried the horn. Messrs W. Henderson and D. Thurman have been appointed whippers-in since the article was written.

Charles Dowson, who served a number of foxhound packs following a successful career as a jockey, joined the Royal Rock as huntsman in 1964.

Since the article was written the Royal Rock are – owing to roadbuilding on the Wirral – taking their hounds more often into north Wales.

Vale of White Horse

EARL BATHURST'S AND CRICKLADE IN ONE

Knowing the immediate and unqualified harmony with which the VWH (Earl Bathurst's) and VWH (Cricklade) amalgamated eight seasons ago, and seeing them last week with all their separate identities and loyalties obviously long jettisoned in favour of the new hunt, one almost forgot that their early background was steeped in wrangle and bitterness.

The VWH was originally a chip of the Old Berkshire, a typical rambling eighteenth-century hunt country, sprawling into five counties, with Burford, Oxford, Marlborough, Malmesbury and Cirencester all within its perimeter. It was founded by the Rev. John Loder in 1760. When no new Master could be found to rule this empire after Mr Codrington's resignation 64 years later, the hunt approached Mr Harvey Coombe, head of the brewing firm, who was then hunting the Old Berkeley (now a part of the Vale of Aylesbury). Coombe agreed to hunt both areas, a remarkable undertaking considering it meant keeping open, single-handed, a tract of land 100 miles or so broad, reaching from Charing Cross to Cirencester. In fact, by his second season he found himself unable to cope, and in 1826 the Earl of Kintore, bringing his own hounds down from Scotland, relieved Mr Coombe of the Old Berkshire country.

In 1830, however, Kintore decided he preferred Scotland and was followed by the Hon. Henry Moreton, the 28-year-old son of the Earl of Ducie. But in spite of Moreton's 'novel custom of taking his hounds to the meet in a van or bus with four post-horses', he found the territory impossibly big. Initially his suggestion that the country should be divided was fiercely opposed; then, on 3 October 1832, the contesting parties agreed to the western portion being placed on loan to Moreton and that '. . . the line should go from Faringdon to Uffington and thence up the bridle road by the White Horse Hill, continuing by the bridle road to Lambourne'. Moreton called this the Vale of White Horse country. After his first season he moved his hounds from Cricklade to Cirencester, into kennels built for him and loaned without rent by the head of a family whose selfless involvement has been a byword in the country ever since – the 4th Earl Bathurst.

In one way the hunt was off to a good start, for Lord Ducie (Moreton inherited in 1835) was one of the great houndsmen of his day, 'thoroughly acquainted', as 'Scrutator' – Mr Horlock – put it, 'with those points, either in foxhound, horse or cattle kind, essential to the perfection of animal structure.' But frail health was one of his handicaps. In 1842 he lent his hounds to Lord Henry Bentinck, who had just taken over the Burton country, in the hope that a season out of the hunting-field would see him fit again. But it was not to be.

84 Sidney Bailey (huntsman since 1966) taking hounds to the first draw from Braydon Hall on the day described by the author.

As I say, the VWH sector was only on loan, so when Ducie retired in 1843 Mr Thornhill Morland, who had taken on the Old Berkshire in 1835 demanded its return, and some angry dialogues ensued. The obstinate, quick-tempered Lord Gifford, who succeeded Ducie, appeared before the magistrates at Faringdon on charges of trespass and breach of the peace before – thanks largely to the conciliatory efforts and good sense of Lord Bathurst – the VWH was recognized in 1844. It was decided the boundary should 'follow the Thames as far as Lechlade and from there the River Cole.' When in 1847, Lord Gifford moved to the HH and the VWH could find no one willing to take over from him, a committee consisting of Lord Andover, Lord Bathurst and Mr

Raymond Cripps (known inevitably as 'the ABC') ran the hunt with John Grant, who had been with Lord Ducie, as huntsman. This was until the arrival in 1850 of the popular Mr Henry Villebois. There then followed a relatively happy period lasting through six Masterships and ending in 1886 during the Mastership of Mr Hoare.

'It was an unlucky day on which Mr C.A.R. Hoare was elected Master of the VWH [in 1879]', the 7th Earl Bathurst recalled; 'for this led to all sorts of social difficulties as well as external friction between the landowners and farmers, which finally led to the division of the country.' Mr Hoare, it seems, combined the role of MFH with *cavaliere servente*. The scandalous rumours grew, until in 1884 the hunt committee gave him notice to quit. But Hoare was a famous benefactor of the farmers, so they were up in arms, and when the committee listened to them, the landowners were furious. But the 6th Earl

85 The late Major Jock Mann. He was senior joint-Master from 1964 until his death in the hunting-field in 1978.

Bathurst, who owned the kennels, simply told the offending Master to find alternative accommodation. Thereupon Hoare brought his hounds to Cricklade, Lord Bathurst bought new hounds and after much unpleasantness and complication the country was divided by a north-east to south-west line with VWH (Cirencester, or Earl Bathurst's) to the north and VWH (Cricklade) to the south. Hoare relinquished the Cricklade two seasons later, and it took Mr Butt Miller, a most dedicated Master and successful hound-breeder, to get the hunt on the right keel. He handed over in 1910 to Lt-Col. Fuller, who was also in office 21 seasons. The 6th and 7th Lords Bathurst between them served even longer Masterships (from 1886 to 1943) for their own hunt.

But for the dramas of 'Charley' Hoare's private life the split would never have happened, and during the following 70 years there were many people who recognised that a reunion was the natural and logical thing for this country. In the post-war years, on the Bathurst side, Mr Gregory Phillips had long recommended it and the present Lord Bathurst (joint-Master since 1949) was sympathetic to the idea, while the prime movers in the Cricklade country were Major E.P. Barker (chairman and a former joint-Master) and his wife (also a joint-Master). The main factors tipping the scales in favour of the re-merger in 1964 were, on both sides, financial pressures and, on the Cricklade side, loss of country due to the growth of Swindon and the extension of the M4. With typical kindness Lord Bathurst gave his hounds to the new hunt. And with Col. M.St.J.V. Gibbs as chairman, and Lord Bathurst, Mrs E.P. Barker, Major J.J. Mann and Mr Gregory Phillips as joint-Masters for the 1964-5 season, everything looked well for the VWH.

Major Mann, who was joint-huntsman of the Cricklade from 1957 to 1961 and on bye-days for the first few seasons after the amalgamation, is now senior joint-Master to three fellow-farmers, Messrs P.J. Hudson, T.J. Dibble and Michael Henriques, and also conducts the hound-breeding policy. The Cricklade kennels at Meysey Hampton, being the more central, were used. Many Cricklade hounds were disposed of, and 26 couple of Lord Bathurst's young hounds (largely bred, incidentally, by Lord Bathurst's mother, Lady Apsley) were taken on the new strength; and, although the Bathurst was a more heavily built hound, these nicked in well at Meysey Hampton. Using Cricklade sires, a number of Bathurst bitches were bred from, and since then the main outcrosses have come from the Beaufort, Berkeley, Carlow, Heythrop and Old Berkshire, the Duke's Falcon '63, Berkeley Soldier '64, Carlow Striver '63, Heythrop Craftsman '62 and Lurcher '67 and the Old Berkshire's Chieftain '68 being the most prominent of these.

They certainly looked impeccably level when they arrived for Major Barrington-Chance's meet at Braydon Hill, near Minety, on the Wednesday of last week. And with 63 brace of foxes killed and an outstanding record of long runs so far this season, everyone expected them to streak away in their customary style. But the scent was much too fickle for that. Drawing Old Copse first, they ran one of a brace a mile south, only to be headed by cars on the Minety Common road. The dismal conditions continuing, they then hunted another over the Derry brook and up to the railway line. Here the pack divided, only three couple going on with the hunted fox to White Lodge. At 12.15 Waits Wood was drawn blank, but they found again at the Fishponds,

and, considering the catchy scent, hunted remarkably fast over this wonderful grass country to the railway by Minety Lower Moor. Here Sydney Bailey (son of Tom, the well-known Heythrop kennelman and the VWH's huntsman for six seasons now) was obliged to dismount and run nearly a mile to be with them, his horse being led round to Pleydell's Farm.

Several foxes were started along the big hedgerows on Mr Peter Hudson's (the joint-Master's) farm and a chorus of unavailing *holloas* was the order of the rest of the afternoon. We did circles round giant yellow tractors carting away Mr Hudson's elms, suffering from the Dutch disease, and the day ended at his Swillbrooks. Seventy followers had set forth from Braydon Hall. The 20 left at Swillbrooks included Major Mann, field Master; his wife and their daughter, Mrs Wills; Col. Gibbs, chairman; Messrs Hudson and Henriques, joint-Masters; Major and Mrs Barker and Mr Phillips, former Masters; Mr D.H. Arkell, one of the three joint-secretaries; Miss Elizabeth Ward, owner of that most celebrated fox stronghold, Red Lodge; and Capt. Caledon Alexander (looking very businesslike in ratcatcher and white armband as gate-shutter for the day); and a dozen or so happy-looking farmers – a most significant factor, for if there is one thing that stands out especially with the Vale of White Horse it is the excellent rapport between the hunt and the farmers.

(3 January 1973)

Mr Martin Scott went from the Tiverton to the VWH as joint-Master and huntsman in 1977. To the very great dismay of the whole country, Major Mann died in the hunting-field in 1978. His place as joint-Master was taken by Mr D.H. Arkell.

The Worcestershire

GOING SINCE THE 1770S

Well over 100 mounted followers, including 20 children, were out with the Worcestershire hounds when I joined them for their very successful day over land belonging to a former joint-Master, Col. Gray-Cheape – the Bentley estate – on 8 February. It was one of those frigid mornings that begin with a blue

haze in the middle distance and turn yellow with the waxing of the midday sun, not generally the sort of weather that keeps a fox's scent on the ground; but a changing one that holds surprises. Moving off at 11.15 from Bank's Farm, where Mr Michael Dufty, the treasurer, was host, they soon had a fox afoot from one of the Colonel's great pheasant strongholds – the Thrift. Leaving the Shadow to his left, he pointed westward for the Hatchett and Bentley House, there saving his brush by crossing the trail of another at 11.45. Still in very catchy scenting conditions, a second fox led them by Church Covert, through Cocksian, then right-handed by Curr Lane and across the plough of Holyoake's until he met the new Redditch-Bromsgrove carriageway, there shaking them off at 12.15.

By this time – riding the 19-year-old bay mare, Cherrybin, a former Badminton horse – I had seen enough of the Worcestershire to know just how well they could speak for their careful Berkeley breeding and for the inspiration of John Kelvey, their quietly energetic huntsman, who came here from the West Warwickshire Farmers' three seasons ago. Indeed there seemed to be only one sorry note in this country – that heralding the departure of the senior joint-Master, Mr Roger Ward (who generously lent me Cherrybin), one of the reasons for it being his recent election to the National Chairmanship of the Pony Club.

Master since 1970, Mr Ward has continued a tradition which commenced two centuries ago, for it was in the mid-1770s that the Worcestershire's first Master, Major Bland, established foxhounds quite close to the present kennels at Fernhill Heath and hunted them over that same nice light earth they know today, till 1812. The Worcestershire Masterships have nearly all been short ones. The year Bland gave up, Lord Foley of Witley, a former Master of the Quorn, stepped in, to found the Foley Hunt Club, but he stayed a mere two seasons, and his successor, Col. Newnham, only three, after which the hunt went into suspended animation until 1820, when T.C. Hornyold took charge. He retired in 1824, but helped Mr John Parker to start a new pack for the 1825–6 season.

Parker, whose affairs were always in a parlous state, kept the Worcestershire going till 1832, when he went as huntsman to a pack of harriers, and according to the hunt historian, Thomas Read Quarrell, then 'eked out a precarious living as a wine merchants' traveller and, about 1870, became an inmate of the Powick Mental Institution'. Thomas Clutton Brock who took up the reins was obliged to resign in 1836, whereupon a sailor, Capt. Chandler, became Master (and 'was most popular and much esteemed by the farmers').

It must have been quite a blow for Brock and his members when in 1838 Robert Stephenson laid the Midland railway between Worcester and Bromsgrove – a far more alarming obstacle than the river Severn, which divides the county in half (but which can at least be swum, as the Marquess of Queensberry proved in his 1870–71 Mastership). Now there is a worse one still – the M5. We were less than five miles east of it on 8 February and only three miles from the line originated by Stephenson. But you would not have known it; the Bentley area is silent and comparatively unspoilt. At 12.30 Kelvey lifted them to Bartles, which they drew blank; but in next-door Hennals they went smartly on to the line of their third fox, who pointed his mask right-handed, over the plough at Foxlydiate and Pump-house Lane, then across the pasture by Norgrove and through Mill Coppice, with plenty of timber jumping for the 70 remaining followers, most of whom were up to see the finish of this run – at Pike's Pool, where they accounted for him at 2.30.

When Candler's Mastership ended in 1846, William Davenport purchased the hounds, to establish the North Staffordshire, while the Worcestershire committee bought a new pack and secured the Hon. Dudley Ward as Master for one season and John Russell Cookes for the following three. With the appointment of Major Thomas Clowes in 1850, it looked as though the hunt would enjoy a somewhat longer reign, but he had to leave when the militia was mobilised at the time of the Crimean War; so J.R. Cookes came in again – alone – until 1857, when Clowes was free to form a joint-Mastership with him, a very successful one. Clowes died in 1865, and Cookes resigned, to be succeeded by Mr Harry Vernon, who ruled by himself for one season and with Mr Henry Allsopp (afterwards Lord Hindlip) for four; and it was during this time that the still very solid and practical kennels at Fernhill were built. Lord Queensberry, who had just given up the Dumfriesshire, put in one season (1870–71), to be followed by Allsopp again, this time with the celebrated Tom Carr as huntsman.

It was now that a division of the county took place, the reason being that the 9th Earl of Coventry (of Croome Court) – who pointed out that 'Gloucestershire had four packs and Worcestershire only one' – was determined to go independent. In 1866 he suggested two packs to hunt Worcestershire six days a week, offering to kennel his own hounds for the southern sector. In 1867 he founded the North Cotswold Hunt, but abandoned this, seven years later, in favour of the 'Earl of Coventry's'. In 1882 this became the Croome (now the Croome and West Warwickshire).

On 8 February, one follower who had been

86 Thomas Woodward's *Gone to Ground* (1844). The hounds are the Worcestershire Messmate and (*behind*) Coventry.

hunting regularly with the Croome told me that Worcestershire had been considerably more fortunate with their country; and certainly, 'in the Bentley area,' it is well opened up and contains considerably more grass than arable. There were plenty of foxes, too. After the kill at Pike's Pool, Kelvey returned to the Thrift, and Mr Barry Heath *holloaed* one away towards Hall's. Hounds lost him by Upper Bentley Farm, but within a few minutes they had another on the move from Hill Lane, and, led by Torture (a particularly useful hound, by Berkeley Tottenham), they were only two or three

feet behind his brush when he went to ground at Tyrrell's at 3.30.

The five Masterships succeeding the Croome division were still short ones: Frederick Ames (1873–6), Charles Morrell (1876–9), Frederick Ames again (1879–96), the Earl of Dudley (1896–1902) and Charles Mills (1902–6). But the Worcestershire did benefit by a 'brilliant phase of continuity' with their huntsman, Will Shepherd, who was said by Quarrell to be 'the greatest expert in the art of hunting hounds ever seen in Worcestershire'. Previously huntsman to the Empress of Austria's private pack at Schönbrunn, Shepherd came to the Worcestershire in 1888 and, declining the offer of the Belvoir horn, served on through the first six seasons of the hunt's longest Mastership (that of Mr Arthur Jones), until he died of pneumonia in 1912. Mr Jones, who is reputed to have bred one of the smartest Belvoir-type packs in Britain, then hunted hounds himself, with Shepherd's son, George, and Tom Vockins, the kennel-huntsman, whipping in.

When Jones resigned in 1929, the hunt secretary, Major H.P. Rushton, took office up to 1937. His joint-Master, Mr Hugh Sumner, carried on alone until 1940, when Mrs Alex Wood gave a hand, and, a

season later, Mrs H.P. Rushton, who nobly commanded from sidesaddle until as late as 1961, being assisted during the period 1948–51 by Major Cadbury, and between 1951 and 1957 by the hunt's good friend, Col. Gray-Cheape, over whose land we rode on 8 February. After that, Mr Ganderton wore the Master's cap till 1966; Mr Pittway and Mrs Rushton's daughter, Mrs Jon Tollit (the rider of no fewer than 171 point-to-point winners), till 1970; then the present senior joint-Master, Mr Roger Ward, with Mr Pittway, till 1973, when the latter was succeeded by Mr Alan Cure.

A fresh triumvirate of Masters has been elected

87 Hounds on the way to draw Bartles, Upper Bentley, when the author was with them on 8 February 1975.

for the 1975–6 season: Mr Michael van Zwanenberg, a joint-secretary since 1971; his business associate, Mr Anthony Sellar (well-known for his work in organising a pool of private horses for the hunt staff); and Mr David Gibbs, a young farmer whose family have been tenants on the Bentley estate for many generations.

These three were still out among the remaining field of 60, when scent improved with the evening chill and hounds found their last fox in Woodgate Gorse at 3.50. Dashing south over Two Tree Hill, he swung left-handed across Forest Farm, to be headed by a group of foot followers on the road; so, piloting them left again, by Leasowes, the Park, the Gardens and Upper Bentley Farm, he skirted the Thrift, pressing on towards Lower Bentley – with the galloping field pointing their horses with special care in the fading light at the timber – until at length he found an earth at Fosters, having given hounds (huddled close and fast to the finish) a six-mile run in two hours. That is the kind of sport the Worcestershire have been showing consistently this season and, given their continuing spirit of sportsmanship, which has endured since the 1770s, the future indeed looks promising for these foxhunters.

(8 February 1975)

Mr D. Gibbs and Mr A.J. Sellar duly formed the new joint-Mastership in 1975 and Mr R.L. Orchard joined them in 1980. J. Creed was put on as huntsman in 1976 and D. Evans as whipper-in in 1978. D. Gatfield succeeded Evans in 1980.

Wales

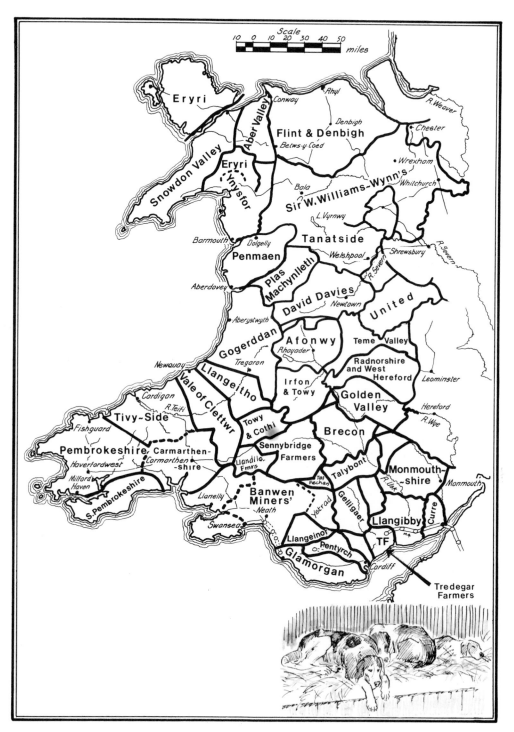

Scale
10 0 10 20 30 40 50
miles

Eryri

Snowdon Valley

Aber Valley

Eryri
Ynysfor

Flint & Denbigh

Conway
Rhyl
Denbigh
Betws-y-Coed
Chester
Wrexham
R. Weaver

Sir W. Williams-Wynn's

Whitchurch
Bala

Penmaen

Tanatside

L. Vyrnwy
Welshpool
Shrewsbury
R. Severn

Barmouth
Dolgelly

Aberdovey

Plas
Machynlleth

David Davies

Newtown

United

R. Severn

Aberystwyth

Gogerddan

Afonwy
Rhayader

Teme Valley

Newquay

Llangeitho

Tregaron

Radnorshire
and West
Hereford

Leominster

Cardigan

Vale of Clettwr

R. Teifi

Irfon
& Towy

Golden
Valley

Hereford
R. Wye

Tivy-Side

Fishguard

Pembrokeshire
Havordfordwest

Carmarthen-
-shire
Carmarthen

Towy
& Cothi

Llandilo.
Fmrs.

Sennybridge
Farmers

Brecon

Milford
Haven

S. Pembrokeshire

Llanelly

Banwen
Miners'

Neath

Taf
Fechan

Talybont

R. Usk

Monmouth-
shire

Monmouth

Swansea

Ystrad

Gelligaer

Llangibby

Curre

Llangeinor

Pentyrch

TF

Glamorgan

Cardiff

Tredegar
Farmers

The Curre

WHITE HOUNDS OF MONMOUTHSHIRE

Nose, cry and perseverance: those are the three great qualities of the Welsh hound. His shortcomings are lack of stamina, and a tendency to independence and babbling, to compensate for which several nineteenth-century Welsh Masters brought infusions of the best English blood to their kennels. But none with such resounding and immortal success as Edward Curre of Itton. In 1896 he went to the head of a heritage that was born in the eighteenth century, for he took over the Chepstow Hunt, which began as harriers under his great-great-grandfather, John Curre. In 1869 the Chepstow, having a very small country, amalgamated with the Llangibby but separated again a decade before Edward Curre took over from Squire Lewis of St Pierre. He re-named the hunt 'Mr Curre's', and was Master for 34 seasons.

'I wanted a hound,' he explained at the end of his career, 'that had drive and voice and speed. I wanted them all of a type, without the woolly Welsh coat – which to me was unsightly – and I wanted them *white*, so that I could see them in the distance; for, even in my country, hounds often ran in places where a horse could not follow, and it would have been difficult to see the darker-coloured ones. But I did not want to lose "the hound of the country". . . . By using stallions from the long-established Welsh packs that possessed the most drive and speed, and crossing the produce with English stud book hounds, which possessed low-scenting qualities, and had plenty of tongue – and, wherever possible, the light colour which I wanted to get, I gradually acquired a type of my own; a type which, as you can see, reproduces itself generation after generation. . . .'

The fuller story is well known to most students of foxhound evolution. Establishing his kennels during the last years of the century with the best Welsh strains – some of John Lawrence's 'killing Llangibby', the Glog and the Neuad Fawr, during the pre-First World War era, Curre crossed these with such influential sires as the Milton Potent 'o1, Belvoir Weaver '06 and Watchman '07, the Duke of Beaufort's Leveller '10, and, most extensively of all, with his favourite, the redoubtable 'hard-as-steel' Four Burrow Whipcord '05. Up to the war, it was Belvoir, Belvoir, Belvoir. Practically every prize-winner at Peterborough was bred from the sacred 'Belvoir Tan'. But owing to over-breeding and over-

emphasis of certain points, the Belvoir had not only become lumbering caricatures of their antecedents, but had lost much of their working qualities: their nose and cry had deteriorated. Hound breeders began to search for a lighter, more active hound.

At this time the Curre blood was becoming famous, and year by year an increasing number of English bitches arrived at the kennels that Sir Edward had built along the road from Itton Court in 1906. The die-hards were horrified: 'The Welsh cross is a blot on the escutcheon, a *mésalliance*,' complained Lord Bathurst, 'a marriage without quarterings'. But the progressives held sway. 'Always on the look-out to improve my hounds,' wrote Ikey Bell, 'I soon paid Sir Edward Curre and his hounds a visit. I was astounded by their cry and their work in the field. . . .' The Curre Fiddler '09 is said to be responsible for Bell's conversion to the Welsh cross, a conversion which marked a salient turning-point in the evolution of the modern hound.

Then that great Anglo-American sportsman, A.H. Higginson, tells how, when he was out with a pack hunted by a 'brilliant amateur', he saw a hound make a hit across some plough when nothing else in the pack would own the line, and was informed that 'it went back to some of Teddy Curre's blood'. He goes on to relate how he owed the success of his own pack in America – the Middlesex – 'to the infusion of Sir Edward Curre's blood. . . . It *made* my pack, I know that. And when I came back to England . . . I found that many of the best working packs in the land used some of the Itton Court stallions. . . .' He could have added that it was originally Curre outcrosses, more than any other, that were responsible for the swing from heavy Belvoir to the foxhound we know today.

The Curre blood permeated nearly all forward-looking kennels in Britain. And the movement has prevailed. After Sir Edward's death in 1930, during his widow's 25-year Mastership when the hunt was known as 'Lady Curre's', Major Forsyth-Forrest and others adhered faithfully to the founder's breeding policy. In 1956, when Lady Curre died and the hunt went subscription – it was probably the last to do so – Mr J.G. O'M. Meade (the father of Richard, of eventing fame) took over the Mastership and, helped by the huntsman, Reg Dale, also the breeding. And, although both he and Mrs Meade will relinquish

88 Sir Edward Curre with his hounds at the opening meet at Itton Court, Monmouthshire, in 1928. The Curre remained a private pack until 1956.

89 George Headdon, the huntsman, showing off six litter-sisters (the progeny of Saucy '64 by Linesman '67) for the author in March 1973.

their share in the present triumvirate on 1 May next, and leave Mr F.M. Broome to be joined in the Mastership by his son David, the world showjumping champion, fortunately for the Curre, the Meades will continue to fashion the shape of these unique white hounds of Monmouthshire.

It was hot and dry when we met at Itton Court on the Tuesday of last week, and drawing through Orles, past Coldbath House and up to Itton Common, with green on the larch and pollen on the catkins, one might easily have spent that clear scentless day without hearing so much as a whimper of the celebrated cry. And, indeed, a couple of hours went by before they could get on terms with a fox. Lifting them from the waterworks area, George Headdon, their huntsman, tried Crosshands (Coed Llwyn-y-Celyn), then Gilbrook Wood, where they accounted for a fox. Two broke from the Grove and ran on to the Coetgae, one turning back into covert, but the other steered them over to Hale Wood, right through there and on to Gethley, while we had a nice long canter over the vivid pasture and hunt jumps of Mr Meade's land and, at last, a splendid sample of the Curre chorus.

Scent was poor in covert, and although they lost him in Gethley Wood, it had been fascinating to watch these rather short-legged, close-coupled and unusually agile hounds wriggle and persevere through the thorn and bramble brakes of the conifer plantations in which this part of Wales abounds. And considering it is such a tiny country, it was heartening to find so much widespread determination that the hunt shall remain independent – and shall never cease to breed the stamp of hound Sir Edward bred, hounds whose blood has suffused every corner of the world of foxhunting for the past half century.

(27 March 1973)

Mr Dennis Price and Mr and Mrs Trefor Beverley-Jones joined Mr Broome in the Mastership in 1977, while Charlie White relieved George Headdon as huntsman in 1976. In 1980 a new joint-Mastership was formed, composed of Messrs Broome and Wayne Kathrens and Mrs Diana Brown.

The David Davies

CONSTANCY IN MONTGOMERYSHIRE

The country hunted by the David Davies, which lies astride the river Severn in South Montgomeryshire, is a most charming one to ride over. The springy sheep pasture of the grass and bracken moorland heights are divided into expansive hedged enclosures with plenty of gaps and gates and hunt jumps; and so are the softer cattle fields surrounding the isolated farmsteads in the valleys below. About one-fifth of the county is sacrificed to conifer plantations. The going can be tricky in the dingles and hillside woods, so you need a compact, sure-footed horse, and one with enough quality to carry you through six or seven hours of climbing and descending; for only when it is too black to see his white hounds will Lord Davies, joint-Master and huntsman, blow his horn for home.

His grandfather, the 1st Lord Davies, who founded this hunt, was the same; only a chance earth or total darkness saved his foxes. At first sight you may think that conditions are generally unaltered since his day, for it is a wonderfully unspoilt bit of country. But, besides the forestry, there is twice the wire, and where the old pasture has been ploughed and re-seeded there are high densities of sheep to foil the scent. Riding with this famous pack on 24 November, I wondered what David Davies would think if he saw them now. For his unique hounds were full of English and Fell blood, now they are almost pure Welsh.

What was he aiming to fashion, I wondered, when in 1905, aged 25, he gathered at Plas Dinan what was described as 'the most cosmopolitan pack in Wales', with drafts from Atherstone, Belvoir, Berkeley, Blencathra, Dartmoor, Fitzwilliam, Meynell and Sir Watkin William Wynn's, besides as many pure Welsh? We know that, like Sir Edward Curre, he was out to breed a fundamentally Welsh hound, retaining the priceless Welsh nose, tongue and drive, and combining those qualities with English constitution and stamina, and pack sense. Like Sir

90 The hunt's founder, David Davies. In 1932, the year in which he was created Baron Davies, he became so preoccupied with his political aspirations that he decided to put his hounds up for auction.

Edward, he wanted a white hound that could be seen at a distance; unlike him he was determined to keep the broken coat. The result was a triumph.

David Davies also had the Montgomery beagles and the Hawkstone otterhounds, and at one time his beautifully laid-out kennels housed 220 hounds and terriers. In 1908 he took five couples to his Canadian ranch to hunt coyote. Wherever he hunted, he always wanted to be up at dawn and home well after dark. He was also an MP, an active philanthropist and busy man of affairs, and although he was a clever breeder whom many English Masters in search of good Welsh cross visited, he was never able to devote sufficient time to his kennels. By 1932, the year he was created Baron Davies, he became even more deeply engrossed in his scheme for an international peace-keeping force than in his local affairs, and he decided to sell all his hounds.

The dog-hounds soon went, and many of the bitches, too; but when Lord Davies returned from abroad and saw the last remaining four and a half

91 Lord Davies, joint-Master and huntsman, leading hounds away from Oakley Park, Montgomeryshire, on 24 November 1973, the day described by the author.

couple of bitches waiting for auction he had a change of heart. He could neither bear to see them go nor the strain, which he had so carefully nurtured, die. There was also a strong and unanimous appeal from the farmers that the hunt they had come to love should be kept going. Davies therefore invited one of his enthusiastic young followers, Mr Peter Lewis, to come in as deputy Master. Lewis agreed to take charge on a dismounted basis with the help of his

sister, Medina, and Miss Mari Jones, as whippers-in. They began with the happy presage of a fox killed after an eight-mile point from their opening meet. They lost the services of Jack Davies, one of the most colourful characters in Wales, who began with Lord Davies in 1913. But, to fill his shoes, they got in the devoted and redoubtable Tom Bound.

Although subscriptions have been taken since the Second World War, the David Davies has remained a private pack. After Lord Davies' death in 1944 and his elder son being killed in action in the same year, Lady Davies was Master until she died in 1948, when the 2nd Lady Davies kept them on behalf of

92 A typical stallion hound: the David Davies Bristol.

her son, the present Master. In the same year David Davies' third son, Islwyn, became joint-Master, and carried the horn until 1963. He remains joint-Master with his nephew, who acts as a huntsman on Saturdays, while David Jones, the kennel-huntsman, hunts hounds on the dismounted days of Mondays and Wednesdays. David Jones succeeded Ted Lewis, who had served the hunt with unswerving dedication for exactly 30 years.

Like all good Welsh hounds, the David Davies cast well by themselves, indeed they hate interference, and knowing the country well, and given reasonable visibility, the dismounted huntsman can keep hounds well in sight and earshot, even on a breast-high scent, by clambering from hilltop to hilltop. I had this sort of view from the horse which Lord Davies kindly lent me on 24 November. Moving off at 11.00 a.m. and followed by the usual preponderance of this hunt's Wembley-famous Pony Club branch, they soon roused a fox in the park trees and ran him to ground in a two-mile circle near the spot where they found him. Lord Davies then lifted them a mile north to Dolgwenith Wood, and when they hunted their second through Bwlch and Pant-y-Malfod Wood, I began to make some assessment of their style.

It was very windy in the middle of the day and scent was poor, but when they spoke to it, it was with that deep organ-like cry that so many English Masters have tried to infuse in their own hounds' breeding over the past half-century. They seemed to pick up the cold scent, as the Welsh breed should, yet were too often unable to persevere with it. They drew well, but their very independent character showed at the cast when, sometimes, one or two couples would regain the line and say so, while the remainder were obstinately determined to find out for themselves. Even for a Welsh hound, the David Davies seem small, light-boned and narrow, and one wondered whether they could have the constitution to close up, in this daunting country, to three or four long-distance foxes in a day.

From that four and a half couple of bitches and the litter of one of them, saved by Lord Davies in 1932, successive Masters have bred out the English strain, and during the past 40 years even the Welsh outcrosses have been too few and far between. So there has been a tendency to inbreeding. The great Blencathra Trueman was probably the strongest outside influence on the 1st Lord Davies' stamp of hound, and instinct tells the present Masters that a Fell cross would prove the best solution now. But they are not certain.

Montgomeryshire only compares with the Lake District in terms of gradient. Lord Davies has a Welsh-Blencathra cross in kennels now and will be watching his performance. But whether they go to one of the Fell packs, to the College Valley, the Cotley or the Curre, theirs is likely to be an English outcross.

At 4.00 p.m. the wind dropped, being replaced by a snap in the air, and with a holding scent these hounds streaked away on the brush of their last fox from the thick brambles in Coed-Meiriog, hunted him with their lovely chorus by Hornby Dingle, through the length of Cwm-y-gath, by Cloys-bank and past Red House and Pen-y-coed. They checked on Drummers Hill, but found him again at Bryn-Bedw.

It was almost pitch black when they lost their last inside Cwm-y-gath, and for us only just light enough to steer the four-mile ride to the road where the hound van was waiting. With the combination of Lord Davies, David Jones and their amateur whipper-in, Neville Owen, always eager to be there till nightfall, there is no restraining influence, so they told me, on David Davies hunting days, but what pleasure this hunt gives to South Montgomeryshire's host of sportsmen – horsemen and foot followers, too.

(24 November 1973)

The Hon. Islwyn Davies retired from the joint-Mastership in 1976.

Since the article was written the David Davies has bred a litter by Eskdale and Ennerdale Bendigo, which has proved very successful. Lord Davies has also bred up the size of his pure Welsh entries.

The Flint and Denbigh

HUNTING IN THE NORTH WELSH TRADITION

Not often do you see such a strong contingent of boys and girls as turned out with the Flint and Denbigh at Plas Heaton, Mr Richard Heaton's meet, on 4 January. Of the 66 mounted followers that day, more than 30 were children enjoying their last week's hunting before the Easter term. Shepherded by an enthusiastic cadre of 17- to 20-year-old associate members, as many as 110 Pony Club supporters at one time have attended meets in these two thinly populated counties. Lying snugly between the Conway and the Dee, the Flint and Denbigh country is one of small enclosures in steeply undulating farmland with a good share of grass, and big dingles, freely distributed and well routed, that lead on, in the climbing south, to a wide expanse of open hill and moorland; not, by and large, a galloping country, but a nicely mixed playground for child riders.

We soon learnt of another reason for the Flint and Denbigh's showing of self-assured young. The Pony Club's district commissioner here is the Hon. Mrs Peter Hotham (the joint-Master, whose special responsibility is the kennels). She knows every one of them, and their ponies, too. They respond to her as to no one else. And, as Mrs Hotham herself said when hounds moved away across Mr Heaton's estate to draw the Terrace copse, the future of foxhunting leans very heavily upon the following and spirit of the Pony Club, particularly upon those members who are farmers' sons and daughters.

Mrs Hotham's joint-Mastership reminds you, too, that it depends almost as much – and, nowhere more than in sparsely populated North Wales – upon heritage. For she was a Williams-Wynn, the sister of the present Sir Watkin; and it is this family that largely provides the strong tie existing between the Flint and Denbigh and Sir Watkin Williams-Wynn's Hunt. Ever since the first foxhunting Sir Watkin kept a pack at the family home of Wynnstay in the mid-eighteenth century, the name Wynn has predominated in the hunting tradition of Shropshire and North Wales. Mrs Hotham's uncle ruled at Wynnstay for no less than 58 seasons (1886–1944), while her father had commanded the Flint and Denbigh for 48 (1888–1946), to be succeeded by her brother for 15 seasons (1946–51), for 12 of which he hunted hounds. (Appropriately enough he moved on to guide the hunt that bears his name.) And it was Mrs Hotham's grandmother who, in the 1890s, converted the farm buildings at Cefn, St Asaph, into the present kennels.

But the Wynns lend a still more ancient link. For they were one of the four prominent families providing sport at Flintshire's Holywell Hunt Club, an institution that survived from 1770 till 1852, and the one that gave birth to the hunt. Here they met – the Grosvenors and Mostyns, Myttons and Wynns – with their hounds and horses, gaily fining each other for such heinous crimes as failing to attend dinners, wearing the wrong coat, and marrying without the others' permission; here crazy Squire Jack Mytton, a regular attendant of that club, first raced his famous Halston; and here, between 1800 and 1833, came Sir Richard Puleston, an early huntsman of the Williams-Wynn country ('one of the first gentlemen to hunt hounds', as Nimrod observed), hacking up from Llanrhaiadr Hall, near Denbigh. Then, in the late 1820s, Sir Thomas Mostyn, the much-loved Master of the Bicester (though rather volatile, in spite of Nimrod's remark that 'there are few better qualified to be at the head of a pack of foxhounds than Sir Thomas'), having watched with growing admiration the sporting potential of his native north Wales, brought his hounds up from Oxfordshire to kennel them at Mostyn Hall, Flintshire; and to hunt all the country from the Conway to the Dee, more or less the east-west tract covered by the Flint and Denbigh today.

93 The joint-Masters at the meet at Plas Heaton, Denbighshire, where the author joined them on 4 January 1972. *Left to right*: Mr R.J. Heaton (the host), Mr W.O.D. Tilley, Mr D.H. Fetherstonhaugh, and the Hon. Mrs Peter Hotham.

Not that it was known as the Flint and Denbigh in those days. Edward (afterwards 2nd Baron) Mostyn, who took over *in toto* on his father's death, with the Hon. Pryce Lloyd managing the kennels, called them 'Lord Mostyn's foxhounds'. Like his father, and like the present Lord and Lady Mostyn (owner-trainers of Battle Royal) he was devoted to the turf as well as the hunting-field. But when he died in 1852, a hiatus occurred. Sir Richard Williams Vaughan, who had inherited the famous home-bred Rûg hounds from his uncle, Col. Howel Vaughan, then hunted part of Lord Mostyn's country. But there was no resident pack in the Flint and Denbigh country again until 1867, when two officers of the Household Brigade, Col. Wynne (Grenadiers) and Capt. Rowley Conwy (2nd Life Guards) got together a scratch pack, purchasing five couples from the New Forest and six from the Brigade Drag, all of which were replaced, in 1869, by drafts from the Cheshire, Linlithgow and Stirlingshire, Bramham Moor and Duke of Buccleuch's; and this blood lasted in the Flint and Denbigh at least until the 1920s. The new Masters were immensely popular, and tall Rowley Conwy was described as 'one of the finest and bravest riders of his day. . . . It was a famous and regular sight to see him jump massive places with big drops the other side, often with a hand on the back of his saddle calling out "it's all right!" as he disappeared down the bank.'

The hunt was first called the Flint and Denbigh by H.R. Hughes, successor to Col. Wynne in 1876, and ancestor of the senior contemporary joint-Master, Mr David Fetherstonhaugh. A decade later on the scene came Mr R.W. Williams-Wynn, afterwards 9th baronet, Mrs Hotham's father. This Williams-Wynn was joined between 1912–27 by Lt-Col. E.W. Griffith, another joint-Master, whose descendant was out on 4 January – Mr Michael Griffith, the point-to-point rider, over much of whose land, between Plas Heaton and Trefnant, we rode that day.

Half a century ago, Col. Griffith (a former field Master of the Belvoir) liked rather heavy 24-inch hounds (he went to the Atherstone, Belvoir and Warwickshire), and this was indeed much the type we saw last week at Plas Heaton: big powerful hounds, mostly of Wynnstay, Puckeridge and Braes of Derwent breeding. The country is too enclosed for a really fast hound. We saw from their scars how terribly they suffered from barbed wire, and for this reason the Flint and Denbigh are now likely to be bred on lighter lines. But this must not be at the price of nose: there are numerous woods in their dale

94 R. Jones, M.M., who has been huntsman since 1967.

country, they hunt from covert to covert; and it is a cold-scenting country, especially on the limestone ridge running north-west from Denbigh.

Scenting conditions on the Tuesday of last week could not have been much worse. But this did nothing to deter Bob Jones, a tremendous enthusiast who has been huntsman to no less than five packs of hounds, since winning his Military Medal with the Royal Welch Fusiliers in the Burma Campaign. He has no professional whipper-in, but is regularly assisted by another competent and colourful personality, farmer and nagsman, Jim Pendleton.

The fox they followed from Mr Heaton's Terrace soon found an earth. So did the one they ran at 12.15 from Cae Drain to the top end of Garn Dingle. And this was an unhappy reminder of the death, in his early forties a fortnight ago, of one of this estate's most effective earthstoppers, Alun Davies. His sort of know-how is not easy to replace. With a scanty scent, open earths were more to be deplored. But Bob Jones has nothing if not perseverance. He pressed on towards Trefnant, leaving Pen-cae-du, Green Uchaf, Nant-y-Patrick and Berth-Ewig drawn blank; then round to the south, and same again with Greenfield Gorse, Plas Newydd, Crest Mawr and Fox Hall Larches. On a clear day, from this stretch of the Clwyd Valley, you can see the jagged ruins of thirteenth-century Denbigh Castle and the ships steaming along the Irish Sea. On 4 January the fog was upon us: we could scarcely see the next dingle.

(4 January 1972)

A new joint-Mastership was formed in 1978. Mr R.J. Heaton, the Hon. Mrs Peter Hotham, Major B. Williams-Wynn and Mr D. Fetherstonhaugh.

The Gogerddan

BRITAIN'S OLDEST FAMILY HUNT?

Majorie Lady Pryse became joint-Master of the Gogerddan in 1930 and has been sole Master and huntsman since her husband, Sir Lewes, died in 1946. She lives two or three miles north-east of Aberystwyth, the kennels being adjacent to her hilltop farmhouse, Ffynnon Caradog ('Caradog's Well'). It is not known whether Caradog, or Caradoc – a pre-Norman Welsh prince and an ancestor of the Pryses – resided on the site of Gogerddan, which lies in the lawn-smooth valley below Ffynnon; but certainly the Pryses, and their forbears, the Llwyds or Lloyds, Lords of Cardigan, nearly always faithful servants of the Crown and the most renowned veneries of west Wales, lived there for at least 1000 years. The big house, its cubic shapes now painted a pale, clinical grey, its drives packed with officials' cars, has been the Welsh Plant Research Centre since 1956, and does not readily come to life in the mind's eye as the headquarters of what is probably the oldest family hunt in Britain.

But reading of ancient dynasties that have preserved their sporting traditions down the ages, it is fascinating to picture the succeeding generations starting out for the chase, or better still perhaps, regaled in Sunday best, showing their visitors the kennels. At Gogerddan (pronounced Gog*ert*han, and once spelt so, too) you might have seen Plantagenet David Llwyd and his guests in hooded cloaks – caught back at the shoulders to reveal bright-coloured smocks and close-fitting hose – admiring lean, shaggy hounds, their blood a cross of the old Celtic and the Bresse, brought in by the Norman monks; Llwyd's grandson, Sir Richard ap Rhys and his son, John Pryse, Councillor of the Marches, in Tudor ruffs and pantaloons and John's heir, Sir Richard – whose receipt for a draft of hounds in 1601 is still in the family's possession – in close-brimmed Jacobean hat and forked doublet. Sir Thomas, the third holder of that baronetcy (who died from a hunting fall), would have been in a broad, white-lawn collar and cavalier boots; and his nephew, Sir Carbery, wearing a frock coat and periwig and a great ostrich feather in his hat, and with perhaps grander kennels and a larger pack of those broken-coated hounds to show off, because lead mines were discovered on his estate, rendering him very rich indeed.

Lewis Pryse, born in 1716, another whose great diversion was hunting, acquired through marriage the New Woodstock property in Oxfordshire, and

his only surviving child and heir, Margaret, added
Buscot Park, Berkshire, to the Pryse estates by
marrying Edward Loveden. The Pryses – or Lovedens now – had estates in Pembrokeshire, too, and
owned Cilgerran Castle. But Gogerddan remained
their principal seat, and it was the green hills and
thick, steep-sided cwms rising from Cardigan Bay
that rang all winter through to their horn and hound
song. The whole county was their hunting-ground.

The Lovedens' son, who changed his name to
Pryse Pryse, was Cardinganshire's MP, as well as a
very active landowner, but that did not prevent him
making full use of three packs: foxhounds, harriers
and English Old Southern foulmart, or polecat,
hounds. A diary entry shows that on at least one
occasion he had all three out, one after the other, on a
single day, accounting for a sample of each quarry.
On other mornings he would be up at 4.00 a.m. for
flighting, coursing till noon, then out with the
hounds in search of a three o'clock fox.

Pryse Pryse's son, who, to confuse us further,
reverted to the name of Loveden, held the Mastership from 1849 to 1855, and was succeeded by his
son, Pryse Pryse, who was created a baronet in 1866.
Sir Pryse's uncle, Col. E.L. Pryse, took the hounds
in 1859, but, until 1864, shared the county with
Capt. Herbert Vaughan, who hunted a second pack
from South Cardiganshire. When Col. Pryse died, in
1888, the Master's cap was worn for five seasons by
the baronet's eldest son. In 1894, with kennels still at
Gogerddan, Vaughan Davies, afterwards Lord
Ystwyth, assumed the Mastership for three years;
then old Sir Pryse returned to the helm. His son,
who acted as his huntsman, died in 1900 at the age of
41, from a fox-bite that went bad on him, and one
feels his obituarist might have been referring to
many different Pryses when he wrote: 'He loved to
associate with the country folk and the simple
villagers . . . he loved the woods, the mountains and
the fields, and he loved to chase the hare and the fox
with a love that was inherited.'

The only non-hunting gap in the history of
Gogerddan House appears to be the season 1906–7,
when Vaughan Davies kept the hounds at Tan-y-
Bwych; but that summer, the next Pryse son, Sir
Edward, a former Master of the Tivyside, took on
the family hunt and ran it at his own expense until
his death in 1918, when his brother and inheritor,
Lewes, assumed the Master's cap.

Sir Lewes' successors moved to Carmarthenshire,
and his widow, the present Master and huntsman,
now nearly 70, does not have the support necessary
to carry on in the old style. She is reduced to eight

and a half couple and is her own kennel-huntsman
(her whipper-in, Will Jenkins, suffered a coronary
and must not go too hard). Lady Pryse stopped
riding when her trusted mare retired with arthritic
shoulders two seasons ago, although to make a
special occasion she did borrow a horse last month
for the Boxing Day meet, and 40 mounted followers
turned out to honour her; but, as she told me rather
ruefully, her hounds only recognised her when she
dismounted. Anyhow, a lot of the Gogerddan
country is too steep for horses.

Nant Eos (meaning Brook of the Nightingales),
the house south of Aberystwyth, at which the
Gogerddan met when I joined them on 10 January,
was rebuilt by Inigo Jones and probably offers the
finest setting in the country for a meet of hounds.
The surrounding hills, steep, wild and lonely, were
unusually vivid for the time of year, for there had
been no hard frost, and the spring growth was
through early, a bad sign for grazing. They were
saturated, too, from the previous night's storm, and
it was feared the foxes would have kept underground. There are not enough of them, anyway,
Lady Pryse explained, because the Forestry Commission, which owns most of the land now, offers
such a good price for a brush, and the farmers and
shepherds shoot them relentlessly, many being
cruelly wounded.

All the same, after drawing Nant Eos park and the
hedgerows beyond it, blank, they pushed up an
outlier in the thick brambles at the foot of one of the
Commission's woods, springing after him over the
pasture with a glorious cry, four litter-brothers-and-
sisters of College Valley breeding, being in the lead,
Ringdove, Rouser, Regal and Ranter. (There was
also one noticeable lagger – black-and-tan Chantress, a present from Sir Rupert Buchanan-Jardine;
she had found her way into the flesh hovel during the
night, I was told, and filled herself so full of meat she
could do no more than amble along now. But she did
accelerate as the afternoon drew on!)

Their quarry set his mask down a thickly copsed
stream-bed, which made going difficult for the
followers; but, after 20 minutes they were out on the
grass again, moving more slowly now, for the wind
was up and scent getting patchy.

Lady Pryse's pack has one particularly difficult
and unpleasant local obstacle to negotiate: pig
netting, some three-feet high, with a strand of
barbed wire six inches above that, and several
hounds were gashed on their thighs by these fences.
(It was a nasty one for followers, too.) But when the
scent regained its pungency, they put down their

95 Marjorie, Lady Pryse (Master since 1946) with some of her hounds on the author's day with the Gogerddan on 10 January 1976.

heads with vim, and I was much impressed by the Gogerddan's great dash and speed and by the style with which they breasted the jumps, and was not surprised to see them soon up with their fox, catching him in a willow-thicket, about 45 minutes from the find.

Lady Pryse cheered them straight on to the next draw, but they could not find again, and at 3.30 she called them for home. Climbing over those Cardig-anshire hills on 10 January was indeed a delight. Despite increasing afforestation, the Gogerddan country is still mostly open pasture, with not much hedge enclosure, thinly populated and very little developed. It has echoed to the present Master's *huic holloa* for 44 seasons now, but the great pity is that there is no Pryse to follow her in a tradition that has probably lasted over 1000 years. Let us hope, at least, that someone worthy of that tradition will step in when the need arises.

(10 January 1976)

The Radnorshire and West Herefordshire

A WELSH BORDER PACK

Rich pasture, close-cropped and steeply undulating, is the principal feature of the borders of Wales and West Herefordshire. This is intersected by massive hedges, while the general pattern is liberally broken up by thick hillside copses, running down to swift-flowing rivulets. The population is sparse, and the game shooting not too highly organised. In such a country foxes thrive and are not easy for hounds to catch. Yet here the fox, which is now an honoured foe, was once counted as no better than a skulking pest, with a pelt worth a bob or two to his exterminator. In the parish register of the Radnorshire village of Pilleth (where, in 1402, Sir Edmund Mortimer was defeated by the great Glendower) are listed such charges as these:

AD 1704   For killing a fox 1–0
AD 1714   Paid Ed Lucas for digging out a fox 1–0
AD 1721   For ale when fox was killed 2–6
AD 1724   Mary Vaughan for expenses at killing 6 foxes 12–0

And so the foxes here were stalked and trapped and waylaid, until the hound-hunting fashion spread west and, in the early nineteenth century, young Squire Cliffe of West Herefordshire organised a trencher pack to hunt the precipitous hills bordering Radnorshire. Next on record, half a century later, Capt. Bevan built kennels at Presteigne and aimed at producing a hound to match this hill-and-dale country. He bought drafts from two of the earliest Welsh packs, the Vale of Aeron and the Gogerddan, some of which were descended from hounds kept by the Abbot of Strata Florida in pre-Reformation times, the earliest Welsh hounds recorded. It was mostly the progeny of an old bitch given to Capt. Bevan by the 8th Duke of Beaufort and crossed with these traditional Welsh, that the country was hunted in the latter part of the nineteenth century. And thus was born the Radnorshire and West Herefordshire hunt.

For the opposition which Capt. Bevan suffered modern foxhunters would warmly sympathise. It came from the pheasant-covert owners, who would not have him near. And it was not until 1868, and the advent of the powerful personality of Col. Price of Castle Weir, a retired officer of the 35th Regiment, who well knew the two sports could be reconciled, that the restrictions were removed. Meanwhile Col. Price maintained Capt. Bevan's policy of crossing pedigree English with pure-bred Welsh, and built up a very effective working pack, to which he carried the horn for 24 seasons.

A day such as 5 March 1873 must have driven such a perfectionist as Col. Price half mad. The Victorian diarist, the Rev. Francis Kilvert, recorded on the 7th that 'when old Tom Evans, the tailor, formerly a huntsman to harriers, heard the horn of the Radnorshire and West Herefordshire along the hill on Wednesday, the old hunting instinct in him awoke like a giant refreshed. He scrambled on to his old pony and rode furiously into the middle of the pack, hat in hand, hopping and holloaing and laying hounds on to the scent as of yore. Col. Price, the MFH, was greatly enraged. "Man, man!," he shouted, "where are you going, man? Come from those hounds!". But the tailor, maddened with the chase, was deaf to all entreaties. He careered along among the hounds, holloaing and waving his hat till the enraged MFH charged him and knocked the tailor and pony head over heels. Nothing daunted, however, the tailor scrambled onto his beast again and was second in at the death, close to the heels of the MFH. . . .'

But such traumas apparently did little to urge the departure of Col. Price. It was not until 1892 that he handed over to Mr Salisbury Thomas, and 1896, the year that Mr Herbert Peel took over, that he sold his 22 couples to the committee.

'Peel found that the pack were very riotous and wild,' says a hunt historian, 'so he introduced hounds from Cheshire, his native country; but this was not a success, for they had not enough tongue for the Radnor country.' Peel's successors therefore reverted to Capt. Bevan's time-honoured breeding: then, in 1910, arrived the stamp of Radnor and West hound that is seen in their kennels today.

In that year Messrs T.P.P. Powell and Ralph Baskerville retired from the Mastership, handing over to Mr John Curre, brother of Sir Edward, the inheritor of the famous Monmouthshire pack in which the forceful Welsh tongue and nose were skilfully interwoven with the best hard-driving English strains, producing the light-built hound with the pale lemon-and-white coat that has been so famous in the countryside around Chepstow for more than a century. John Curre bred from his brother's hounds to make the new Radnor and West.

96 Mr P.J. Davenport, acting Master of the Radnor and West since 1978. He has also been honorary secretary since 1967.

And that, with a College Valley outcross to produce extra drive for these border gradients was the hound we saw when Mr Robin Cursham, joint-Master and huntsman, unboxed by Mr Jones's Lower Farm in Huntington, a mile or so to the English side of the border, on Monday, 6 December.

Here, one distinguished foot-follower took up the historical thread. This was Mrs Edward Longueville, the widow of Major Longueville, who was Master for 45 years. 'My husband took his first pack of hounds to the South African war, as a subaltern in the Coldstream' she recalled at the meet; 'he hunted the little steinbock deer, coursing them first with greyhound, then laying on the foxhounds when the greyhounds were tired . . . that was his main experience before he accepted the Radnor and West's horn in 1919. . . .' Carefully nurturing the Curre type, with an occasional outcross from Sir Watkin Williams-Wynn's, Major Longueville continued in office until 1964, being joined in the Mastership in 1952, by Sir Derrick Bailey and, in 1957, by Miss Griselda Dunne, aunt of the present joint-Master, Capt. Thomas Dunne.

At 11.00 a.m. Capt. Dunne led us off behind hounds to Church Coppice, which was drawn blank. Then we rode the lane to Mr Tom Williams's Lodge Wood where a fox dashed from a bracken bank a mile southwards, and went to ground. Up came John Morgan, celebrated locally for his formidable terriers and his talent for divining earths with a twist of wire. In went his terrier and out shot the fox, flying north again, through Lodge Wood, across this firm if precipitous border grazing land and up to Forest Wood where the scent petered out. But Mr Cursham drew that covert from the west and the one they now found may have been the original fox. Anyway they went up to Mr Bayliss' covert, circling via Upper Hergest, back to ground in Forest Wood, where they gave him best. The next fox, which was found by the ruins of the Norman Huntington Castle, headed for the south bank of the Gladestry brook and gave us a nice hunt, still without a corner of plough to be seen, through Huntington Park, Lodge Wood and Church Coppice, until cattle foiled the scent at Hill Gate.

So great was the local enthusiasm, that there seemed to be a farmer, armed with binoculars, at every gate and wayside lane. At 3.30 they were commenting hopefully on the sharpening temperature. And sure enough once hounds found their third fox amid the gorse of Gobe bank, they ran in a close swift huddle as they chased him over the Gladestry brook and on to Hergest ridge by Upper Rabber, giving us a wonderful view and sample of their resounding Welsh chorus. For two hours they pursued this fox; but then, as they careered towards the outskirts of Kington, the light faded so that we could not see the turnings, let alone where our horses trod, and Mr Cursham called them off. It was a most thrilling hunt, across a hill country mercifully unspoiled by modern agriculture and amenity; and one felt that if the likes of Col. Price and John Curre were alive, they would unreservedly praise the style and speed with which the Radnor and West stick to the line of their quarry today.

(6 December 1971)

Mr P.J. Davenport and Mr E.E.T. Evans formed a new joint-Mastership in 1972. Mr Davenport then shared the Mastership with Mr E.J.V. Thomas until 1979, when Mr M.L. Ewart took over.

N. Stubbings was put on as huntsman in 1975 and was relieved by D. Gaylard, in 1979.

Sir Watkin Williams-Wynn's

THE HERITAGE OF WYNNSTAY

Foxhunting and the name of Williams-Wynn are synonymous, while the excellence in hound-breeding and the dramatic sport shown in and around Shropshire during the past 130 years have been largely due to the dedication of the heirs of that family. Although the present pack was not founded until the 6th baronet came of age in 1842, the hunting tradition of the Wynns can be traced to the middle of the eighteenth century when the first Sir Watkin, a Jacobite who deprived himself of three foxhunting seasons after joining Prince Charles at Derby in the '45, kept a pack at his family seat of Wynnstay, and was killed from a hunting fall in 1749.

The three succeeding baronets, though keener on their racing studs, all kept packs, hunting mostly bag-foxes and hares. Foxes were rare animals in those days. It took a few generations to realise that hunting bag-foxes was a sure way to keep them rare. The hounds were slow; their voices lacked music.

It was Squire Leche of Carden, in Cheshire, who took the foxhunting in earnest in this area. But it was his friend and neighbour in Shropshire, Sir Richard Puleston, who put hound-breeding on that part of the map. Sir Richard watched the strains with infinite care, favouring Hugo Meynell's, with Lord Monson's and Lord Sefton's as second choice. 'He tried to combine strength with beauty and steadiness with high mettle,' wrote his biographer; 'the first qualities he considered were fine noses and stout runners'. The huge headstone which he had erected over the grave of his favourite hound Dromo, a product of the Meynell and Monson kennels, exemplified his dedication: 'Alas, poor Dromo!' runs its inscription; 'Reynard with dread oft heard his awful name. Died September, 1809'. It was the descendants of the likes of Dromo that were largely to influence the founding of the Wynnstay pack 30 years later.

Sir Richard hunted Shropshire for 40 years, and according to Cecil in his *Records of the Chase*, he was considered to be the best judge of foxhounds of his time. Breeding competition was keen, and it was during his Mastership, in 1829, that the Shropshire, the Woore and the Cheshire each sent seven couples to Shavington for a trial of speed between the three packs. Two thousand horsemen turned out, 700 of them in scarlet. In the 30-minute unchecked hunt that followed, one of the innumerable legends of the eccentric Squire Jack Mytton was born. A vast ditch containing a post-and-rails fence stopped the field. 'Out of the way you fellows,' yelled Mytton, 'here goes for the honour of the Shropshire.' His 'Hit or Miss' mare fell and rolled on him. Streaming with blood, the indomitable Mytton was, of course, up in a trice, leading the 2000 to the finish. Mytton or no Mytton, the Cheshire hounds won the day.

The 6th Sir Watkin Williams-Wynn followed Sir Richard Puleston's example when he resigned from the Life Guards to manage his estates in 1843. And it was a Puleston draft together with the finely bred pack of Harleston Leche, the old squire's son, that were bought for his use. Fifty-five couples arrived at the new kennels at Wynnstay, alongside 60 high-quality horses. So for the next 43 seasons, in princely style and entirely at his own expense, Sir Watkin hunted widely across Shropshire, Cheshire, Denbigh and Flint. His country included most of Sir Richard Puleston's and all Harleston Leche's, 'the cream of Shropshire and a very fine portion of the Chester Vale'.

Sir Watkin would have nothing but the best. That also went for the succession of huntsmen he appointed. There was 'Merry John' Walker, who came to the Wynnstay after 18 seasons with the Fife. 'Walker went for all the best foxhound blood in England, the Belvoir strain being his most highly favoured', we are told. He seems to have enjoyed a pretty liberal hand in the breeding at Wynnstay, too. Perhaps that is why he turned down £500 a year to join Lord Suffield at the Quorn. Following Walker,

there was Charles Payne, who had whipped in to both Quorn and Pytchley, and he was succeeded by Frank Goodall, a member of the family that probably produced more hunt servants than any other.

Sir Watkin died in 1885, being succeeded by his son, who continued as MFH until he died in 1944. In spite of the worsening burden of taxation he was determined to provide sport for his friends and neighbours on the grand scale, entirely at his own expense. The tradition of high-grade huntsmen was continued by this Master, for whom such formidable names as Harry Maiden, Walter Morgan and Fred Robinson carried the horn, drawing the coverts between Chester, Wrexham, Oswestry and Ellesmere with consistent aplomb. Sir Watkin bought Lord Ferrers' and Lord Portsmouth's packs for Wynnstay, mixing them with the blood of the Warwickshire, Belvoir, Oakley and Milton, and the Wynnstay kennels soon gained the reputation of housing 'the most superbly bred pack in the provinces of England'.

The 7th Sir Watkin Williams-Wynn's record must be a hard one to beat. For he was MFH and owner of a pack of superb hounds for no less than 58 years. 'In the hunting field he was a fearsome disciplinarian,' recalled Sir Watkin during my visit, 'and the farmers would do anything for him.' Sir Watkin's father, brother of the 7th baronet, was for 50 seasons master of the Flint and Denbigh, which Sir Watkin himself hunted for 12 seasons. In 1957, he joined Mr R.L. Matson (who has done so much to restore the condition of the hunt after two World Wars) at Wynnstay, and now shares the Mastership with Mrs P.W. Ockleston. Sir Watkins Williams-Wynn's has been a subscription pack since 1946.

He keeps the traditional type at Wynnstay: a short-backed well-ribbed hound. He is sceptical of the contemporary emphasis laid on speed. 'There is a lot of difference between hounds that *run* fast and hounds that *hunt* fast. Mine hunt fast,' he told me. With this factor of hound quality is another contributing to the success of the hunt: a wonderful, if somewhat heavy, grass country, given over to intensive dairy farming, with a variety of jumpable fences to every field. Plough is scarcely seen, and, apart from the river Dee which divides the country north and south, there are no barriers here.

After a rotten scenting day on Christmas Eve, and in spite of dense fog, Mr Philip Warburton-Lee and Capt. Timothy Ritson, the hunt secretaries, collected caps from 80 optimistic followers when hounds met at Malpas on the Cheshire side on 26 December. Indeed, motorists coming from every

97 Lt-Col. Sir Watkin Williams-Wynn and his son, Mr David Williams-Wynn. Sir Watkin first entered the Mastership in 1957 and his son in 1971.

quarter were still reporting fog at midday, when quite spontaneously, the sun broke through and Sir Watkin gave the word for the first draw, a kale field on the fringe of Mr Dawson's farm.

A big fox showed hounds the way over Dickley brook to Cholmondeley Castle, there running to ground after a good hour's hunt, a nice pipe-opener for the sensational run that was to follow. C. Wilkin, their clever huntsman, lifted hounds at Bickley Hall,

where at 3.30 p.m. he drew a second field of kale and found a second fox. This one led Sir Watkin's hounds at a hard pace south of Bickley Moss, over the Whitchurch-Tarporley road and into the water-meadows of Cholmondeley Meres (which he abandoned in the same moment as a magnificent flock of 400 geese, providing a momentary sideline of entertainment).

Passing Long Acres Farm and Wrenbury and going left-handed by Chorley Stock, the followers left 30 good fences and five miles of impeccable grassland behind them. They also gained exhilarating views of these hounds with their fine melody, their speed in casting wide at their checks, and their closely huddled movement as they stuck close to the brush of the second fox. But, pushed on into Long Plantations in the dusk, they could make no more of him and Wilkin called them off. This hunt, which lasted just under two hours, covered 10–12 miles as hounds ran, including a four-mile point.

'Oh, Sir Watkin's stout hounds make the sweetest of sounds when a good fox is holloaed away,' enthused a nineteenth-century poet. His lilt was well and truly echoed on Boxing Day in the Cheshire side of the country.

(26 December 1969)

The Hon. Neville Hill-Trevor joined Sir Watkin and Mrs Ockleston in the Mastership in 1970. When Mrs Ockleston retired in 1971, David Williams-Wynn joined his father and Mr Hill-Trevor. Mrs Philip Warburton-Lee made up a quaternity in 1975. The four of them continued until 1978 when Messrs Hill-Trevor and Williams-Wynn and Mrs Warburton-Lee all resigned, Sir Watkin being supported from 1978 by Mr Roger Hewitt.

C. Lauder was put on as huntsman in 1972.

The North

Berwick

North
Northum-
berland

College
Valley

Milvain
(Percy)

West
Percy

Percy

Amble

Border

Morpeth

Morpeth

North
Tyne

Gretna

Bewcastle

Haltwhistle

Tynedale

Newcastle

Corbridge

Carlisle

Brampton

Haydon

Braes
of
Derwent

A1(M)

A68

Durham

Cumberland

Wigton

Kirkoswald

Hartlepool

Cumberland
Farmers

Keswick

South
Durham

Melbreak

Whitehaven

Blencathra

Ullswater

Appleby

R.Tees

Barnard
Castle

Saltburn

Cleveland

Whitby

Egremont

M6

A66

Zetland

A1(M)

Richmond

Hurworth

Farn-
dale

Goath-
land

Staintonvale

Eskdale &
Ennerdale

Ambleside

Tebay

Lunesdale

R.Swale

Bilsdale

Pickering

Derwent

Scarborough

Neutral

Coniston

Hawes

A684

Bedale

Thirsk
Masham

Sinnington

R.Derwent

N.Lonsdale

R.Lune

Kirkby
Lonsdale

West
of
Yore

Middleton &
Middleton East

Bridlington

(North)
York

Skipton

Harrogate
Ilkley

&

Stamford Bridge

Hornsea

Pendle
Forest &
Craven

Colne

Wetherby

Ainsty
(South)

Market Weighton

Beverley

M55

Burnley

Bradford

Bramham
Moor

R.Wharfe

Leeds

Selby

Loaned
to Y.&A.(S)
by Holp.

Holderness

Blackburn

Hull

M6

A56

M62

M62

Pontefract

M1

Badsworth

A1(M)

Barnsley

Pennine

Scale
10 0 10 20 30 40 50
miles

The Badsworth

SQUIRE BRIGHT'S VENTURE

Coming from the Midlands to the Vale of York as they proceeded north military forces and other travellers were bound to pass by Pontefract and Wentbridge. Caesar's cohorts, the Conqueror's knights, the men who went to destroy the monastries at King Henry's bidding, had all tramped through this apex vale. The reduction of Pontefract Castle was a key factor in Cromwell's domination of the north. But if centres of communication get more than their share of the tempest in times of strife, they thrive in peace, for they are easily accessible, they sprout ordered coaching points, trade is brisk at the confluence and the farmer can market his wares with easy journeys and at alluring prices. The squirarchy around this juncture was always prosperous, and so it became a natural breeding-ground for the Wentbridge hunting fraternity which grew up in the seventeenth century, prospered under Whig and Tory, and in 1720, prompted Pontefract's MP, Squire Thomas Bright, to build kennels at his home, Badsworth Hall, abandon the amateurishness of trencher-fed harrier-cum-foxhound in full favour of the fox, and thus establish what was to become the Badsworth Hunt.

There was a happy-go-lucky spirit about it all in the eighteenth century. The Masterships of Sir Godfrey Wentworth and two successive Sir Rowland Winns were followed by those remarkably ubiquitous 2nd and 3rd Earls of Darlington of Raby Hunt fame. Not content merely with their Durham coverts they took over the Badsworth country 80 miles south, hunting there intensively for seven or eight weeks at a stretch, travelling back and forth to Raby with their entire establishment. From Ben Marshall's celebrated portrait and the buoyant verses of Martin Hawke we gain a ready image of the 3rd Earl:

My friends in black collars nearly beat out of sight,
And Badsworth's old heroes in sorrowful plight . . .
Then first in the burst see dashing away,
Taking all in his stroke on Ralpho the grey,
With persuaders in flank comes Darlington's peer,
His chin sticking out and his cap on one ear.

Where the strictures of Nimrod's pen worried the paragons of Melton, they left the bloods of Badsworth stone cold. The smart reporter announced his intention to hunt them well in advance; but arriving on a pouring wet day in March 1826, he found that,

headed by their Master, the Hon. Edward ('Money-to-burn', as he was nicknamed) Petre, they had all been dancing in York the previous evening: '. . . and instead of meeting, as I'd expected, a large field, with many of whom I should have been acquainted, Jack Richards, the huntsman, was the only man out to whom I could say "how d'ye do?" . . . What I saw of the Badsworth pack did not much captivate my sight. I thought them rather coarse,' complained poor Nimrod, neglected and soaked to the skin.

Although the Mastership of Lord Hawke, Petre's successor, lasted 43 years, no great thought was given to the Badsworth breeding until the arrival in 1876 of the great hound expert Mr C.B.E. Wright, who brought drafts from the Grafton, Belvoir, Oakley and Milton; bred the famous Peterborough winner, Badsworth Advocate; raised his pack to a fine pinnacle – and was glad to hand over to another keen hound-breeder Mr John Fullerton, who was Master through the Edwardian era. But, with the exception of the reigns of that great hound and horse breeder and clever amateur huntsman, Major Lionel Holliday (1922–31), and Mr John King (1949–58), now Master of the Belvoir, the Badsworth have suffered in this century from short Masterships. We read such names in *Baily's* list as Major Gordon Foster (well known throughout Yorkshire for the sport he showed), Col. Ralph Warde-Aldam, Lord Allendale (who kept the country open during the war), Col. 'Mouse' Townsend, Mr Milton Asquith and Capt. Colin MacAndrew (who afterwards made such a name for himself with the Zetland); but we see little perpetuity in the hound-breeding.

Then, in 1962, the hunt was fortunate enough to secure Col. Warde-Aldam's stepson, Lt-Col. Max Gordon, as huntsman in a joint-Mastership with Miss Eileen Asquith, Milton Asquith's daughter. A Badsworth member since boyhood and formerly Master and huntsman of the Royal Horse Guards hounds, Col. Gordon set himself the task of building up a really useful working pack. In this he was well advised by the late Col. Thomas Slingsby, who also did much to guide the Sinnington in their breeding. Col. Gordon acquired three couples of litter-sisters of Four Burrow breeding by the Sinnington's Candid '57 out of their Marvel '56, thereby producing a fresh stamp of foxhound for this country, a light-

98 Lt-Col. C.G.M. Gordon, joint-Master, 1962–71. He also
hunted hounds throughout his tenure.

boned hound with an exceptionally good cry.

When Bert Taylor, their kennel-huntsman of 40
years' experience, unboxed hounds at Notton on the
west side of the country, close by the hazardous A61,
on Thursday, 5 February, a sharp, strong ground
wind combined with sunshine to promise a poor
scenting day. Nevertheless, at Col. Gordon's first
draw, Ridings Wood, hounds found immediately
and persevered through the catchy climate to Woolley Dam Bog, running on into New Milton Dam
Woods, encouraged all the way by their Master
(despite the restricting neck support which is obliged to wear as the result of a war wound). Foxes
were rife, and scent barely existent in the coverts, and
hounds were led in spurts to a bog near Bleakley
Dyke. Here they got a good start on a vixen and as
soon as they hunted her you sensed that this nicely

matched pack would be there at the end. Faithful to
their promise, running her in close formation with
remorseless speed and great voice through Owler
Wood, they raced on to Woolley Dam, where they
killed – a well deserved reward for their tenacity in
such adverse conditions, and a happy reflection on
the seven years of devotion given by Col. Gordon
and Bert Taylor, and the joint-Masters, Miss Eileen
Asquith and Mr Philip Scott.

(5 February 1970)

*Mr A.B. Harrop succeeded Col. Gordon and Miss
Asquith in the Mastership in 1971, but stayed only for
one season, and a committee governed the affairs of the
hunt until 1973 when Mr G.W. Cressey was appointed.
Mr Scott re-entered the Mastership in 1976, and
Messrs J. Firth and W. Askew joined him in 1977.*

*J. Batterbee, who succeeded B. Taylor as huntsman
in 1973, was followed by Stanley Cocksedge in 1978.*

The Bedale

WHERE FREEMAN FIRST CARRIED THE HORN

Joining the Bedale for their traditional opening meet at Bedale Hall on Monday, 28 October, reminded me that this is one of the half-dozen corners deeply immersed in the history of Yorkshire foxhunting, and if the name does not quite rank with Cranborne, Melton or Tarporley, it may well have been connected with the chase for as long as any of them. How did the heritage begin? Perhaps with the seventeenth-century Duke of Bolton, who built Bolton Hall, refused to speak for weeks on end 'lest he should swallow bad air', composed *The Wensleydale Fox Hunt*, always hunted his foxes by night – by torchlight – and whose Mecca was the Vale of Bedale. But whether or not this was a hunting man's paradise before Bolton's time, it was essentially from the 3rd Earl of Darlington (afterwards 1st Duke of Cleveland) and his Raby Hunt, a century and more later, that the Bedale country as we know it emerged.

The Raby empire extended north of Durham and, from 1787 to 1832, comprised at least all the country now hunted by the Zetland, Bedale and Hurworth, and most of the York and Ainsty. Darlington started a craze in the North Country for hunt clubs, and it could only be a matter of time before Raby members, living in the grassy openness of the Bedale area, should found one. This happened in 1816. The following year, Darlington's daughter, Lady Augusta Vane, married a well-known foxhunter called Mark Milbank, of Thorp Perrow, Bedale, and in 1832 the Earl made over the Raby's southern – or Bedale – sector to his son-in-law, thus creating a new hunt. And it was the 141st opening meet that Bedale Hall witnessed, when Capt. Malcolm Sherwin – joint-Master and huntsman since 1972, when he took over from Capt. Vaux – brought hounds there on 28 October.

Major R.O'C. Moorsom (who became hunt secretary after Col. Hill-Walker's 20-year innings, in 1970) counted a field of 65 –about 30 fewer than usual for the opening meet, a discrepancy owing, I was told, to the fact that many Bedale members had entered their horses for the Zetland cross-country event the previous day, coupled with the farmers' season being so late. Besides contributing £1000 a year to the hunt between them, incidentally, the Bedale's 30 hunting farmers elect six members to the dozen-strong hunt committee, an arrangement that gains whole-hearted support from Capt. Sherwin –

himself a beef farmer. At 11.15 he led hounds over the A684 and up to their first draw, Bedale Wood, precariously adjacent to a railway line and less than two miles from the A1, and I tried to imagine what this country was like before its tarmac and wire appeared and 'Milbank went where he liked', as 'The Druid' put it.

In 1856, after 24 seasons, Milbank handed over the Master's cap to the Hon. Ernest Duncombe. But, like his predecessor, Duncombe was a very successful politician and gave up his time-consuming sporting office in 1867, when he became the 1st Earl of Feversham – at the same time inheriting estates in the Sinnington country. With the introduction of the breech-loading gun, the country seems to have become particularly popular for pheasant-shooting, and hence for fox destruction, and John Booth, one of Duncombe's keenest followers, claimed to have ridden '500 miles without touching the line of a fox'. When Duncombe's hounds went up for auction, it was Booth who bought them. Although he rode at 17 stone, the new Master proved an excellent man to hounds and carried the horn five days a fortnight with a guarantee of £1000 a year. He also planted a large number of gorse coverts, and went about the business of fox preservation with a will.

There is no lack of foxes in the country now: the hunt killed 30½ brace last season – the best tally since the 1920s and nearly all above ground – and this autumn they had disposed of 12½ brace of cubs by 28 October. The trouble with my day was the weather. A howling gale the previous night kept most foxes tight underground, and there they remained on the blustery Monday. So strong was the blast that hounds were hunting the scent 50 yards off course of the one that was *holloaed* away from Bedale Wood. But working on it, tight as leeches, they hunted him for 40 minutes and over two miles – as far as Holtby Hall, we following, with heads into the north wind, across pasture intersected by several of the 200 bridges maintained by the hunt to cross the 'stells', or drainage ditches, for which this country is renowned.

It is a good firm grass country; it always was. 'The Bedale country is one of the best adapted for foxhunting in the north of England', enthused a *Field* correspondent in 1878. That was the year in which John Booth handed over to Major Henry

99 Capt. M.S. Sherwin (joint-Master and huntsman, 1972–7).

Dent. He stayed for six seasons, being followed by Mr George Elliot, MP, for four, and Capt. Wilson-Todd for eight, before the committee induced him to return for a short second term (1896–8). The 10th Duke of Leeds, of Hornby Castle, a very large land and covert owner, then came in for six seasons and operated very much in the spirit of his ancestor, the 6th Duke (who kept a rival pack to Darlington's, and was the senior founder-member of the Bedale Hunt Club). In 1902 and 1903 the Duke bought the bulk of the unentered Belvoir draft, 23 couple in the first year and $16\frac{1}{2}$ in the second.

He also built the New Kennels at Low Street, Little Fencote, where they still stand, and he kept sufficient hounds there to hunt a fourth day a week. But he had bad luck: mange broke out in the country, he himself caught scarlet fever and suffered several breaking falls, and he had to pension off his old huntsman, Fred Holland, who had served through 21 seasons and under six Masterships, and Holland's replacement was not a success. The Duke gave up in 1904, and after a lot of casting about, the committee found a very fine sportsman to relieve him: Mr John J. Moubray, of Perthshire, who was married to John Booth's niece and who had already hunted regularly from a base in the country.

One of the first measures Moubray took was to engage as his huntsman the budding Frank Freeman, first whipper-in of the North Cheshire, who had been taught his trade by such experts as Will Dale (Brocklesby), Frank Goodall (Kildare) and Ben Capell (Belvoir). Freeman took over from an indifferent huntsman and inherited a situation of few foxes and lot of third-season hounds, virtually unentered to fox and riotous to anything else. But, in the words of his biographer, Major Paget, 'he taught this pack to hunt foxes and to spread themselves in a wide circle without hanging on to his horse's heels, and to mark a fox to ground. This was one of the most uphill performances that has probably ever fallen to the lot of a huntsman. . . .' Unfortunately for the Bedale, however, Lord Annaly, who has been described as 'the greatest field Master of all time', got to hear of the genius and lured him to the Pytchley, where his unique career ended the day our present Queen was out in 1931.

Moubray, who had an 18-year reign as the Master of the Bedale (and whose daughter, Miss Eileen Moubray, was, until quite recently, chairman of the hunt committee) certainly knew how to pick them. He put on clever Sam Gillson from the South and West Wilts, and when he lost him, Peter Farelly, a former Quorn whipper-in. Both were triumphs. In 1920 Lady Masham was Master until her sudden death in 1924. Two seasons later, Major William Burdon took both the command and the horn until 1934, being joined in the last two years of his Mastership by Mr J.M. Barwick, who carried on until the war. In 1945 an excellent hound-breeder, Capt. Henry Farrar, took the Bedale cap, continuing as Master and huntsman until 1953, when he died while hunting the Northern Counties Otterhounds. The committee then persuaded Major Fife to act as Master, with Frank Ingram as huntsman, until Mr Jeremy Graham, another fine amateur huntsman came in – for three seasons on his own, and two with Major J.N. Howie and Mr James Ramsden, MP. It was Mr Ramsden who, in 1962, revived the West of Yore, the country originally loaned by the Bedale – to Mr W.E. Burrill – in 1932.

Although the West of Yore still retain a quite separate identity, with their own hound lists and hunt membership, their hounds are kept at the Bedale kennels, and Capt. Sherwin and Mr Michael Abrahams, the two senior Joint-Masters, simply

100 Mr W.P. Nunneley (joint-Master and huntsman, 1977–9).

exchange their roles of huntsman and field Master for West of Yore days.

At 12.45 hounds were cheered into Langhorne Whin, where one of a brace was *holloaed* away by Mrs Michael Abraham (whose husband so kindly mounted me on his champion hunter, liver-chestnut Henry). And in spite of the 40 m.p.h. wind, we enjoyed another brisk canter across Mr Jonathan Ropner's land to Hunter's Hill, where they lost on the road, and where second horses were waiting. They drew Hunter's Hill covert blank, and the same with the Duck Decoy in Hornby Park, where the only smell was roe deer. We were on General Clutterbuck's home ground now, and this 80-year-old pillar of the hunt committee, who had been well in front of the field, apologised for no foxes at Hornby. Miss Susan Fife, the third joint-Master, then led us from Chain Pond north to New Covert where, after a final valiant try at 3.15 p.m., Capt. Sherwin blew for home.

(28 October 1974)

Mr William Nunneley took over as joint-Master and huntsman in 1977, and carried on single-handed during the 1978–9 season, after which he retired.

A new joint-Mastership was formed for the 1979–80 season, consisting of Mr David Dick, Sir John Ropner and Sir Stephen Furness, a nephew of the celebrated Miss Furness (MFH, Hurworth, 1936–71).

Capt. Sandy Henderson has been honorary secretary since 1978.

The Bramham Moor

FOXHOUNDS OF THE WEST RIDING

No one welcomed last Friday night's heavy downpour in the West Riding of Yorkshire more than Tom Cody, huntsman of the Bramham Moor. For the opening meet was scheduled for Saturday and few parts of the country are so afflicted with a cold-scenting reputation as this. The Bramham accounted for 15 brace during the cub-hunting season, about a cub a day; the litters proved exceptionally big, and had the autumn not been so dry, many another Bramham tyro would certainly have lost his brush.

The sun that followed the rain last Saturday may have been unwelcome to the hunt staff, but it did produce a golden-leaf dazzle for Major James Gillam's meet at Healaugh. By tradition now, Major Gillam (whose wife, the daughter of that celebrated Badsworth Master, Major Lionel Holliday, was herself Master of the York and Ainsty, North, from 1959–69) traditionally opens the Bramham hospitality in his knoll-top village between York and Leeds. The Gillams can always reckon on over 100 followers crowding the lane that passes between Healaugh Old Hall and the elegant Norman church of St John's and it was a lengthy mounted cavalcade that, at 11.15 a.m. took the path leading south-westwards to Dews Wood and the first draw.

That covert has echoed to Tom Cody's *leu in* in early November for 18 seasons in succession. It was in Coronation year, 1953, that he gave up whipping in to the Whaddon Chase to take the Bramham horn, and thus continued this hunt's fine tradition of long tenures at the kennels. Charles Treadwell's 23 seasons with Squire George Lane-Fox ended in 1865. Turpin, who came from the Fife in 1869 to relieve Stephen Goodall, guided the Bramham to 133 kills in the first of his seven successful seasons, before handing over to Sir Watkin Williams-Wynn's first whipper-in, Tom Smith, who went on to serve 31 years with George Lane-Fox. And a piece of praise given to Tom Smith, so they say, might well be attributed to Tom Cody: 'he was a fine huntsman, good man to hounds and wonderfully patient with a cold scent; he showed extraordinary sport, he was courteous to a degree and was friends with everyone with whom he came in contact. . . .'

Here at Dewes Wood we saw Tom, ably supported in the role of whipper-in by Mr Stanley Wilkinson, one of the joint-Masters, who has fol-lowed the Bramham for 40 years; and by Stewart Blackburn, a very energetic young hunt servant and a fine horseman, who came up from the North Warwickshire two seasons ago. This good foxhold-ing covert did not fail the trio. One raced by the east shore of the great swamp to the south of Dewes, suddenly enlivening the sky with squadrons of mallard as we galloped behind. A mass of russet leaves were brisked across the water; a north wind had started and scent was sketchy, but you soon saw how well the Bramham hounds worked out the faint trace.

'The breeding of hounds ought not to be merely a question of appearance and dash', said Squire George Lane-Fox, who was Master from 1848 to 1896; 'they should also be the offspring of stallions and matrons of time-honoured residence in the kennels.' But the inexorable spread of plough in a naturally cold-scenting country has prompted twentieth-century Masters to place nose as the first priority at the kennels at Hope Hall. For many years, Lord Halifax advised on the breeding of this pack. Over half are of Middleton parentage and 15 are by Puckeridge sires: hounds from another cold-scenting country that had had to adapt to extensive plough, although at a much earlier period.

Now, after a few minutes, they pushed this first fox into a drain, but quickly found another, which, with characteristic tenacity, they pursued south by Whin Covert to Woodhouse Farm. Here he was turned westwards to Shire Oaks, then lost in the nearly gale-force wind; but not before he had given the field a lot of nice gallops and jumping. They drew a blank in the nearby plantation, and Major George Lane-Fox, of Bramham Park, the field Master, now led us south to Healaugh Manor where second horses were waiting.

The followers that wear the famous silver button inscribed with a fox and the single word 'Forward!' are more than happy to have a Lane-Fox in command again. It was some time between 1740 and 1750 that James Fox-Lane, a son of the 2nd Lord Bingley, founded the hunt and staged his meets across an area at least twice the size of the present country – until 1770, when it was taken over successively by Lord Darlington (of Raby Hunt Club fame); Sir Thomas Gascoigne (who went on to become first Master of the Middleton); Sir William

101 Lord Bingley (formerly Lt-Col. Lane-Fox) who was joint-Master, 1921–2 and 1935–45.

102 Miss Carolyn Dunkley jumping Catterton brook, near Healaugh on 6 November 1971.

Vavasour, Sir Rowland Winn (another former Badsworth Master); and Mr Edward Lascelles, 1st Earl of Harewood. James Lane-Fox, the close friend of Peter Beckford and Hugo Meynell, who had meanwhile succeeded to the Branham estates, took over the Mastership in 1798, building new kennels at Wothersome.

Then a diary note for 13 January 1819 informs us that 'Lord Lascelles took possession of the hounds this day'. He commanded until 1841. The 3rd Earl of Harewood, who relieved him, was followed in 1848, by the longest tenure of Bramham Masterships, that of the previously mentioned Mr George Lane-Fox (the present field Master's great-great-grandfather) who ruled with considerable wisdom, humour and success for 48 seasons. Thereafter a succession of Lane-Foxes and Lascelleses filled the post until 1945, but were not represented again until Major Lane-Fox's retirement from the Household Cavalry in 1970.

After a long cold search in Healaugh Manor Gardens, less than a mile from Tadcaster, a fox was bolted north-eastwards for Shire Oaks and Whin Covert, but although the wind then dropped, they failed to get on terms with him, and Tom Cody lifted them back to Healaugh village and the fish-pond to the north. Here they started three foxes, one of which was headed in the village, a second being hunted with great tongue over the Healaugh-Catterton road to Whin Covert, where he was given best at 4.00 p.m., when hounds were sounded home from this stimulating curtain-raiser to their 1971-2 season.

You feel in the Bramham country that community whole-heartedness about foxhunting which is so characteristic of rural Yorkshire, and which somehow gives you the certainty, in spite of the gradual and dismal trend towards the convergence of Leeds and Harrogate, that the Bramham citadel, bounded by the Nidd to the north, the Aire to the south, the Ouse to the east and Moors to the west, will be happily and successfully hunted as long as this sport remains part of the British way of life.

(6 November 1971)

Mr Wilkinson retired from the Mastership in 1971, and Major Lane-Fox in 1974. Mr Jack Gillam came into it in 1973, being joined in 1975 by Mr David McCloy. Major Lane-Fox rejoined in 1980.

Tom Cody retired as huntsman at the end of the 1975-6 season, being relieved by Stewart Blackburn. George Adams was appointed first whipper-in, and Mr Gillam's son, Robert, has been an amateur whipper-in since 1976.

The College Valley

SIR ALFRED GOODSON'S PACK

When, 64 years ago, the first Sir Alfred Goodson, Devonshire and Cheshire landowner and Master of the Haldon Harriers, asked his son Alfred (or Bill as he was, and is, generally known) where he would like to do his farming apprenticeship, the reply was, 'where your ewes come from'. And the answer to that was the Cheviots. So, in 1909, Sir Alfred secured a place for the young man on the boundaries of Roxburghshire and Northumberland. Soon, finding the moorland and mountains closer to his heart than the rich south-western enclosures of his childhood, the farm student did not look back, and what excited him more than anything else in the Border country was the music and the drive of old Jacob Robson's hounds.

A little before the Great War his father bought him the Border farm of Kilham. And soon a yeomanry subaltern was whiling away his off-duty hours on the Somme imagining the cattle and the hounds he would breed for that far-away land, that rather poor scenting country where the white grasses and mossy turf competed with bracken and heather and scree on the naked mountainside of the Border.

So when the conflict with the Kaiser was over he set to and bred Aberdeen Angus cattle and Cheviot sheep; and he bred harriers and beagles and hunted them with his friend and neighbouring estate owner, Capt. Claud Lambton. Hare hunting was good fun; but the two young cattle-farmers were sad about one thing: the way in which foxes were disposed of in their country. For this country lay at the apex of three hunts, all of which more or less neglected it:

103 Capt. A.L. Goodson (*left*) and Capt. the Hon. Claud Lambton at their Puppy Show in 1928.

the Border, the Duke of Buccleuch's and the North Northumberland. Here the foxes were shot, and more often wounded than killed, by shepherds, or caught in shares set by the rabbit-catchers, and cruelly maimed. So when the Border Hunt agreed to surrender their unwanted north-eastern sector. Captains Goodson and Lambton got together a pack of hounds and hunted the valleys of Bowmont Water and College Burn on a regular basis and soon afterwards, the North Northumberland and the Duke of Buccleuch's lent them the steep-sided valleys of their own southern corners.

It was a close duo. Capt. Lambton acted as field Master, saw to the foxes and organised the country,

while Capt. Goodson was the huntsman and breeder of hounds. He was a born breeder. He had bred bantams and racing pigeons from the age of six, and as 'Dalesman' (C.N. de Courcy Parry) was later to put it: 'this courteous and charming gentleman possesses that uncanny feeling or touch with all animals that enables him to breed the very best. . . .' Hounds from Jacob Robson's Border kennels – mostly fell, with judicious outcrosses from the Duke of Buccleuch's – formed the basis of Capt. Goodson's pack. The best of these were put to a Goathland bitch, Rosebud '21 (by the celebrated Morpeth Random) that took Capt. Goodson's fancy, and another from that kennels called Friendly; also Bramham Chorus. The Friendly and Chorus lines did not prevail, but 95 per cent of the pack still go back to the foundation bitch, Goathland Rosebud.

104 Sir Alfred and Lady Goodson with (*right*) the Hon. Claud Lambton on the occasion of the author's day hunting in December 1972.

In the beginning they were catching 15 brace of foxes a season. Well before 1930 the annual tally for this small country averaged 60 brace.

Attracted by the legend, many of the great foxhunting names, who were to become firm friends of warm and witty Bill Goodson, visited Kilham for a glimpse of the quality hounds he had bred: Lord Knutsford, Sir Peter Farquhar, Ikey Bell, Bill Scott. They saw and they were very impressed. When Ikey Bell watched the College Valley in action, he confided that he wished he had used fell rather than Welsh blood when he bred the South and West Wilts – the pack which were to mark the turning-point in the shape and size and weight of the modern foxhound. So if Bell had seen the College Valley a bit earlier, today's fashionable grass and plough country hounds might have had a different conformation and character; they might well have carried their knees further back, stood more squarely on the hint of a hare foot, been longer in the humerus and snipier in the head, and shown a greater degree of independence.

'The College Valley are mostly white in colour, full of quality and very level in appearance,' wrote Sir John Buchanan-Jardine in 1936; 'they are considered by many people who have seen them to be the fastest pack in Great Britain; certainly they account for a very high percentage of foxes and show great sport. . . .' 'Dalesman' went further: 'Goodson's white hounds are without any shadow of

105 Mr Martin Letts, joint-Master and huntsman on Easter Tor.

doubt the best pack to catch foxes in the hills of any in the world'.

Sir Alfred Goodson (he inherited the baronetcy from his Devonian father in 1940) insists on tongue first; then on nose and drive. College Valley Raglan, Racer and Barber, his three and most used sires, were well endowed with these qualities. With stamina, too. For as Sir Alfred says, neither tongue, nose nor drive are of any avail without great constitution and the ability to go all-out on a long day. And as I saw for myself on the Tuesday of last week, the College Valley have that special fell hound facility for casting themselves on over difficult stretches of ground, for knowing they can expect no scent on shale, and that drenched bracken obliterates it.

The first of the four foxes they killed in College Valley that wet and windy day was much too slow for them. After moving off from the meet at Hethpool at 11.00 a.m., Martin Letts, formerly Master of both the Northern Counties and the Eastern Counties Otterhounds, and of the Bolebroke Beagles, now one of the best hill-huntsmen there is (and that day providing the only touch of scarlet on the landscape), cheered them on to the bracken slopes of Easter Tor. Spreading like some huge quick net, within two minutes they unkennelled their first and killed him in full view of us. Then hunting southwards they chased their second behind some rocks short of Newton Tors. In went the terrier; out came the quarry; but within 200 yards, in his panic, he somersaulted over a rock and was swiftly accounted for – again right in view.

Keeping near the valley roadside we enjoyed our grandstand vista; but with a hailstorm horizontal in our faces we did not see much of fox number three which was bolted from a great earth at Hare Law stones and killed after another sharp run. At 12.30 they put up a brace in the wooded glen south of Hare Law, then changed on to an old fox whose scent vanished on the scree of Southernknowe. North now with a second veteran past Hare Law and Easter Tor; then a vixen from Torlee House to an earth at Kirk Newton, for after the soaking night and the hail they mostly preferred it underground.

But by 2.15 the sun was shining; thorn trees threw long shadows over the coppery bracken; Michael Inness (ex-joint-Master of the Wensleydale Harriers), the acting whipper-in, riding along the crest of Easter Tor, cut a tiny silhouette, against the now blue sky. On the road below Sir Alfred lit a pipe, leaned against his Range Rover and trained his binoculars towards a feature high above the swollen burn – Yeavering Bell. The one they discovered there gave them a two-hour run with a five-mile point and a fourth kill in the open. What a joy it was to watch this last hound hunt, the pack a white and level ribbon, accompanied by a triumphant chorus snaking far away through the bracken and thin dun grasses, veering tight on the fox at every turn, without a murmur from Mr Letts.

The College Valley are indeed fortunate to have this dedicated young joint-Master and huntsman. He is married to Lady Goodson's grand-daughter, Eildon, herself a splendid horsewoman, and a useful whipper-in, too. And as kennel-huntsman they have Mark Evans, whose father had joined Captains Goodson and Lambton in the same capacity in 1924. Thus the saga of the College Valley Hunt, which began in 1908 and blossomed in the 1920s, continues to unfold, and brightly.

(12 December 1972)

The Holcombe Harriers

JAMES I GAVE THEM SCARLET

The visitor's immediate impression of the Holcombe is the warm glow of their Lancashire welcome, at once drawing him into their fraternity, so that he almost feels that he wears their button for his day with them. He is also quickly conscious of the followers' happy and unqualified devotion to their sport and, therefore, their persistence in keeping every available yard of their (technically) huge country open. That determination is essential, for they have already lost much.

What was once the unspoiled Forest of Lancaster, a close pattern of wood and warren, richly stocked with deer, pig and hare, is now divided by the M6 and the parallel M61 into two separate territories: to the east, the heather, bracken and boggy sheep pasture of Pennine moorland, between Burnley, Blackburn and Bolton, where hares are stout and strong, and there are stone walls to be jumped and hidden mine shafts and tunnels to be avoided; and beyond that, towards Southport, the cotton-mill, quarry and mine-studded coastal plain, much blemished by suburbia and new towns. Little over a third of this tract is huntable, and each year a fraction less remains.

But what landowner or farmer could refuse admission to such an amicable and considerate band of harehunters, I wondered, as we trotted away from the Rigbye Arms at Wrightington, on 6 November, and the huntsman, Alec Sneddon, led us by Hunter's Hill on to the old sheep pasture of Mr Monks's Bannister Hall tenancy. Pride of heritage is of course, another strong factor in the Holcombe's record of success. How many ancient hunt countries have like this one a focal point that has never changed? Packs of hounds have probably been kennelled around Holcombe, a few miles north-east of Bolton, for over 500 years. But the Holcombe Hunt identify themselves more strictly from August 1617, when James I, on the invitation of his young courtier, Sir Gilbert Hoghton, stayed at Hoghton Tower, near Blackburn.

'The King hunting: a great companie', the Lancashire diarist, Sir Nicholas Assheton, recorded for 17 August. 'Killed afore dinner a brace of staggs. Verie hott, so he went into dinner. We attend the Lords table . . . in the afternoon Hunted ye Hare.' And, in the words of the hunt historian, 'the deep-mouthed Holcombe hounds . . . so pleased the King

106 John Jackson, huntsman, 1867–99. Although the Masters and followers have always ridden, the hunt staff were on foot until the 1920s.

107 Mr Newton Bacon. He has been Master, or joint-Master, since 1965.

that they were sought out for special notice and their owner graciously given the Royal Warrant to hunt over 12 townships, and the privilege of wearing the scarlet livery of the King'. (Three centuries were to elapse before another monarch saw them at Hoghton: they were brought there for George V's inspection in 1913.)

James also conferred on them the gold embellishment that went with the red of the Royal Buckhounds, and the harehunters afterwards preserved this honour in the old gold collar and waistcoat of their evening dress, which they still wear. At first it felt a trifle strange – instead of the customary harrier green – to be among scarlet-coated horsemen as you watched the hare hunted around Bannister Hall Farm. Not that, in the muggy, scentless climate of 6 November we saw much more than snatchy bursts. And there were too many hares for hound concentration. (Normally, by November, one or two hare drives would have disposed of the surplus, but owing to the late harvest these had not been staged.) But when Mr Newton Bacon, the senior joint-Master, and Mr Peter Georgeson, his field Master, led us by Mr Dandie's land, past a great sandstone quarry to Mrs Clayton's, it began drizzling. This seemed to keep their noses closer to the ground, and, just across from Stony Lane, they raced up to one and rolled her over on the stubble.

The succession of holders of Mr Bacon's appointment can be traced to the period of James I's visit, when Sir Thomas Barton, of Quarton, was named as

'Master of the Holcombe Hunt', but presumably the hunt remained staghounds or boarhounds until a century later, by which time the country was more or less cleared of its forests.

Hounds were later kennelled at Holcombe Hey House, which was the home of the de Traffords, then of the Brandwoods. The hunt historian reckons that 'Lawrence Brandwood was one of the first Masters of the Holcombe after its inauguration as a subscription hunt in 1708. Then there was a Townshend Brandwood, and after his death in 1770, the hounds were removed to Holcombe village.'

Between the 1790s and 1830s the hunt seems to have been first in the hands of families called Baron of Walshaw, Halstead of Nuttall Hall, and Booth, of Holcombe Brook, before passing to Thomas Hargreaves. After Thomas Gorton's 19-year reign (1840–59), a committee presided until George Ashworth agreed to run the hunt for five seasons from 1866. (At about this stage several other hare-hunts, some with famous names, such as the Bury and the Bolton, merged with the Holcombe.) The most prominent names in the role of Masters during the past century have been Ashworth, Hardcastle, Mucklow and Walker. Walter Mucklow was Master from 1881–99, and it was his grandson, Major G.D. Mucklow, who succeeded Dr Leather and Major Gibson Hughes in 1957, and handed over the Master's cap to Mr Bacon – formerly a North Staffs follower for 25 years – nine seasons ago.

After that first kill, Alec Sneddon cast where the maize had been harvested on Parbold Hall Farm and then across Mr Sneesby's Boggart House Farm. At this stage a tragedy took place: an excellent three-season hound called Groper, careering on to the B5239, was hit and died of his injuries. (But, thankfully, this is the first road disaster for as long as eight seasons.)

The Holcombe hounds were the old miniature Gascon type up to 1925, when they converted to stud book harriers, of which Charles Garnett, who was hunt secretary (1900–17) commented: 'They get away quicker than the old-fashioned harrier; they are I think, easier to turn, and when scent is good they are easier to ride to, as they push a hare more, and consequently you get straighter runs. But their great fault is that they have too much drive. . . .' That is why, in the late 1920s, the hunt servants began to hunt mounted, as the Master and followers had done for centuries. But the old Gascony blood was brought back in the 1960s, with outcrosses from the West Lodge Bassets, and no one who sees the Holcombe at work today would call them flashy. Now Mr Bacon and Alec Sneedon go mainly to the Cambridgeshire, High Peak, Pendle Forest and Windermere.

As we turned away from the disastrous B5239, we faced hounds hunting a hare towards us, which they quickly killed; and scarcely leaving a moment to dispose of her, they cast themselves north again in search of another. Throughout 6 November, the Holcombe Harriers showed wonderful pertinacity in poor conditions, a resolution like that of the hunt members who, with their innate spirit of sport for sport's sake, are steadfastly determined that neither urbanisation, nor roads, nor costs will diminish their institution, which has flourished so happily since the days of the Tudors.

(6 November 1974)

The 1981–2 season opened with a joint-Mastership composed of Messrs P. Georgeson and T. Bracewell and Mrs M. Burton.

Alec Sneddon continued as huntsman.

The Middleton

THE HERITAGE OF BIRDSALL

'The kennels at Birdsall are as good as any in England', claimed the 1871 *Baily's*; 'they are situated under cover so that a huntsman can draw his hounds for inspection in any weather'. Built by the 8th Lord Middleton they had been up 13 years then, and with their solid Palladian features, clear cut '1858' inscription and massive grey flagstones, they look much now as they must have looked a century ago. Situated 20 miles north-east of York and five miles south-east of Malton, the kennels are more or less at the centre of this big country, measuring 43 by 23 miles. Birdsall is the seat too, of the present Lord

Middleton, and the hub and spiritual home of the hunt to which the Willoughby family have given their titular name these last 140 years.

The Middleton is a rather steep, but gently rolling farm country, and Nimrod, describing a visit in 1823, wrote 'the place appeared to me to be more adapted to a picnic party of pleasure on a summer's evening than a fixture of foxhounds . . . the road to it led through most picturesque scenery, much resembling parts of North Wales'. There is an air of romance about Birdsall and its surrounding wolds, and it is somehow fitting that the Willoughbys should have arrived here as they did, in that spirit. One night early in the eighteenth century, Thomas Willoughby, second son of the 1st Lord Middleton, whose estates were in Lincolnshire, Nottinghamshire and Warwickshire, was caught in a fierce snowstorm as he rode through the night from Hull to Malton. Coming to Birdsall brow he spotted a light in the valley below. By arduous degrees he led his horse to this hopeful signal amid the tempest. A groom relieved him of it; a footman answered his hammering, quickly heaving the door against the driving snow. And there to greet him in the glow of the hall, and to change his life, was the beautiful Birdsall heiress, Elizabeth Sotheby. Through the marriage that followed this encounter, Thomas Willoughby brought into his family these estates on the Yorkshire wolds, which his son Henry, who became 5th Baron Middleton on the failure of his elder brother's line, united with the other Middleton lands. It was the 6th Baron who, in 1832, gave the hunt the name 'Lord Middleton's'.

But the area was steeped in the tradition of hunting and racing long before that happened, for it included such sporting families as the Howards (Earls of Carlisle) of Castle Howard; the Sykeses, who 'kennelled a pack of hunting dogs' at Sledmere, near Driffield; the Osbaldestons, kinsmen of 'the Squire', who lived at Hunmanby; the Dukes of Devonshire with estates at Londesborough; and the Thorntons, led by that eccentric adventurer-sportsman, Col. Thornton, who claimed to have hunted wolves as well as foxes between York and Malton.

The Middleton Hunt itself, however, really begins with Sir Thomas Gascoigne who, with the successful pack he bought from Mr Watson of Old Malton, seems to have established the country approximately in its present shape between 1764 and 1773. The Duke of Hamilton took over in that year for two seasons; James Lane-Fox, then carried on until 1788 when he succeeded to his family pack at

Bramham; and Lord Mexborough followed for a similarly short tour, handing over to his cousin Henry Bumper Savile who, in 1786, made way for Sir Walter Vavasour. When, two seasons later, the Mastership could not be suitably refilled, a committee of three was formed, and this included the first Willoughby to be associated with the hunt. He was then Master from 1789 to 1792 and his fellow committee member, Mr Legard, for two seasons after that.

The 'Middleton' then went through a rather anonymous period, being merged with the Holderness during the last years of the eighteenth century, and taken in by Charles Duncombe, who became the 1st Lord Feversham and who hunted the whole of East Yorkshire for the first few years of the nineteenth century. But from 1804 till 1832, apparently, the Sykeses of Sledmere had Gascoigne's old boundaries firmly re-established. Sir Mark Masterman Sykes, having bought Duncombe's hounds, was the first of this era, and his brother, Sir Tatton, was a good man to follow him. With 200 racehorses in training Sir Tatton founded what was described as 'the premier stud of the Empire' and, according to Nimrod, showed 'humility of demeanour to all ranks'. He hunted hounds till well past his 70th year.

The Middleton dynasty, which began with the two-season Mastership (1832–4) of the 6th Baron, was broken by Sir Tatton Sykes's second Mastership (1834–53), and continued with Henry Willoughby, afterwards 8th Baron (1853–77), and the 9th Baron (1877–1920). 'For 24 years,' writes a biographer of the 8th Baron, 'the Middleton hunt, the improvement of the pack, and the sport and pleasure he gave to the country, were obviously one of the main concerns of his life. So they were to his successor, who added to his interests the encouragement of both light and heavy horse breeding on the best lines, and progress in agricultural methods. . . .'

In 1921, the year after the 9th Lord Middleton's 44 years as MFH finished, the hunt became known as 'the Middleton'. And, well set up with the continuing use of Birdsall, a guarantee of £3000 and Bert Thatcher, followed by Dick Thatcher, as thoroughly reliable huntsmen, Lord Grimthorpe and Lt-Col. Malcolm Borwick had command. The seeds of division between the Middleton and Middleton East were sown in the 1921–2 season when Col. Borwick, and Capt. T.L. Wickham-Boynton, who had been his whipper-in, split the pack to hunt separately.

Col. Borwick was followed on the east side for five

108 The late Earl of Halifax. His Mastership began in 1946. He was also a former Chairman of the Masters of Foxhounds' Association.

years by Lord Grimthorpe. Then, in 1927, the official split between east and west took place, with Col. Borwick at the head of the Middleton and Capt. Wickham-Boynton of the Middleton East. This segregation lasted until 1953 when the committee of the East, whose Master was then Mr E.W. Wrigley, agreed with the Middleton that a reunion would be expedient.

Meanwhile, 20 seasons previously, in 1932, when Viscount Halifax, after returning from his Vice-royalty of India, joined Lord Grimthorpe in the Mastership of the Middleton, the Wood family influence began. It has now endured for half a century. As the Hon. Charles Wood, the present Earl of Halifax, before going off to the war, shared the Mastership with Lord Grimthorpe, and after the war with his father, the late Earl. Now his joint-Masters are Mr W.D. Pinkney, who has been with him since 1958; Lady Anne Fitzalan-Howard, the Duke of Norfolk's eldest daughter, who came in ten years later; and Capt. the Hon. Nicholas Crossley, who hunts hounds on Fridays, and on alternate Mondays and Wednesdays, which days he shares with Dennis Sturgeon, the kennel-huntsman, who carries the horn on Saturdays, when the central and best of the Middleton country is hunted.

The hunt are indeed fortunate to have as their senior joint-Master such a shrewd and experienced houndsman as Lord Halifax. Although this is a lovely country and a generally good riding one, from the hound point of view it is mixed and rugged, and does not hold scent too well. Lord Halifax has the hound for it. Every bitch at Birdsall goes back on tail female to Warwickshire Comfort 1822, the Middleton foundation bitch, and Lord Halifax adheres strictly to her lines. The second influence dates back to Col. Borwick's departure for the Pytchley in 1931, when he took several Middleton bitches with him. Since that year the Middleton and Pytchley have been closely bred. Lord Halifax, an admirer of Sir Peter Farquhar's work, also made good use of the Portman Lorimer and Freeman in the 1950s; and, afterwards, such widely admired sires as Heythrop Brigand '54, Tipperary Growler '64, the Duke of Beaufort's Beadle '66 and Warwickshire Partner '68 made their mark at Birdsall.

On the Monday of last week, when hounds met at Mr Jackson's farmhouse at Whenby, and 30 followers paid their cap to the dismounted and convalescent secretary, Maj-Gen. H.T. Alexander, the sun was shining fierce as in June and, not surprisingly, the two morning hunts – the first from Spellar to Bransby High Wood and the second from Foulrice Beck to Foulrice Farm – were fun, but slow and inconspicuous. Then, as so often happens after a hot blank hunting day, when the sun began to sink and a nip came in the air, scent picked up; and when Capt. Crossley drew Farlington High Wood, where they found at once, a sharp hunt ensued. Cantering over the Golden Flatts, with Cornborough Hall on our

109 Across Golden Flatts, near Whenby, Yorkshire, on the day described by the author. *Left to right*: The Hon. Lady Parkinson, Lady Brooksbank, and Mr John Ford, who was acting as whipper-in.

left and the gaunt ruins of that once great Yorkshire stronghold, Sherriff Hutton Castle, looming on our right, we crossed the road: and with hounds going rather too fast for the field over this wiry tract, we finished in High Stittenham Wood, where they marked to ground at an old artificial drain, completing a very enjoyable three and a half mile point.

(19 February 1973)

Mr J.K. Mansfield joined Lord Halifax in the Mastership in 1974, and Mr D.J.S. Herring, in 1978. Col. Crossley went to the Derwent as joint-Master and huntsman, in 1976, and Lady Anne Fitzalan-Howard

and Mr Pinkney have also since retired from the Middleton Mastership.

At the end of the 1978–9 season Mr Herring resigned and Lord Halifax and Mr Mansfield were joined by Mr Nunneley from the Bedale.

Dennis Sturgeon retired in 1978 and was succeeded as kennel-huntsman by Tony Edwards who had been with the Tyndedale.

The Hon. Mrs M. Willoughby has also joined the Mastership which makes it the first time since 1921 that a member of the Middleton family has been Master. Lt. Colonel the Hon. R.N. Crossley rejoined the Mastership in 1980.

The Sinnington

PLAYGROUND OF A CAROLEAN DUKE

However devious the political record of George Villiers, Duke of Buckingham (1628–87), may have been, in the hunting-field he was reputed to be 'bold, generous and as hard a rider as you'd find in England'. With remarkable ubiquity, this favourite of Charles II hunted the whole of what is now the Sinnington country as well as the extensive areas of Bransdale and Farndale. And it may be fairly claimed that the North Yorkshireman's celebrated passion for the chase and deep foxhunting tradition partly stem from the positive lead given by the controversial Buckingham – who, in 1687, died at Kirbymoorside from a fever brought on by a wet hunting day.

In 1695 Helmsley Castle was bought from Buckingham's executors by the Duncombe family. And with the active patronage of the Duncombes, combined with the support given by their yeomen farmers, the dare-devil Sinnington Hunt Club was founded, a fraternity steeped in the Buckingham spirit. 'When a fox was killed,' we are told, '*Io Trumpho*! was the cry, adjournment was made to the nearest inn and, dinner being served, the libations were of a strenuous character. Every member, not in at the kill, was fined 5s, every member not attending the dinner 2s 6d. Then a gift of 5s was made to the churchwardens of the parish in which a fox was killed.'

Although the Duncombes have influenced the Sinnington more than any other family, the Ken-dalls of Ness Hall, holding the Mastership without a break from 1765–1875, come close second. For no less than 46 years of this period (1776–1822) the Kendalls' huntsman was James Goldie who (relates a Regency recorder), 'would seem not only to have hunted like a wolf, but been as jealous as a hawk, and strangers hunting with the pack were marked by him to be ridden down. . . .' But under the later Kendalls, who mostly carried the horn themselves, the Sinnington presented a more hospitable image. And judging by some faithful records that were kept, an equally devoted one.

'One of the best runs the great Mr Tom Kendall had,' says the sporting author, Scarth Dixon, of the last of the Kendall Masters, 'was in 1861, and so impressed had he been with it that, on his return home, he wrote an account of it on the fly-leaf of a novel when it was fresh in his memory, thus giving that volume (which was only of a moderate degree of merit), a value which of itself it could never have possessed. . . . After a hunt of 14 miles the fox had been lost in Kirbymoorside. He had crept up the roof of a low thatched cottage and, crouching close to the chimney, was unseen in the twilight. He remained beside the warm chimney all night, his footmarks as he made his ascent and descent, as well as his lair near the chimney, being distinctly traced in the snow on the roof next morning. . . .'

Few hunts can have been so fortunate as the Sinnington in the success and popularity of their

110 Major Guy Cunard taking a typical Ryedale brush-and-ditch combination. Major Cunard, who rode 268 point-to-point winners, went on to train at Malton.

Masters. Following the Kendall reign, came Thomas Parrington, founder of the Peterborough hound show and agent to the Earl of Feversham (the principal title granted to the Duncombes); Clayton Swann, who, in 1891, concentrated the hounds in kennels from trencher feeding; then Penn Sherbrooke, another outstanding huntsman and hound-breeder. The 2nd Earl of Feversham, who was killed in action in 1916, was followed by Major Gordon Foster, who came up from the Badsworth, and who many people would claim as the finest amateur huntsman of his day. The Duncome tradition

persisting, the 3rd Earl of Feversham took both the Mastership and the horn in 1934 and except for the war years, when he was away commanding a cavalry regiment, he remained in office until his death in 1963. Lady Feversham, who joined her husband as joint-Master in 1950, now shares the command with Brig. Heathcoat-Amory, Major Shaw and Lord Westbury, who is huntsman.

This singularly strong team and its followers enjoy a varied and fairly unspoilt country, the north and west of which consists of dales running to moorland, while the remainder is made up of Ryedale and the Vale of Pickering. To compete with the wide variety of obstacles and gradients a well-built hound of the traditional stamp has proved the most successful, and much credit must be given to

111 Terrier men: Tom Oldfield and Keith Preston.

the late Col. Slingsby, who was mostly responsible for the stallion hound selection since Major Foster's day (his most quoted slogan was 'never use a stallion hound that comes from a better scenting country than your own'.) The best stallion influence in this very stylish-looking pack was the celebrated Pytchley Vandyke '62.

Last Thursday, 28 January, hounds met at Great Habton where the hunt supporters had danced the night before till the early hours for a 21st birthday celebration, and where the pilot jet of the Home Oil of Canada Company's well burned perpetually like some medieval beacon, providing visiting foxhunters with an ever-present landmark. It was foggy and still when, at 11.15 a.m. – after Mr Hugh Murray Wells of Ness Hall, the Hunt Secretary, had

collected caps in aid of the Hunt Servants' Benefit Fund – Lord Westbury cheered hounds into Habton Whin; not quite 12.00 when they killed a dog-fox inside the covert, and only a moment after when they ran a second fox westward, via Mr Seager's Rakes Farm to Shottern Hall, immediately impressing the visitor with their speed and pack drive. They followed their fox back to Habton Whin, and there losing him traced a stale line to Habton Grange, where he sprang up in the rough. Scent was good and they were soon on terms; Lord Westbury could leave them alone with confidence.

Away they flew, southwards over the numerous becks, checking briefly at Garforth Hall, and picking up the line again by Lund Forest. Here, obstructed by the new drainage works, the field lost touch until signalled by the *holloas* of the car followers by Kirby Misperton Zoo (where an audience of ostriches and

112 The joint-Masters at the meet at Great Habton, Yorkshire, where the author joined them on 28 January 1971. The Countess of Feversham with (*left to right*) Major John Shaw, Capt. Lord Westbury and Brig. Roderick Heathcoat-Amory.

wallabies looked strangely incongruous in the Yorkshire mist). Now plainly tired, he escaped past White Lily Farm, piloting hounds to the village of Great Barugh. Mistakenly, they cast over the road, but Major Shaw, the field Master – who had navigated the field to this point with remarkable accuracy – viewed him (cunningly crouched, rather like Tom Kendall's chimney-fancier in 1861) in a garden. Calling hounds back, Lord Westbury started him up again and, after a final mile ran him into a culvert in Little Habton, where they killed. This had been a hound hunt in the classic style: three and a

half hours and 14 miles as hounds ran. Such buoyant days with the Sinnington are by no means unusual. But, in the world of foxhunting, such a reputation for high-class sport, coupled with the aura of three centuries' tradition, is indeed rare.

(28 January 1971)

After Lord Westbury's resignation as joint-Master and huntsman, in 1974, the hunt's affairs were controlled by a committee for a couple of seasons. Then, in 1976, Mr and Mrs Willie Poole joined Lady Feversham in the Mastership, Mr Poole hunting hounds, with B. Dobson as kennel-huntsman. In 1979 Mr P.M. Lyon made a quaternity of the Mastership. In 1976, Lt-Colonel C.G.M. Gordon, a former Master of the Badsworth, took over as hunt secretary.

Lakeland

The Blencathra

JOHN PEEL'S COUNTRY

The Blencathra carried off the four top prizes at the 1971 Rydal Show; their Trueman '68 was champion hound; and when they appeared at the Salutation Inn, just a few minutes' walk from their kennels in Threlkeld, Cumberland, on Wednesday, 13 October, for their opening meet, there was no doubting their quality. They wore the waspy loins and cagey ribs that all good fell-hounds show in season. A month ago, cossetted by individual hunt supporters at summer trencher-feeding, they were as sleek as could be. Since when they have been in hard training. For with more than an ounce of fat on their flanks, they will not dominate the shaly gradient nor persevere against the strong fox. Johnny Richardson, their huntsman, likes them lean and bony. Porridge is their staple diet; the small meat ration is reserved for Friday evenings. 'Give them any more than that', promises Richardson 'and they'll pant, and lap at every beck; they'll be left behind.' He

113 Blencathra Trueman '68. He was by the College Valley Raglan '63 out of Bleu Crystal '63.

114 John Peel. Born in Caldbeck in 1777, he hunted the Blencathra country for 56 consecutive years.

ribbon, ragged and mercurial, contouring the hills towards Borrowdale. For John Crozier, the son of John Peel's great friend, who founded the Blencathra in 1840, bred from Peel's pack. And the blood of legendary 'Briton' and 'Peely' flows in their veins today. As the nineteenth-century historian, Claude E. Benson put it: 'The strain of Peel's hounds is thick in the Threlkeld pack; Crozier *père* was his friend, Crozier *fils* was his pupil'.

These harsh mountains are saturated with Peel's spirit. It haunts the slate outcrops and the burns; it is on the note of the huntsman's horn and the tongue of his hounds; it pervades the farmers' cottages and the fields where their sheep graze; it filled the chant which these Blencathra dalesmen sang so lustily when last week's hunt was over:

'Twas the sound of his horn called me from my bed,
And the cry of his hounds has me oft-times led,
For Peel's view halloa would awaken the dead
Or a fox from his lair in the morning. . .

The tall, bony Cumbrian innkeeper 'with his coat so gray', who was born in the dour wool town of Caldbeck in 1777, hunted these hills between October and May for 56 consecutive years. And right up to his end in 1854, when he was 78, 60-mile unchecked runs far into the mountains were not unusual for him. In Cumberland he was a legend long before the song was written. 'There was no scarlet about the Cumberland huntsmen of those days,' said a friend of his; 'Peel used to wear a grey coat with buttons at the back, what we call a lap coat. Tall and straight, a bit of a rough diamond, and as cute and keen a man as ever dealt in horse-flesh, he had a good heart under his grey coat, and was a friend of every farmer in a country that was overrun with foxes. He rode the shortest stirrup ever I saw a huntsman have; his knees were very nearly up with the saddle of Dunny, the brown cross-bred he usually rode when I saw him: clean leg, plenty of bone, a fast Cumberland nag. But more generally John Peel was to be seen on his feet, striding. . . .'

Only five men have controlled this country since Peel: John Crozier (1840–1903), James Lowther, a former Speaker of the House of Commons (1903–17), R.J. Holdsworth (1919–37), John Tatters (1937–45) and, for the last 26 years, Sir Percy Hope. In tribute to the immensely popular John Crozier, whose tenure – 64 seasons – was even longer

knows what puts the edge on a pack of hounds; he knows what it feels like to be chased, too. He took over the Blencathra just after Hitler's war. Like a grey hill fox, tough and rangy, he was soon on the run from a prison camp after his capture at Tobruk.

But for the opening meet, with Johnny Richardson only just out of hospital, it was Stanley Mattinson, now in his 11th season as whipper-in, who carried the horn; and Sir Percy Hope, at 86 celebrating a quarter-century of Mastership, who led them away from Threlkeld. By 9.30, Stanley had them in the Blencathra foothills, hunting a drag over Saddleback, a stale line, but not quite too dull for their sharp noses. Having heard how well they live up to their great heritage, visitors gave their full attention as these hounds composed their white

115 Stanley Mattinson, who was acting huntsman for Johnny Richardson on Saddleback from the meet at Threlkeld on the author's Blencathra day.

than Peel's, another of the great Cumbrian hunting songs was composed:

We'll drink success to Crozier
In bumpers all around,
The Prince of Mountain Sportsmen,
The Master of the Hounds!
The brave pack of Blencathra
Is free alike to all;
The peasant from the cottage,
And the Squire from the Hall.

That is a wonderful thing about fell-hunting: there can be no suspicion it is monopolised by scarlet cavaliers. For a few shillings it is for everyone, and always has been. 'Nothing much, for that matter, has changed in these hills,' remarked Sir Percy's fellow-octogenarian, Reg Folder, on 13 October. Reg Folder, who knew John Crozier, was first appointed to the hunt committee in 1926. Even the slate quarry and the road below Borrowdale must have looked much the same from the top in Queen Victoria's day. Only the traffic roaring from Keswick to Penrith is new. And the huddle of stationary cars, dark specks on the grass verge, always immediately below the point where hounds are running: a helpful guide to lost followers, perhaps 2000 feet up and two mountain spurs behind the hunt.

As the hounds turned east through Minesghyll, Doddick Ghyll, White House Ghyll and Scalesfell, I felt the scene to be a good replica of a Peel hunt: hound music over russet bracken, and blaeberry, broken up here and there by inky larch trees and stone walls. From the tops you could see across the Solway to the hills of Dumfriesshire. It was to these tops that hounds now headed. For they found in Southerfell, raced him high over Saddleback and down Knowecrag to the waterworks beyond Broken End. For six miles, resembling a string of piebalds on some hectic marathon steeplechase, they mounted the slippery gradients with unfaltering speed. Then, beginning to climb Lonscale Crag, they ran him to ground in a rocky crevice. In went Gyp, the terrier, and after 15 minutes their fox was bolted and killed by this unerring mixed pack, just 200 yards down the fellside:

D'ye ken that bitch whose tongue was death?
D'ye ken her sons of peerless faith?
D'ye ken that a fox, with his last breath,
Cursed them all as he died in the morning?
Yes I ken John Peel and Ruby, too,
Ranter and Royal and Bellman as true,
From the drag to the chase, from the chase to the view,
From the view to the death in the morning.

(13 October 1971)

A new Mastership, composed of Mr P.L. Davidson and Mr G.B. Graham, QC, was appointed in 1973. Mr H. Ralph became hunt secretary in the same year. B. Todhunter relieved S. Mattinson as whipper-in in 1973.

The Coniston

FELL HOUNDS OVER WINDERMERE

When at 9.20 a.m. last Thursday, 24 September, 17 couples of the Coniston hounds flew with fine music from the bracken of Kirkstone valley for the rock-strewn gradient of Red Screes, 1500 feet above the sea, two minutes behind their fox, it was the first time for five months they had known real exercise. For they had been only a week in kennels, at Ambleside, from their sedentary summer existence, for which each hound had lodged trencher-fed with a separate farmer. And, watching them through binoculars from a stone eminence high above sun-dazzled Windermere, Mr Bruce Logan, their Master, doubted they would stick the line much longer: they were unfit, he reckoned, while a generous heat was drying up the dew-held scent.

How many times, I wondered, has a Logan stood thus apprehensively upon the fells over Windermere, scrutinising the performance of his hounds the first day of the season? It was his great-great-great uncle, Anthony Gaskarth of Coniston Hall, a farmer and a butcher too, who – after angrily seizing two hounds from a Duddon client in payment of a meat debt in 1825 – bred up the forbears of this celebrated pack. Then they were trencher-fed the whole year

116 Mr Bruce Logan, Master from 1954 to 1978.

round, converging at the meet from neighbouring farms at the sound of Gaskarth's horn. Their first kennels were built at Coniston in the 1850s, but it was not until 1881, when the Rev. E.M. Reynolds succeeded as Master, that the Coniston were removed to their present home at Greenbank, Ambleside. In 1908, John and Bruce Logan, Gaskarth's great-nephews, arranged to amalgamate their private hunt with the Coniston, forming a new subscription pack with the old name. When John Logan died, his brother continued as Master for 32 years, being succeeded in 1941 by Robert Logan, who was in turn followed by his son, Bruce, the present Master, in 1954. Therefore the Coniston possess in no small measure that thread of family tradition so precious to hunt administration and hound-breeding.

'That was a wonderful season to take over,' recalled Mr Logan, eyeing his hounds as they raced, tightly bunched, higher and higher up the rock-strewn hill. 'We killed 52 brace then, the all-time record. And that's the veteran responsible,' he pointed, with his crook to a red-coated, leather-gaitered figure, 700 yards away – Anthony Chapman, the huntsman.

The Chapman family boast as strong a Coniston tradition as the Logans. Anthony's great-great uncle, Tom Chapman, came from Patterdale to be huntsman in the 1850s, founding a reputation not easy to follow. 'He's the best huntsman in England,' wrote a visiting reporter towards the end of Tom's term, 'if you'd seen him chanting hounds as they were questing it would have fair lifted the cap off your head; it went to your very soul, there was such grand music in his tones. When he was huntsman at Patterdale he was courting a girl at Kendal, whom he afterwards married. He often left the Patterdale kennels at 10 o'clock at night after a day's hunting, to walk the 20 miles to Kendal to see his sweetheart, then walk back the next day. That's the stuff that Chapmans are made of. . . .' Tom's son Harrison and his nephew, Anthony (the present Anthony's grandfather), divided their time between the Windermere Harriers and the Coniston. George Chapman, taking over in 1908, enjoyed not only 24 seasons but also the pleasure of seeing his 19-year-old son Anthony as whipper-in, just after handing over the horn to Ernest Parker in 1932.

'Presented by the supporters in appreciation of his

117 Anthony Chapman began his Coniston career as whipper-in in 1932 and retired in 1976 after carrying the horn for 32 years.

great achievement', reads the silver collar of the whip Anthony Chapman now carries, which was given to him after achieving his tally of 52 brace in the 1954–5 season. A fell huntsman that can kill foxes is indeed a hero to the farmers. Nor would any disagree with J.W. Allen, the large-scale sheep farmer, who is chairman of the Westmorland Agricultural Executive Committee. 'Hunting is literally the only effective form of fox control we have in the fells'. He says; 'that is why these packs hunt well on through lambing, into May'.

It was 9.35 when – with hounds close and fast behind him – this big fox, with the long easy stride of the mountain breed, ran into a borran high up on the scree of Ravenscrag, a natural hollow under the loose rock. Chris Ogilvie, the whipper-in, pre-positioned as usual in the high ground, was soon there with his three terriers. They are brindled, silky-coated little dogs, some with Border in their blood, some with Bedlington. But the basic breed of Lakeland working terrier was man's servant, so they say, before the Romans came. They play a key role in fell-hunting and will keep a fox at bay all day and all night unless they bolt him. This time, at 9.50, they bolted him.

Tempest '68 and Wonder '67 were first at his brush, the others tight behind him. Earlier in the summer Tempest was proclaimed champion hound at Lorton, while just a fortnight ago Wonder triumphed in the bitch class at Cumberland's Loweswater show. They were the sort of leaders needed to defeat this fox now steering straight up the shaly face. In common with all good fell hounds they show certain distinct qualities: an extreme lightness to compete with slopes and walls, a long pastern to minimize concussion, a sound hare foot to grip the rocks, a big well-placed shoulder for mountain strength and a very well let-down hock for speed, combined with a superlative nose and a loud cry. From where I stood by the Kirkstone Pass at that moment, it looked as though they were galloping a vertical scramble. But then he circled down, making towards the rocky chaos of Petts quarries. He knew a safe borran there.

'Civilization's done nothing to change these hills,' remarked Mr Tom Preston, a retired farmer whose first day's fell hunting was in the 1890s, as he watched this dramatic hunt with a steady eye. 'They're just as God made them. Except for the walls and they've been up a century and a half,' he added. 'We're luckier than the Lunesdale,' commented another. 'With the M6 extension opening next month and cutting straight through them. The Ullswater will have that M6 right on their flank, too.

It's a nasty business this motorway construction'.

'That road'll mean more holiday-makers out,' put in Mr Gordon Gregory, the hunt secretary, 'fell-hunting's a spectator sport now, advertised by the Holiday Association and the National Parks. Motorways cut both ways. Up to a few years ago you never got visitors in the hunting season, now they're up here all the year round.'

Half a dozen strangers from the hotels of Windermere and Ambleside watched with the regular hunt supporters as this fox found his second borran at 10.00 a.m., a little below Petts quarries; such a jungle of boulders that Chapman decided to leave him and cast in the valley for another. But the sun was intense, scent seemed to be quite dried up, and drawing a blank, he returned at 10.50 with the terriers to the borran. All hands went to pull away the rocks – Chris Ogilvie, Gordon Gregory, three farmers, two quarrymen – but in vain. It seemed, from the distant echo of the terriers' yapping, that this fox had found a cavern at least 20 feet down. Anthony Chapman took out his horn and sounded 'home' from this 38th opening hunt of his fine career – rightly pleased with his 1970–71 curtain raiser.

(24 September 1970)

Mr Gordon Gregory took over the Mastership on Mr Logan's retirement in 1978, while Mark Forster relieved Anthony Chapman in 1976 as huntsman. Then, on 1 July 1979, Mark Forster's place was taken by Chris Ogilvie.

Mr D.K. Williams has held the post of secretary since 1980.

The Eskdale and Ennerdale

IN THE STEPS OF 'LAAL TOMMY'

In the whole world of sport, from tiddly-winks to ocean racing, probably no greater pride, in either their old heroes or their contemporary gladiators, is expressed than that felt by the fell hunters of Lakeland. And the hunt hero of each is, without question, second to none. 'Could anyone seriously suggest', ask the Blencathra, 'that a finer man ever drew breath than John Peel, who hunted our country for 56 seasons, still following his hounds on 40-mile chases till the age of 78? And, if you want a runner-up, take John Crozier, our founder, and Master for 64 seasons'.

'For real good men', claim the Melbreak, 'there's none to beat our Benson or our Iredale'. But Melbreak sportsmen would scarcely say that above a whisper in an Ullswater pub, when the 'tatie' goes round and the ballads begin; for there Joe Bowman was the champion of *all* Cumbria for *all* time. . . . 'Bowman?' enquire the Coniston, with a headshake. 'Peel? Oh yes, we've heard of them, but they were not a patch on our Tom Chapman, who has always been labelled "greatest of them all".'

But in the bright rumbustious gallery of famous fell-hunters, whose was the most spectacular career? I believe 'Laal [little] Tommy' Dobson's was as remarkable as any. Born in 1826 at Staveley, by the southern tip of Lake Windermere, young Dobson is said to have 'yearned for the fell tops and the sight and sound of hounds on the line of a strong fox since childhood'; and from the beginning of his apprenticeship as a bobbin-turner and wood craftsman in West Cumbria, he kept under his workbench a useful couple of hounds called Cruiser and Charmer, which, two days a week, he joined forces with the four or five, belonging to farmer friends, for 'a day after Reynard'. The genius of Dobson, who always hunted hounds himself, was recognised early. One imagines a short, wiry youth with a ruddy, puckish face, a boy of scant words, but of immense personality and humour, whose soul was where the 'greyhound foxes' of Scafell, Black Combe and Ennerdale lived. On his own hounds' rest-days, he whipped in for four seasons to the Kendal otterhounds. And toasts to 'Laal Tommy' were soon echoing around the Lakeland inns in company with the great.

He was the founder of the Eskdale and Ennerdale Hunt, and it came about like this. At one time and another, between the 1780s and 1850s, three hunts, all run by the squirarchy, flourished in this country: the Ennerdale, the Wasdale and the Eskdale. Mr Lamplugh Irton, of Irton Hall, is the first name recorded with a pack in the Eskdale area; then Capt. Parker and Admiral Scott kept hounds at Ennerdale, and these apparently were taken on by Mr Huddlestone, of Gosforth, who, with colourful 'Auld Will' Ritson, hunted more in the Wasdale area. These Wasdale hounds later came under the Mastership of Mr Rawson, of Wasdale Hall, and Squire Lewthwaite, of Woodhow, but, when they gave up in the 1850s, that was the end of the old regular packs, the gap being filled only by the combined trencher-fed forces of 'Laal Tommy', 'Auld Will' Ritson and another stalwart called Tom Lindsay.

Within a few years, everything – hounds, terriers, kennels and management – was in 'Laal' Tommy's hands'. In 1883 a committee of supporters announced the birth of a new county hunt – the Eskdale and Ennerdale – 'Laal Tommy', retaining ownership of the hounds. It was in 1900, at the age of 74, that he was appointed Master. When he died, ten years later, a characteristic dirge was composed for him, the first and last verses of which go like this:

There's gloom on the mountains, and gloom in the valleys
Where sparkling Esk rolls by mead, wood, fell and brae,
And grief fills the hearts of the foxhunting dalesmen,
For death has called Tommy, their Master, away . . .

Let the winds blow shrill blasts o'er the grave of the
* hunter,*
Let sly foxes howl; hounds dejectedly whine;
Fond mem'ries of 'Laal Tommy' Dobson forever
We'll deep in our heart of hearts dearly enshrine.

On hunting days, back in the eighties, a very small boy could be seen close on Tommy's footsteps, and often, at the end of a long day, up on the old huntsman's shoulders. The same boy would be back at the kennels, helping Dobson with the hounds' feed, then sitting on his knee listening to accounts of marathon runs of long ago. When 'Laal Tommy' was appointed Master in 1900, he made that boy, Willie Porter, huntsman, and in 1910, just before he died, left him all the hounds and terriers. Willie carried on as Master for 42 years. His son, Jack Porter, was huntsman till 1944, then handing over to Arthur Irving, and, in 1952, succeeding Willie as Master, the post he still holds. In natural course, in 1958, Jack Porter's son, Edmund, began whipping in to Irving, and took over as huntsman in 1963. Had 'Laal Tommy' married and had a son, would there be Dobsons hunting hounds today? The conjecture is of little significance; for he did something still

118 'Laal Tommy' Dobson with (*right*) Willie Porter in 1900. Mr J.W. Porter, who became Master in 1952, is Willie Porter's son.

119 Edmund Porter, the huntsman, who is the Master's son, with hounds marking to ground at Cotta during the author's E and E day in October 1974.

more remarkable: he initiated the Porter dynasty.

Edmund Porter was out on Black Combe, the peninsular massif cutting down between the Duddon estuary and the sea, when I joined them on 19 October, hounds being temporarily kennelled at Parkhead, the home of Mr Brockbank, the hunt chairman, for a full week's hunting in that area. Black Combe is not the loftiest part of this most rugged of all fell-hunt countries; that distinction belongs to Scafell. Nor does it hold the fox-killing record: that goes to Ennerdale, where they disposed of another eight in the middle of the month. But it is the most open, and therefore the freest and fastest and, in a way, the best from a spectator's view. After unboxing at Whicham at 9.30 a.m., hounds first sought their drag in the bracken of Parsonage Breast, then up through Whicham Hall Ghyll, Rabbits' Crags and Ralliss Ghyll, until at last at 11.00, they found a fox on Black Combe scree. Pushing him to the summit and down the crags again to Horse Back, where they broke straight through the middle of a close herd of sheep, they ran him to ground, after 15 minutes, at Cotla.

Leaving a terrier, a favourite called Turk, to mark him, the huntsman lifted hounds close to Whitbeck on the west coast road. Scent was good, and there they found a second, a big yellow one with a huge stride, which led them back like fleeting drops of cream over the shaly top giving another 20 minutes of the best; then he chose a borran refuge on Cotla, not 400 yards from his companion's. It was 2.30 p.m. now and, after an abortive hunt towards the valley and the long line of car followers (who had, apparently, enjoyed wonderful views for most of the day) on the A595, Edmund Porter decided to concert all energies on to bolting the first fox. They pulled away some stones, they tried to widen the gap, they hoped the terrier would turn on his tail. But all in vain. And as they moved away towards home, through the bent-grass and the blaeberry to the bracken slopes below, more than one farmer shook his head ruefully, as though to say that there were two more lamb-killers who got away with it.

But not many lamb-killers are reprieved when the E and E find them. The hunt destroys nearly 100 most seasons. Jack Porter holds the record with his 1943–4 tally: 107. Edmund came close to that, in 1971–2, with 104. And here is further 'proof of the pudding'; the E and E carried off the highly prized 'best group of five' (best entered and unentered bitch, best brood bitch and best entered and unentered dog-hound) at this year's Rydal show.

They also won the 'best group of four' at the Lorton, Sedbergh, Loweswater and Eskdale shows. The Ullswater Hunt used much E and E blood in Willie Porter's time, so now we find Edmund Porter going mainly to the Ullswater for his outcrosses. He is also, perhaps, the leading name among the fell hunts as a breeder of successful working terriers. As for the hunt's backing, they now count 600 on their subscribers' list and 500 in the hunt supporters' club. So I left with the feeling that the fortunes of the Eskdale and Ennerdale under three generations of Porters would more than have satisfied the hopeful dreams of 'Laal Tommy'.

(9 October 1974)

Since the article was written Mr Porter informed me that the E and E accounted for 131 foxes in the 1974–5 season, which he believes is a record for a fell pack.

The Lunesdale

HUNTERS OF THE PENNINE FELLS

Sedbergh, which has been described as the spiritual centre of the Lunesdale Hunt, overlooks that little valley where the Lune, flowing down towards Lancaster, is met by its tributary, the Rawthey, whose source is found on the Pennines, below the peak of Baugh Fell. If you follow the A683 a couple of miles up the Rawthey valley you come to a signpost 'Hole House', and that is where the Lunesdale kennels have been these last seven years. Previously the hunt rented some farm buildings at Orton, 12 miles north, but when it was announced that the M6 would pass less than a mile away, the committee decided the site was too close for comfort.

Fell-hunters, traditionally regarding their country as sacrosanct, saw the motorway as a dreadful intrusion and, apart from the eyesore and the hazard, it has dealt one irrevocable blow, for it virtually deprived them of a four-to-eight mile strip along their western boundary. But in a country 40 miles by 40, to the visitor that does not seem a crippling sacrifice; and still, to cover their broad and rugged territory, they make about 15 two-to-six day visits to farms in outlying areas in the course of each season.

For our day, 20 March, hounds were operating from the kennels, and John Nicholson, who has been their huntsman for 13 years and was whip (never 'whipper-in') for another 14 years before that, had 35 (not 17 couple) ready to move off at 8.30 a.m. This is, perhaps, the most level and quality-looking of all

120 John Nicholson has carried the horn since 1963.

the fell packs; at any rate, during the past three or four years, they have been prominent among the prize-winners at the Lakeland shows, and, with Dally, they are holding many championship trophies. The hounds are mostly of Ullswater breeding.

The Lunesdale take a good measure of their heritage from neighbouring Ullswater, the hunt which once held the rights over most of these hills. That is not to say that the Lunesdale country lacks its own traditions, for, during the eighteenth and nineteenth centuries at least, it contained a succession of private scratch packs. The oldest evidence we saw of this were two posters, dated 1849 and 1851. 'Staveley Hunt. Mr Higginson informs his friends and the Public that his HUNT will take place on Friday. The Dogs will throw off near the Abbey Hotel at Nine o'clock in the Morning. . . . Fox Hunt, Sedbergh: Mr William Lupton . . . will give his annual Fox Hunt (Being the last of the present season) on Friday, the 4th day of April next. Three Packs of Hounds are fully expected to meet together, and a brilliant run may be calculated on. . . .'

During the second half of the nineteenth century the Ullswater hunted the Sedbergh fells regularly, but in 1905, Messrs William Blathgate and Matthew Sedgwick founded the Sedbergh Foxhounds, with Mr Charles Taylor as Master and Mr Sedgwick as his deputy and honorary huntsman, and a gift of three hounds from the Ullswater. Shortly after the end of the First World War, 'the Lunesdale hunt' was formed by Mr Thomas Robinson, of Bainsbank; this absorbed the Sedbergh, giving birth to a new hunt, the Sedbergh and Lunesdale. The S and L went into suspended animation in the 1920s, but was revived for the 1929–30 season, with Mr Harold Hodgson, the well-known auctioneer, as chairman; and Mr Robinson as honorary huntsman and joint-Master, with Miss Lees of Burton Hall, Carnforth. In 1936 the hunt was renamed as the Lunesdale Foxhounds. The hunt was just kept going during the last war, and was re-organised in 1945, with the help of Mr Douglas Todd, a local journalist.

The present chairman of the Lunesdale is Mr Harold Watson, an Ullswater stalwart by birth and upbringing, with an excellent eye for a hound. He was a Cumbria policeman until 1959. His committee, which must hold the size record for the hunting world – 52, including 26 hill farmers – prefer not to appoint a Master. Mr Watson is also joint-secretary, a post he shares with Mr Oliver Berry (brother of the former joint-Master of both the Woodland Pytchley and the Fitzwilliam, who wrote *The Times* hunting reports, in the 1930s – Mr Michael Berry). Oliver

Berry combines his Lunesdale duties with those of secretary of the Central Committee of Fell Packs.

He now met us at the kennels, and we followed hounds to Bluecaster bridge, where Mr Watson and some of the followers were waiting, others having made their way direct to vantage points on the hilltops. In the fell-hunt tradition these hounds will go trencher-fed at the end of this month – or by mid-May, it depends on lamb-worrying calls – remaining with their walkers until early September, when they re-assemble, sleek and spruce, for the Lunesdale hound, terrier, sheep and sheepdog show. And on 20 March, at Bluecaster bridge, several hounds recognised their walkers and broke away from the pack to give them a wet and boisterous welcome. One of these walkers, John Dixon, who was John Nicholson's whip for ten years, had around his feet three of the Lakeland terriers, which play such an important role in fell-hunting; another was Wilson Hardisty, a dominant figure at sheepdog trials and brother of Harry, of Melbreak fame; another was octogenarian Tom Sedgwick, nephew of the Sedbergh's co-founder; and another a chartered accountant, David Fell, the treasurer. The previous night's entertainment was a particularly important occasion for Mr Fell and the finances, a dance featuring the final of the contest for the Lunesdale Beauty Queen, which raised £300 for the hunt, 600 people having attended.

John Nicholson thus got to bed at 3.00, and was up at 5.00, but he did not look it as he strode away towards Uldale and went in search of a fox on Baugh Fell. We took out our field-glasses and watched him and his hounds – tiny dots against the white grass hillside – circle north on the foothills of the Wild Boar Fell (swine outnumbered fox by more than 100 to one when the Pennines were all forest). In the fierce north wind of 20 March scent was blown to the heavens, but John knew a 'smittle spot' (a likely place), the wooded Taythes Ghyll, where foxes shelter and lie up after their night's hunting. Perhaps, if the scent was recently laid, hounds might, even in this tempest, trace the drag to his kennel and there 'put him off', as they call it. Walkers, expecting some contact with their summer charges, marched swiftly to Taythes and began egging them on, the fell-hunter's expression for 'cheering' being 'Good lad, Ranger! . . . Good lass, Tango! Goo-arn!' Then if their hound 'gave mouth' – 'Hark forrard!' A single hound did give mouth, and the remainder were soon behind her, a string of tan, white and black on the fellside. 'They'll lose'n on

121 The Lunesdale hounds feeding at the end of the day described by the author.

t'hill in t'wind,' one walker predicted.

If you can imagine a steep and barren bleached-grass moorland, without a sign of human habitation or activity, except for an occasional flock of sheep and, once in a while, a stone wall – which these hounds jump like gazelles – you begin with a basic idea of typical Lunesdale country. In the weather of 20 March it took on a tundra quality: the gale doubled flat the bent-grass and cotton-grass; the tiny waterfalls marking the becks were a stalactite pattern of icicles; your feet crunched into the soft ice covering the yellow-green sphagnum moss, the bogs were frozen over, and the high tops were silvered with snow. 'What way?' The familiar fell-hunter's request rang out from the direction of a rocky outcrop 400 yards away. But you need not reply, for, suddenly, round the shoulder of the silent hill, came a piebald and skewbald vortex of hounds, flashing in circles, telling you they had lost that drag from Taythes Ghyll.

John Nicholson swung westward now, with his relentless fell huntsman's stride, long and easy, and just as fast, whether uphill or on the flat; and with him, Michael Fernhead, his 17-year-old whip (who, not content with all this, walks eight miles from home to the kennels and back every day). John did not touch his horn to summon hounds that had cast on, but with one short call – 'Come on!' – had them with him again. Sometimes there was a yelp from a clever old hound, saying he had a remote and momentary whiff of fox, and then you saw 34 heads lift, 34 pairs of ears cock and turn, to converge on the discoverer, like filings to a magnet.

One drag led them to a pattern of holes (they do not speak of 'earths'), and three followers went sharply to the spot with their terriers. Fell-hunters love the 'bolt': it is the moment for terrier-owners to show off their charges, where hound speed may be seen close-to, and an occasion to catch up and recuperate and chat. Then, when the terrier goes down, the cry is given: 'Stand back, stand back, give fox a chance!' But on gusty 20 March the black-and-tan Lakelands scuttled down unavailingly, and a disappointed John tramped on towards Ravenstonedale (the name of the 1976 'Miss Lunesdale's' village), south along a 'trod' (a sheep track) on Harter Fell, crossing, our map told us, the Cumbria-Yorkshire border, and finally surrendering to the ungenerous weather at 2.30. That was not too early for many of them as we knew from their mutters of 'Best go home and do up', a reference to evening jobs on the farm.

Being on an eastern limb from the Lakes there is less to impinge on the Lunesdale's sporting character, less tourism, less publicity, less interference. They are very independent and understandably jealous of their unique heritage, and of their sport too. When on Sunday morning it was announced to a group of them that the Coniston had also endured a blank Saturday, we noticed a bright, knowing glint in their collective eye as they shook their heads in sympathy.

(20 March 1976)

Mrs Susan Harrison became joint-secretary with Mr Berry in 1978.

The Melbreak

LAKELAND'S OLDEST HUNT

The sun was warm enough to produce a mid-summery haze on the fells when the Melbreak met at Kirkstile Inn last Saturday. To the visitor this looked ominous for scent. But Harry Hardisty, their huntsman, who arrived prompt at 9.30 a.m. with 35 hounds, seemed confident enough; for a drenching dew was seen on the rich meadows between Crummock Water and Loweswater, and out of a total of nine trial excursions leading up to this their opening meet, the Melbreak had accounted for no fewer than eight foxes since 21 September, mostly in precisely similar conditions. And the quarrymen and roadmen (and such shepherds and farmers who were not enticed by the rival attraction of the agricultural sale at Lorton) turning out to follow him, appeared as proud of the pack as Harry.

Indeed fell-hunting forms almost as close a part of the true Lakelander's life as his flocks or herds or the slate he extracts from the hillside or the pick he wields.

We do not know when the tradition began, for the early records are thin. But when Hutchinson wrote this note on the inhabitants of Loweswater in his *History of Cumberland*, published in 1794, one assumes the roots were already deep: 'The people live in harmony and they express contentment. The peasantry have one enjoyment here, which is prohibited to most men of their class. Through the liberality of their lords a hound is kept in nearly every house. Two or three qualified inhabitants take licence to kill game and command the pack. As soon as harvest is in, an honest cobbler shifts his garb and becomes huntsman, and every second or third morning collects the dogs and calls the sportsmen to the field; the cottagers climb the mountainside where they can view the chase, and without much exertion enjoy the pleasure of the hunt; after which they retire with cheerful minds and invigorated constitutions to their peaceful homes.'

It was in 1807 that William Pearson of Bannockrout first kept some nine couple of hounds for the amusement of his friends, and called his hunt the Melbreak. But what of the other fell-hunts? We know that John Peel hunted the Derwentwater and Skiddaw countries as well as what is now the Cumberland country from 1798, but the Blencathra, who claim descent from him, were not born till John Crozier came on the scene in 1840. The Coniston began life about the same time, the Eskdale and Ennerdale in the 1850s, the Ullswater not until 1880 and the Lunesdale only 40 years ago. So the Melbreak are the oldest.

Pearson died, aged 49, in 1816, and John Hudson, 'Yeoman of Kirkhead', we are told, took command for the next 38 seasons. And in the year he retired the Melbreak's original huntsman died. '. . . At Scalehill, in Brackenthwaite, on October 14, 1854, William Collingwood – "old Collin" – aged 84, hunted hounds upwards of 50 years,' ran the local press announcement. John Nicholson followed Hudson till 1865, then the greatly admired John Benson took office – for a decade with Robinson Mitchell and afterwards on his own till 1916 when he presented the pack to a committee 'for the benefit of the country'. Benson was said to be the only man living who was known to have hunted with John Peel ('of whom he claimed to have a vivid recollection', adds his obituarist). In 1917 Major E.A. Iredale began his long innings, in

harness with Dan Robinson and a second Robinson Mitchell, prompting, in 1919, this typical lilt in a Cumbrian drinking song:

The Masters today are three sportsmen
The first is Captain Iredale:
He has not only hunted with foxhounds
He helped to hunt Germans as well.
And all of the three are respected
For one's Mr Dan from Foulsyke,
And the other is Robinson Mitchell,
The squire that lives at High Dyke.

From 1928 till 1965 – the year in which he died and the present Master, Mr Frank Coates, took over – Iredale remained in sole command; and earlier this month his image was brought sharply into focus again for the Melbreak stalwarts. In the major's memory his nephew, Capt. Tim Iredale, presented a silver fox, set on a salver, for 'the best turned out huntsman with two foxhounds and two terriers from the six fell packs'. It was Harry Hardisty, whipper-in to the Melbreak from 1946 and huntsman since 1951, who carried the trophy home.

A grandson of that great fell-hunter, Josh Hardisty, Harry's houndsmanship is in the blood. He understands what makes fox catchers click and he knows just when and where the best Cumbrian outcrosses are to be secured. The breeding of the Melbreak is left to him. And when he led off from Kirkstile last Saturday, his 17 couples, every rib showing, loins like whippets and coats with silvery sheen, looked every inch as though they had striven for, and earned their eight foxes on the recent warming-up days.

While Harry drew the bracken around the rocky outcrops of Crabtree, we joined the deputy Master, Mr J.E. Musgrave, then climbed past Highcress up on to Low Fell and put up two bright russet foxes on our way. 'There are plenty of them,' remarked Major David Style, an ex-paratrooper who combines – quite invaluably, from all accounts – the secretaryships of both the Melbreak and the Central Committee of Fell Packs with the leadership of a mountain rescue team and daily business in Workington; 'but see how strong and well they look – it's the survival of the fittest in the Melbreak – and the Melbreak is the *most* precipitous of the Lakeland hunt countries.'

Meanwhile, having hunted a drag from Crabtree, hounds unkennelled their own fox on the south slope of Darling Fell, and when we reached the north-east face of Low Fell, their chanting ribbon suddenly appeared between Smithy and Sourfoot. But, tricking them here, another fox, perhaps one of those we

122 Harry Hardisty, huntsman to the Melbreak with hounds above Crummock Water.

had just seen, crossed the line. Five couple settled for the northern scent which took them left-handed across Whin Fell, Gillbrow and Graythwaite and three miles beyond that. The other 12 couple kept their noses to a line that led them into the Cocker valley between Latherhead and Cold Keld, twice across the river and road south of Loweswater village, Low Park and High Park, way down the coast of Crummock Water and up into the mountains between Buttermere and the Liza river – seven

miles on to 2500 ft. High Crag, where scent ran out on the hot shale.

From our perch on Low Fell the first hour of this marathon provided a grand spectacle. On their breast-high scent in the Cocker valley hounds gave the impression of a tight-knit huddle of white fleetfoot midgets, expanding and closing very briefly when they checked; and with the sun dazzling on Crummock Water, the ling and gorse bright with mauve and yellow and the animation of hound music in the valley, one was not surprised to see 30 visitors dotting the hillside with eager binoculars and a dozen more by their cars on the road below. Some of these come up annually and follow a different pack each day, for fell-hunting has become a highly popular diversion in Cumbria. The English Lake Counties Tourist Association broadcasts their meets.

It is earnest business too. The role of huntsman was a reserved occupation in the last war; the hunts are still regarded by the Ministry of Agriculture as 'fox destruction societies' and are duly rewarded for handing in the brushes. When, last Friday, I asked Mr J.S.R. Chard, adviser on wildlife to the Forestry Commission, whether there are too many foxes on Grizedale, he replied: 'No – thanks to the fell packs (particularly, on that side' to the Melbreak) they are always kept down. We take no other action; hunting is clearly the most effective and most natural way to control foxes.' Nor would the shepherds of Loweswater disagree with that: the fox is at once their enemy and their guide, their villain and their hero. And the Melbreak Hunt is their eternal delight:

When chill October bares the fells,
And red the brackens lie
'Tis grand to see the gallant hounds,
Sweep past us in full cry.

(14 October 1972)

Mr R.H. Nicholson succeeded Major Style as hunt secretary in 1974 and, at the same time, R. Bland succeeded H. Hardisty as huntsman.

Mr Peter Caddy was appointed joint-honorary secretary in 1979.

The Ullswater

FELL HOUNDS OF HELVELLYN

Few Ullswater veterans have ever witnessed such a large turnout as appeared for the opening meet of the hunt's 101st season at the Royal Hotel, Dockray, on 20 October. It was over 250, the majority of them local and regular hunt supporters, shepherds and publicans, farmers and solicitors, quarrymen and doctors, for whom the pack is their pride, the symbol of their brotherhood and their delight. On the dot of 10.00 a.m. that happy majority, with its sprinkling of enterprising visitors, began to follow huntsman Dennis Barrow on to Gowbarrow Fell; then they deployed on the heights to put themselves at the best advantage should hounds hit off the drag of a fox. This happened at 10.10.

From a few hundred feet up you soon saw what had become of the *minority* – the motor-car brigade. Bumper-to-bumper they congested the road below: a sorry spectacle, not only because they impeded other road-users and were fairly sure to head any fox pointing off the fell, but also because they and their passengers lose much of the aura of fell-hunting. For how, boxed up on the A592, could anyone experience the real thrill, sport apart, of being in the Lake District: the exhilarating climbs, the sensation of gazing from great heights to the deep waters of broad, smooth lakes and across, from the same level, at the scudding cloud shadows on the purple and gold of the opposite mountains?

Then there are the ever-changing contrasts of colour and scene, only known to the genuine foot follower: here bracken (which slows hounds up so badly) bronzed from the frost, and jumbles of boulders (where the cavernous borrans that serve as fox refuges are concealed); here Herdwick and Swaledale sheep, grazing on dew-drenched grass, with buzzards and crows circling above them, hoping they will die; and there, round the shoulder of the fell, past an outcrop of that thickly lichened volcanic stone, which makes Cumbria what it is, to an expanse of heather from which, with their tuneful scream, grouse intermittently explode and quickly vanish. Here perhaps, the heather and bracken give way to bog, to sphagnum moss, a rosy-verdant squelch, with cotton-grass and bent-grass flying against the wind; and then, around another bend, into a steep-sided ghyll, with lone and stunted hawthorn and ash trees contriving a life from the stone, and tinkling waterfalls to mark the ascent. Car followers have none of this, nor the self-satisfaction of physical exertion, nor the melody of hounds and huntsman.

Every time you hear the sounds of a fell hunt, you sense they belong, as much as the buzzards' cries, to the hill. They mark the spirit that binds the

123 Joe Bowman, huntsman, 1879–1911 and 1914–23.

dalesman to the fell as no other force has ever done. They echo back down the ages. And around Ullswater, probably as far back as any other, Clarke's *Ancient History*, written in the eighteenth century, shows the district to be one of the principal traditional hunting centres of the north. No one really knows how long ago the shepherds and farmers here began to keep foxhounds at home and join forces on certain days to wage war on the raiders that took their lambs and chickens.

A century and a half ago, Squire Taylor kennelled his Matterdale hounds at Baldhow, then Squire Hasell kept a pack at Dalemains; and the Patterdale hounds, which were descended from John Peel's and which numbered the legendary Tom Chapman and Joe Dawson among their huntsmen, came to Grassthwaite Howe. In 1873, prompted by easier communications and access and the need to economise, the Baldhow and Patterdale united to form a new hunt, the Ullswater, with kennels at Patterdale Hall, and with Lord Lonsdale, the 'Yellow Earl', at the head of its list of subscribers. He was busy with the Cottesmore at the time and sent up a present of five couples of his thick-boned, straight-legged hounds from Barleythorpe. They ran, apparently as good as gold with the local breed. His family, the Lowthers, and the Hasells, became the principal backers of the Ullswater. Mr J.W. Marshall was first Master and Mr J.E. Hasell second. Abe Pattinson carried the horn in the beginning, and the hunt's first drinking song, the pioneer of countless drinking songs, inevitably chants his praises.

What heroes are the great fell huntsmen! No other figures rank anywhere near as high in the estimation of the country folk. And none higher than John Bowman – 'Old Hunty' – as he was called – who followed Abe in 1879 and hunted these hounds till 1911, and again after recovering from illness and injury, from 1914 to 1923 – a total of 40 seasons. Bowman towers over the Ullswater story as Peel looms behind the Blencathra. It was not simply that he ranked, as huntsman and houndsman, in the same flight as Willie Porter of the Eskdale and Ennerdale, Anthony Chapman of the Coniston and Jim Dalton of the Blencathra, but he was a grand mixer and humorist too, and the leader of the fun when the chase was over and the 'tatie pot' and beer were served and the singing began. And, considering the hunt is the hub of social life in a fell country, such qualities are invaluable.

Bowman's runs were a legend, many of them over 20 miles. Runs like that are very rare now, for the blood of the long-limbed 'greyhound foxes' has

mostly been diluted from mixing with the increased populations of the surrounding lowlanders. The one whose drag they traced on Gowbarrow on 20 October was unkennelled at Yew Crag to be followed on a fair scent up to the Shooting Box. But he was not for the open hill: he wanted nothing better than to return to his lair. So back he ran. They turned him again at Dobbinwood Lodge and, with swift Barmaid, Gaily, Rival and Welcome a shade ahead of the others, they were hard on his brush up to Gowbarrow Combes. There he escaped into a badger's sett, making work for the terriers, while hounds marked.

It was a pity octogenarian ex-huntsman, Joe Wear, who, faithful as ever, had been at the meet, was too frail to reach the scene. His career began in 1923, as whipper-in to Braithwaite Wilson who had taken over the horn from Bowman. Excepting the war period, Joe was huntsman from 1932 till 1970, when Dennis Barrow, with a nine-year apprenticeship as whip to the Coniston behind him, took over. There were 17 applicants for that appointment. Dennis has no whipper-in (or, rather, 'whip' as they always say up there).

Before the opening meet, he had his hounds up on the Pennines' limestone crags, kennelling at Brough for a fortnight. There they caught, among others, a 'greyhound fox' of 18 lb after a great hunt. And marking to ground at that badger's sett on 20 October they certainly looked the part. The Ullswater believe more in the virtues of bone and substance than the other fell-hunts, most of whom seem to favour a ribby look. But, for all their flesh, they are hard. And although they would not win a prize for levelness, they run as compact as a flock of starlings and can be heard two valleys away.

Dennis Barrow is guided by joint-Masters with a profound knowledge of fellhunting: Capt. Anthony Lowther, a great-nephew of 'the Yellow Earl' and a shrewd Lakeland venerer, whose mother was joint-Master from 1934 till 1939, and Mr John Bulman, who hunted the Windermere harriers for 15 seasons. In the 40-year-old kennels at Helvellyn they have, in particular, a number of very useful hounds by Blencathra Ranger and Bewcastle Prowler, and some successful young entries, sired by their own Tramper, a hound of Melbreak breeding.

At about 12.30 p.m., only a minute or so after the terrier went down, this fox at Gowbarrow Combes made another bid for safety. He was a veritable 'homer'. He tried to complete a circle that would return him to the sett. But they killed him in the open, in full view of the field.

124 The Ullswater at the Royal Hotel, Dockray, Cumberland, where the author joined them for the opening meet of the hunt's 101st season. *Left to right*: Mr J.A. Bulman (joint-Master); Joe Wear (huntsman, 1932–40 and 1945–70), Dennis Barrow (huntsman since 1971) and the late Capt. the Hon. A.G. Lowther (joint-Master).

That same day, at Dovescrag, 2600 feet up on the Helvellyn range, there was business of a grimmer nature. Armed with a net, a member of the Ullswater Outward Bound School dangled at a cliff-face to rescue Rascal, a third-season bitch and Rydal prize-winner, who lay starving and shivering on a 12-inch ledge, or 'bink', with a sheer 200-foot drop below her. She had been there three days: for it was on 17 October that the Ullswater's fox piloted them along the cliff top. Only Rascal had the nerve to follow him down the bink. And such was the gale and blinding rain over the next 70 hours that the Outward Bounders could not bring her to safety until the Saturday. In spirit, many an Ullswater veteran was with Rascal on the Helvellyn cliff-face during those three days, and during the hunt of 20 October, too. After Rascal was saved and Dennis took his pack home to Helvellyn, glasses were filled, as they have been filled after hunting days since the Royal Hotel first stood, and the old pub tremored with old songs until far into the night:

We're away to the meet and a'hunting we'll go,
For nothing's so sweet as the glad tally-ho,
With the Ullswater hounds we'll travel along,
Awaking the country with laughter and song.
*   The Fires on the hearth*
*   And good cheer abounds,*
*   We'll drink to Joe Bowman,*
*   And his Ullswater hounds . . .*

(20 October 1973)

Mr John Bulman retired from the Mastership in 1974, Capt. Anthony Lowther carried on alone until 1979 when he was joined by Lady Jane Benson. Capt. Lowther died in 1980.

Scotland

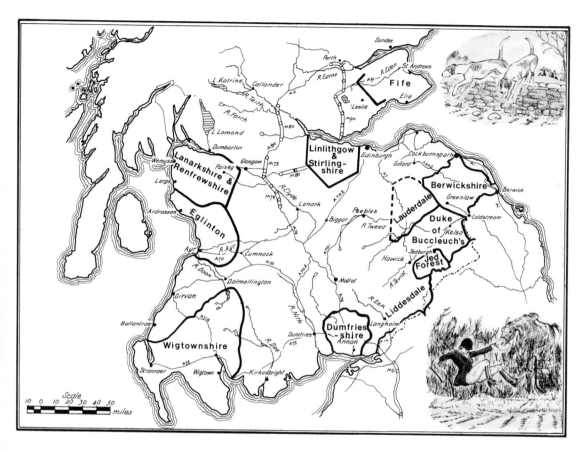

Dundee
Perth
R. Eden
St. Andrews
L. Katrine
Callander
R. Earns
A91
Fife
R. Teith
A9
Elie
R. Forth
'Leslie
L. Lomond
M90
M80
Linlithgow
&
Stirling-
shire
Dumbarton
A80
Edinburgh
Cockburnspath
Wemyss
Glasgow
M73
Gifford
A1
Lanarkshire &
Renfrewshire
Paisley
M80
A68
Berwickshire
Berwick
Largs
M8
Greenlaw
Ardrossan
Eglinton
M74
Lanark
A702
Lauderdale
Coldstream
R. Clyde
Peebles
Duke
of
Kelso
Buccleuch's
Ayr
A70
Cumnock
A76
Biggar
R. Tweed
Jedburgh
R. Doon
Dalmellington
A702
Hawick
Jed
Forest
Girvan
A714
A701
Moffat
R. Teviot
Ballantrae
R. Nith
A74
R. Esk
Liddesdale
Wigtownshire
R. Dee
Dumfries
Langholm
Stranraer
Wigtown
Kirkudbright
A75
Dumfries-
shire
Annan
M6
Scale
10 0 10 20 30 40 50
miles

The Berwickshire

WHERE SURTEES SENT HIS DAMNED

'Rot ye, Sir! Hanging's too good for ye!' Mr Sponge was informed, having caused Lord Scamperdale a fall. 'You should be condemned to hunt in Berwickshire for the rest of your life!' So much, in the estimation of Surtees, for the sporting qualities of Scotland's south-east corner; which goes to prove, how poorly based his prejudices were, because although the country is inclined to carry scent rather faintly, it is a most beautiful and varied tract, about half of it being low-ground farmland – nearly all owner-occupied now – a third hill-pasture and perhaps a sixth moorland. And when Surtees knew it, 130 years or so ago, it was lovelier still, for it was virtually without plough.

When lambing begins in the middle of February, the Berwickshire steer clear of their lowland and foothills, and hold their meets on the Lammermuirs, where the later-lambing black-faced sheep graze, a landscape of hill folded against hill, copper and purple, interspersed with long white grass, sparkling lochans and burns; conifer woods, well stocked with pheasant and woodcock; and on 8 March, when I enjoyed a day with them, gigantic cumulus climbed an azure sky. It is difficult to imagine a backcloth that could better enhance the tricolour of hounds and the foxhunter's scarlet.

We met at an old manse, Major and Mrs Jock MacKinnon's Craigie Lodge, Longformacus, some six miles north-west of Duns (the only town of consequence in the country), moved off at 11.00 a.m. and drew across the Duke of Roxburghe's Rawburn estate, with Mr David Thomson, joint-Master and huntsman, trying Rathburn, Allergrain, Whin Rig, Dunside, over Dye Water's ford, up to Horse-upcleugh and, at 1.00 p.m. with about seven steep moorland miles behind us, reaching Hill Wood, where a sudden 10-minute torrent of hail sent collars up and horses' heads down and made a muffled sound of that huntsman's renowned *try-hy*!

As Nimrod remarked, 'It appears that Berwickshire has been hunted beyond the memory of man' and, although it is difficult to establish the origin of the county hunt, certainly the 30 happy followers I met on the Lammermuirs that day guard a heritage that has prevailed for at least two centuries. The Earls of Home are known to have hunted the fox there in the seventeenth century, and the Lumsdaines, as Nimrod also recorded, had a

pack at Blanerne from about 1770. George Baillie, of Mellerstain and Jerviswoode, who began to hunt deer, hare and fox in Berwickshire, Roxburghshire and North Northumberland from 1787, formed a new pack in 1791, which he entered to fox only, being the first Scottish sportsman to do so. His sons, George, who became 10th Earl of Haddington, and Robert, inherited these hounds in 1826, and later sold them to Mr Baird. *Baily's Directory*, and other histories, claim this thread for the county hunt, but although their green collar derives from that worn by George Baillie, it is really the Duke of Buccleuch's who find their origin in his establishment, for the 5th Duke, who founded the ancestral hunt, bought Baird's hounds around 1830.

You look more plausibly for the start of the Berwickshire to the centre of the present county – to Dunse (now Duns) Castle, from which Mr William Hay (a Tweeddale Hay) hunted both the Scottish and English sides of the Tweed Valley from about the year of Waterloo. It was upon his foundation that in 1840 two other large landowners – Mr Robertson, on the Northumberland side and Lord Elcho (afterwards 9th Earl of Wemyss and March) on the Berwickshire side – started hunts in these vivid dales.

Elcho, who had previously hunted a pack of harriers and was one of the great sportsmen of that golden age, is cited by Nimrod as having, in a single day, killed two hares, both at the end of very long runs, ridden with the Duke of Buccleuch to see a record point in the afternoon, and then fished nine salmon from the Tweed before dinner. 'Who can beat Elcho when *he* gets a start?' was a classic question in the shires, where he hunted as a young man. He also took his hounds to East Lothian, but abandoned that county in about 1850, when he bought the Hon. F. W. Lambton's pack to hunt what are now the North Northumberland and Percy countries, in addition to the Berwickshire.

When Lord Elcho retired at the end of 27 seasons, in 1867, the 'Berwickshire and East Lothian' was organised under Lord Haddington and his brother, Robert Baillie-Hamilton, while Mr Askew hunted the southern sector until 1871, when he handed on the horn to Sir John Marjoribanks. Following five years of that regime, Haddington and his brother established the Berwickshire country much as it is

125 The field at Longformacus following the lawn meet given by Major and Mrs Jock Mackinnon at Craigie Lodge when the author rode with them on 8 March 1975.

today, keeping it open in high style for ten seasons. F.W. Lambton, who had been hunting the Northumberland side, retired in 1888, when Major James Hunter, a 9th Lancer who followed Marjoribanks in Berwickshire, reunited the whole country as 'the Northumberland and Berwickshire' remaining in command until the close of the 1896–7 season. It was Hunter's successor and close friend, Sir James Miller – the owner of Derby, Oaks, 1000 Guineas and Cesarewitch winners, and another highly popular Master – who converted that thick, stone-steading at Brieryhill, Duns, into the fine kennels that still serve the hunt so well.

Then came Mr Frederick Usher (1906–10), Sir John Hume Campbell, of Marchmont (1910–12), Lt-Col. Gray Cheape (who died as commander of the Worcestershire Yeomanry when the *Leashow Castle* was torpedoed), Col. C.T. Menzies (1915–19), and Mr J.L. Greig, of Eccles (1919–22). It was now that Moffat Thomson, of Lambden (father of the present senior joint-Master), began his eight-year innings, hunting the bitches only to begin with, then

both packs up to 1930, when Mrs Menzies, who had kept the hunt going during her husband's absence in the war, wore the Master's cap again until 1939. For the Second World War's opening season Mrs Menzies handed over to a trio – Major C.W.H. Baillie (a nephew of Sir James Miller), Capt. H.R. Trotter and her son, John Menzies. Bert Stevens (who was killed with the Lanarkshire and Renfrewshire earlier this month) was their huntsman.

Another brave Diana then took the Master's cap and the horn until 1946 – Miss Annette Usher, daughter of the Edwardian Master. One raconteur says of this remarkable woman that, during the war, 'after several hours of cleaning kennels, feeding and exercising hounds and horses, she mounted her bicycle and pedalled to Lintlaw farm, where she destroyed an ailing beast, skinned it, quartered it, buried the offal and transported the fleshy quarters across her handlebars, back to Brieryhill, before commencing the evening's routine work. . . .'

After she left to assume the Mastership of the Linlithgow and Stirlingshire (following her uncle there), Major Trotter, whose hound-breeding policy was to help produce such excellent sport in the forties and fifties, returned to the Berwickshire, to be joined by Mr Stenard Landale (1948–51), Major Baillie (1951–8); and Majors Burdon and Horne (1958–9). The last two named carried on together up to 1961. Then Major Horne, with Leslie Moss as huntsman, was in sole command till 1967, when Mr David Thomson agreed to take charge, provided he could hunt hounds, too. He was joined by his fellow-farmer and racehorse owner, Mr Robson Tullie, in 1971.

After that hailstorm at Hill Wood, with the cry of curlew and grouse blown across a brightened sky, and blue hares – as many as I have ever seen – in their winter white, frisking across the heather like napkins in a gale, Mr Thomson rode on over Cranshaws (a property of the former Master, Mr Landale), up Little Hill and Dog Law and across the Whiteadder's ford by St Agnes, until at last, at 2.15, they found in the Forestry Commission's Harehead. And with a weak scent, this fine pack – whose breeding, over the years, has been on the same lines as the Duke of Buccleuch's – pressed their quarry with great song via Blackcleugh, Greenhope, Tod Lea and Smiddy Hill, until they lost him in the gorse whins at Fellcleugh, to make a three-mile point and all of five miles as hounds ran.

This is a most precipitous area, with many hidden sheep drains, holes and bogs – a dozen followers were thrown on the flat that day (though none over the hunt jumps, for the construction of which the senior joint-secretary, Lt-Col. John Trotter, is so famous) – and it says much for the pertinacity of these hounds that, in spite of the moderate scenting conditions and liberal sheep foil, they managed to stay so close to their fox throughout. Thus ended one of the Berwickshire's most brilliant seasons of the century. And, considering their warmth and friendliness, I was not surprised to learn that many sportsmen and their children from the Lothians make the southward journey to hunt with them. It is often remarked that Lowland foxhunters (in spite of Surtees) do not know how lucky they are, but appreciation is strong among the Berwickshire sportsmen and women.

(8 March 1975)

Mr Tom Morgan, another farmer and former joint-secretary, joined Mr Thomson in the Mastership in 1975, and Mr Colin Furness came in as joint-secretary at the same time. Mr Tullie also remains in the joint-Mastership.

George Brown who went to the Berwickshire as kennel-huntsman at the same time that Mr Thomson was appointed Master (1967) continues in the same role.

The Duke of Buccleuch's

ANCESTRAL HUNT OF THE BORDER

'It is a country which teaches good riding, being of a give-and-take character. Stone walls and timber predominate, and there is a good deal of rough moorland, but there is also a fair amount of grass, over which hounds run fast'. That description of the Duke of Buccleuch's country, made 70 years ago, holds good today. Thirty-five miles east to west and 25 north to south, devoid of railways, divided by a scanty pattern of roads, none of them motorways, this great tract of the Border – where still the stone walls and timber predominate, provides almost as nice a variety as the horseman could wish for. On Mondays they hunt the green vale north of the Tweed, and east of St Boswell's, where the great sandstone kennels have stood for over a century; Wednesdays the foothill farmland to the west and the Eildon Hills to the north; Thursdays the steeper hills south of Kelso; and Saturdays the high open moors to the west.

Because the counter-attraction of the Cumberland Farmer's point-to-point was to be held on Saturday, it was for the Friday of last week that they organised the Roberton meet. And having unboxed in front of the dramatic enclosed escarpment below Lord Polwarth's Harden House (into which the cattle raiders used to drive and pen their plunder) we spent all day riding over the white grass uplands west of Hawick. And very fair they looked with a flicker of spring green on oak and ash and thorn, the gorse already touched with yellow, and cloud-shadows drifting over the broad and twisting undulations. But in this the severest drought the Border

126 Sir Hugh Arbuthnot, Bt. He was joint-Master and huntsman to the Duke of Buccleuch's hunt from 1964 to 1972.

126 Sir Hugh Arbuthnot, Bt. He was joint-Master and huntsman to the Duke of Buccleuch's hunt from 1964 to 1972.

has suffered for at least a decade, no one dared hope for a scent; and when Sir Hugh Arbuthnot, joint-Master and huntsman since 1964, crossed Borthwick Water and climbed Easter Park Hill, drew through the Chisholme spruce thickets and back by the bridge at Burnfoot, blank all the way, doubts seemed to be confirmed.

Then at about 1.00 p.m. hounds picked up a drag on Borthwick mains, and down went their heads and quicker their pace as they climbed the bracken slopes towards Borthwickshiels. Then there was hunting for the rest of this lovely March day. With scarcely a sign of habitation and only an occasional conifer plantation or electric wire fence to signify the modern world I felt, watching them, that the country must look much the same now as when that most ubiquitous of Scottish foxhunters, George Baillie of Mellerstain, originated the hunting tradition here 200 years ago.

Described by Nimrod as one of the first sportsmen in all Scotland, Baillie was also a distinguished agriculturalist (it was he who, among other initiatives, introduced the Southdown sheep in Scotland) and a most colourful personality. 'Nim North' claimed that every respectable kennel in Scotland contained Mellerstain blood and that 'his establishment is maintained in first-rate style without any subscription. . . . All Baillie's men are very civil, and Andrew Lumsden, the huntsman, uncommonly so'. From the 1780s this huge landowner hunted the fox in Roxburgh, Peebles, Selkirk and parts of Northumberland, Midlothian and Berwickshire. It was from his empire that the Lauderdale and Jed Forest hunts sprang and, most important of all, the Duke of Buccleuch's. For, in 1826, Baillie handed over his hounds to Mr Robert Baird, who already hunted a pack in association with the 4th Duke; and the following season, on the Duke's death, Baird gave his hounds to the 5th Duke.

As hunting folk well know, keeping a successful country is not only a matter of power and money, but one of commanding affection and respect. This was a quality the 5th Duke had in common with George Baillie. He owned 450,000 acres and could ride the stretch from Dalkeith, on the south-east outskirts of Edinburgh, to Dumfries without going off his own property. Loved by his tenants, it was said of him that 'if danger threatened, every sword in the seven counties would leap from its scabbard to protect him or any member of his family'. He was 22 when Baird's hounds came to Dalkeith House, and survived to lead them for 57 seasons, being for some time the oldest MFH in Britain, and having made the hunt a famous institution. As Lord Dalkeith, his son took an increasingly active part, and, in 1884, aged 53, he succeeded to the dukedom and the Mastership. In 1914 this passed to the 7th Duke; and, in the early 1930s to the present Duke of Buccleuch and Queensberry, who was joined, in right tradition, in 1951, by his son, the Earl of Dalkeith.

Since the war, others have shared the command: in 1947 the Duke's cousin, Lt-Col. John Scott, a talented hound-breeder, came in as deputy Master, until 1954; Lord Ellesmere (now Duke of Sutherland) was joint-Master from 1954 to 1964; Maj.-Gen. Younger (a prominent follower last Friday) put in five seasons, ending in 1966, and Mr J.W. Bradley two from 1967 to 1969. But, as I have shown, the Montague-Douglas-Scotts' interest in the hunt has remained unbroken. And so, in 1827, the 5th Duke founded a dynasty which has so far endured for 164 years.

Riding up to the Borthwickbrae policy last Friday we passed the spot where, in 1971, Lord Dalkeith tragically ended his active hunting days when he was paralysed from a fall. There is to be a new regime this season: while Sir Hugh Arbuthnot confines himself to hunting and breeding the hounds, the joint-Mastership will be assumed by the Duchess of Roxburgh, Mr Mark Johnson, the present field Master, and Mr Jack Watherston, a former hunt secretary. And, fortunately for this ancestral hunt, Lord Dalkeith, in spite of his handicap, has consented to come in again and make up a quartet.

Hounds found their second fox in the spruce plantation by the waterworks north of Roberton and led us east of Highchesters hill up to Borthaugh, where they lost him. Riding up close by Tom Smith, kennel-huntsman and first whipper-in, when he was turning them back towards Highchesters for Sir Hugh, I was reminded that the Duke of Buccleuch's have been blessed with two other assets invaluable to any hunt: long terms of office in the posts of huntsman and secretary. Excepting two very short interregnums, the hunt has been served by only four huntsmen: Will Williamson (1827–63); Will Shore (1863–1902), George Summers (1902–46) and Tom Smith who came as huntsman in 1948 and has continued as kennel-huntsman since Sir Hugh Arbuthnot's arrival in 1964.

The 6th Duke said of Williamson that 'had he not been his huntsman, he would certainly have been

Prime Minister; of Shore an Edwardian recorder wrote that a better huntsman and a more conscientious servant could not have been found, and Summers, it was said, was one of the greatest huntsmen of modern times. As for Tom Smith, it need only be remarked that he does due credit in representing the seventh generation of huntsmen in his family, the first four of these – beginning in the eighteenth century, being with the Brocklesby; then his grandfather served with the Bramham Moor and his father with the Dumfriesshire. The secretaries during the last century have been Mr Gideon Pott, D.W.B. Tait, Major Arthur Paton (1918–39), Major T.H.C. Cox (1939–57) and Mr J.G. Watherston (1956–71). Mr Robert Bruce of Pinnacle took over at the beginning of this season.

The vixen hunted from Mabonlaw ran round Pisgah Hill, Woolaw and Smasha Hill and two miles south-east, giving us a fine course of grass and hunt jumps and walls to cross before they caught her. The Duke of Buccleuch's was a pure-bred traditional English pack when Sir Hugh Arbuthnot came up from the Cotswold nine seasons ago. It was his opinion, however, that they had too much bone for this country and so he brought along ten couples of the Beaufort-Portman type. But now, recently using Brocklesby Wrangler '69, he is introducing one pure-bred English line again.

Away they trotted in the evening to draw Hangingshaw Hill, and with the sun slanting golden over acres and acres of the white bent-grass, I turned my horse towards his stables with this abiding impression: how lucky are the men and women who can still follow hounds in these amazingly unspoilt hills.

(16 March 1973)

A new Mastership was formed in 1976, led by the 9th Duke of Buccleuch and Queensberry and also including Mr R. Bruce, Mr W. Murray and Capt. S.T. Clarke, who hunted hounds. Capt. Clarke moved on, in the same capacity, to the South and West Wilts in 1979. Mr Jamie Innes, of New Belses, followed Mr Bruce as secretary. They were followed jointly, in 1980, by Messrs N.P. Cameron and W.L. Stewart. In 1979 Mrs Stobart joined the Mastership, and, in 1980, Mr Innes.

In 1977 Tom Smith retired after 30 years' service, receiving a substantial present from the hunt members and a free house for life from the Duke. Tom's place was filled by Lionel Salter, formerly first whipper-in to the Grove and Rufford. The first whipper-in is George Trotter, who joined the hunt from the North Northumberland.

The Dumfriesshire

SCOTLAND'S BLACK-AND-TANS

There is about the Dumfriesshire a rare and delightful atmosphere of fraternity, a bond between the county sportsmen and their families of which this isolated hunt is at once the chief symbol and primary outlet. The challenge of horsemanship is strong in their veins: their ancestors were incessantly involved in Border feuds, and were largely cattle-thieves – a quite respectable pursuit 400 years ago; and that stretch of the Carlisle-Glasgow road that runs over the Solway Firth and through the Annan Valley had echoed to the sound of frantic hooves centuries before Robert Bruce was born. When the law began to catch up with rustling, the obvious diversion to fill the gap was the chase, and men appeared with reputations like the turbulent seventeenth-century John Irving, known as Jock o' Milk, who, when Lord Torthorwald ran him through with a lance over a cattle dispute, prompted this nice epitaph from the lips of James VI: '. . . yet he had virtues that Jock o'Milk, for he was a tight huntsman and could holloa to hounds till the woods rang again.'

The Annan coverts never ceased ringing to the horn and *holloa* of wild huntsmen like Jock o'Milk. But in the early nineteenth century, it was neighbouring foxhunting squires, lured by the challenge of the fast Dumfriesshire hill foxes and readily responding to the invitations of the local bloods, that took the big packs to this county: men like Wullie Hay of Dunse Castle in Berwickshire, who had been Master of the Warwickshire, Mr Murray of Broughton in Peebleshire and Major St Colomb of the Cumberland and Inglewood Forest Hunt. Then came another Cumberlander, Col. Salkeld, bringing with him as huntsman one of the towering figures in the history of Scottish hunting and the founder of the Dumfriesshire – Joe Graham, to whom, in 1848, we are told, Salkeld 'gave 16 couples of hounds to use for any purpose he pleased'. Graham settled his pack at Lockerbie's Blue Bell Inn. But although the sportsmen of Dumfriesshire agreed to pay up to £240 a season, Graham could not really carry on alone, so it was a lucky stroke that year when Lord Drumlanrig (afterwards 7th Marquess of Queensberry) took over the Mastership, with Graham as huntsman, and the kennels removed to Leafield.

The Dumfriesshire Hunt now firmly established, Graham hunted hounds through the Mastership of Mr Carruthers of Dormont (1856–68), and was first whipper-in and kennel-huntsman to 'Old Q' – the 8th Marquess of Queensberry (1868–9), Mr John Johnstone of Halleaths (1869–80), who came from hunting jackal in Calcutta, and Mr Luis Salkeld (1881–4), who employed the great Jack Peak as huntsman. But 'Old Joe' Graham (who meanwhile had become a racehorse trainer, had a Grand National winner named after him and was perhaps the greatest living legendary figure in the county) took up the horn again under the rule of a committee (1884–9), and Mr Andrew Johnstone of Halleaths (1890–2), until he died after 45 seasons, in 1893, when a monument was erected on Almagill, an obelisk still visible for many miles round, with the inscription: 'And now he has gone far, far away – we shall never hear his voice in the morning'.

How much 'Old Joe' would love to have hunted under Sir Robert Buchanan-Jardine of Castle Milk, a cousin of Andrew Johnstone's, who was joint-Master, with Mr E.J. Brook of Hoddam. Joe Graham told his great admirer 'The Druid' that 'the Jardines are the soul of hunting, and Castle Milk is *our* meet; most like an English meet of any; regular Badminton-lawn business and everything for all.' And how much it would have warmed his heart to see Sir Robert's son, that great hound man, Sir John Buchanan-Jardine, take over in 1921 for a reign of half a century, and his grandson, the present joint-Master, who has carried the horn in the same tradition since 1950.

The development of the Dumfriesshire hound makes one of the most interesting sagas in the history of foxhunting. As the Edwardian observer 'Tantivy' put it, 'Dumfriesshire hunting men have been forced to the conclusion that, due to their stoutness and wild nature, these foxes take a tremendous amount of catching. A *fast* hound is needed'. Col. Salkeld's pack are recorded as being 'a comparatively slow type – heavy, hard, persevering, and accustomed to stick to their line, be it ever so cold'. In the 1880s a bloodhound cross was introduced and, under Andrew Johnstone, greater speed and tongue came out of the breeding. But Col. Charles Brook who had succeeded to the Mastership in 1908, seeing little future for hunting after the First World War, dispensed with most of the old pack, and this gave Sir John Buchanan-Jardine, in 1921, the opportunity to build up from the bottom.

127 The Dumfriesshire Placid '68 by Riddle '60 out of Plentiful '65. 'What emerged was a pure black-and-tan with a tremendous shoulder and depth through the heart, great long-distance speed, a bloodhound's nose and a golden voice, once heard never forgotten: a perfect match for this steep, varied country and its outsize foxes'.

He wanted a pack of pure black-and-tans, possessing a better cry and nose and greater speed than the average English foxhound. He achieved this, firstly by putting selected bitches to a field trial champion bloodhound called Ledburn Boswell. Sir John described a grandson of these experiments, Harlequin, a quarter bloodhound as the best hound in the field that he ever saw. He also acquired a hound of Gascon breeding called Triomphe, and the foundation of his pack was the result of crossing Triomphe with Harlequin's sisters. He then brought in other black-and-tan influences, such as the Brecon Whipcord, which was by the famous Tiverton Whipcord; and Croome Clansman. In 17 or 18 years of selective breeding the white was eliminated. What emerged was a pure black-and-tan with a tremendous shoulder and depth through the heart, great long-distance speed, a bloodhound's nose and a golden voice, once heard never forgotten: a perfect match for this steep, varied country and its outsize foxes.

To the south lie farmland and big woodlands, to the north grass hills and moor. From February onwards they hunt the hill; and Tundergarth, the home of Mr and the Hon. Mrs John Tulloch, three miles east of Lockerbie, one of the best meets in the uplands, was chosen for 13 March. At 11.40 Sir Rupert Buchanan-Jardine drew Mosshead covert. Finding immediately, we were led past Courstein and left-handed into Gimmendie Glen. In spite of poor scenting conditions the black-and-tans with a melody as happy and loud as Christmas cymbals, sped right-handed past Gibson Scale Hill and doubled back up the glen, killing him after 40 minutes – with Capt. John Bell-Irving (hunt chairman and a direct descendant of the legendary Jock o'Milk), Capt. Ronald Cunningham-Jardine (hunt secretary) and Mr John Tulloch, on one of his eventers, close behind Mr David Culham, the new field Master, at the finish. The brush went to Johnnie Tulloch, our host's son.

They picked up the line of their second fox on the side of Burnswark, the site of an old Roman camp,

128 Major Sir Rupert Buchanan-Jardine, Bt. He followed his father as Master and huntsman in 1950. His joint-Master is Mrs Edward Birkbeck, of Kinmount, granddaughter of Col. Charles Brook (Master, 1908–18).

and raced over the hill, through the young Burnswark covert, and past Haregills, Douglas Hall Farm and Newfield, where he got into a drain. But they bolted him and, with a devastating rush, killed in the open, a second Pony Club member – Miranda Bell-Macdonald this time – receiving the brush, and holding it high above her head as she galloped back to her mother with smeared cheeks and an ecstatic cry of 'Tom's blooded me!' And the black-and-tans trotted away to Burnswark old covert, to push up their third fox, run him under the floorboards of Dansrig Farm, bolt him and fly like the wind back to his covert; then right-handed past Mosshead and Tundergarth Mains to Castle Hill covert, where he saved his brush in a cavernous earth.

But *fly* is the word. They take off, these black-and-tans, from six feet before a four-foot wall or wire fence, to breast it at the gallop; you see them streak through tight spruce at the pace of cheetahs; and on a bad scenting day, like 13 March, time and again you are entertained to their quick wide casts – the huntsman leaving it to them – the bell-like music a single instrument where one of them rediscovers the patchy line then suddenly the full orchestra, and away with their unique and lengthy stride. Are they the fastest pack of foxhounds in the world? They would be hard put to it to find challengers to that distinction.

(13 March 1971)

Mr David Culham later relinquished his Mastership, and in 1976, Mrs Edward Birkbeck, of Kinmount, a life-long follower of the hunt and grand-daughter of Col. Charles Brook, joined Sir Rupert in the command.

Peter Reed succeeded Tom Cockerell as kennel-huntsman in 1977.

The Fife

FOXHOUNDS BY THE FIRTH OF FORTH

Although foxhunters of Fife have always regarded the whole county as their domain, they now meet only in a limited area between the Firths of Forth and Tay. Those hills consist of about 40 per cent plough, ten per cent woodland, 25 per cent grass fields, and, on the higher ground – best of all – 25 per cent sheep pasture. Comprising some of the finest hunting country in Britain, this old white grassland drains well, holds scent and is very resilient. It also affords the most beautiful vistas, from pale rolling hills punctuated by stands of Scots pine and Japanese larch, alternating with stretches of golden bracken and massive clumps of gorse, to the silvery gleam of the Firths or the sea. These high tracts are comparatively free, and given their liberal ration of hunt jumps, it is never difficult to be well up when hounds are running. As for roads, you may not even be unlucky enough to see one, let alone have to cross it.

Such was the landscape we rode over from Cdr. and Mrs Humphrey Hutchison-Bradburne's meet at Cunnoquhie House on 9 February. And when a fox was *holloaed* away from the south end of West Hill Wood and we cantered on towards Gowdie and Letham, I soon guessed why – notwithstanding the fact that the face of this terrain has changed considerably over the centuries – it has always been a famous land for venery. Indeed the hunting tradition of the Kingdom of Fife, like that of Cranborne Chase and the New Forest, has been on record since Norman times, when the Macduffs set off from old Falkland Castle with bow and spear into the forests on those fertile lowlands. Up to the seventeenth century hunting with hounds in the Fife peninsular was the chief diversion of the Scottish monarchs sojourning at Falkland Palace; then of the Stuarts.

From the moment foxhunting became the rage in England, the founding of a pack in 'a land so esteemed for the chase' could not be long delayed; and, some 200 years ago, Alexander Scrymgeour Wedderburn, Hereditary Standard Bearer of Scotland and ancestor of the Earls of Dundee, started a hunt at his home, Birkhill. On Wedderburn's resignation in 1789, General Wemyss kept these hounds at Wemyss Castle; in 1800 they passed to Wedderburn's nephew, Mr Gillespie, and two seasons later to John Anstruther Thomson, of Charleton. He retired in 1805, and presented the

hounds to the country, James Home Rigg acting for the committee. In 1821 the Fife joined forces with Lord Kintore's to hunt in Angus, too, with co-operating headquarters at Forfar and Cupar, an arrangement which lasted until 1837 when the county pack went independent again, under the Mastership of Admiral Erskine Wemyss and John Whyte Melville.

Whyte Melville, Anstruther Thomson, Gilmour – those are the greatest names in the saga of the Fife. John Whyte Melville spent two seasons (1827–9) in partnership with Home Rigg, ten with Admiral Erskine Wemyss (1827–39) and another nine (1839–48) in sole command. Col. Anstruther Thomson, son of the 1802–5 Master, a cavalryman of singular initiative and dash and one of the most prominent characters in the history of the sport, first came on the Fife scene in 1849. He returned as Master with the Earl of Rosslyn (1858–9), going on alone from 1859 to 1864 and again from 1873 to 1888, and, achieving much celebrity in between with the Atherstone and the Pytchley.

The Gilmour dynasty began later. The first Sir John assumed the joint-Mastership of the Fife in 1896 with Capt. J.A. Middleton, brother of the famous 'Bay', then carrying on by himself from 1897 until 1902, when his son John inherited the Master's cap. Representing the next generation, in 1954 the present Sir John took control with Lady Kilmany (whose husband is a grandson of Col. Anstruther Thomson) and remained at the helm until 1972. Then, in 1973, his elder son, John, became joint-Master with Major Henry Hutchison, a fellow Fife and Forfar Yeoman and son of Mrs Hutchison-Bradburne, our lawn-meet hostess.

With Mr Gilmour and Major Hutchison in the lead and Lady Kilmany and Sir John close behind in the field of 70, we rode left-handed beyond the Letham Woods as our fox set his mask for Cantyhall, then raced through East Hill Wood and over Collairnie to Balmeadow Hill. Here a brace of fresh foxes jumped up from the gorse, and, with the poor scenting conditions, they had no hope of staying with the first. But I had the impression that these tough hill foxes of Fife are in for a stronger challenge from now on. For with Lord Glenarthur, of the Eglinton, as their adviser, fresh drafts of three couples from that kennels, besides two couples from

129 Some of the 70 followers riding towards West Hill Wood, Cunnoquhie, for the second draw on the day described.

the VWH and two from the Puckeridge and Thurlow, and a closely studied breeding policy, the Masters are reshaping this pack in earnest.

Hounds are still kept at the solid and very practical kennels at Harlswynd, near Cupar, built by Col. Anstruther Thomson in 1874. And there is another reason why 1974 marks a Fife centenary. For it was exactly 100 years ago that a separate pack was formed, under Sir Arthur Halkett, to hunt the west side of the country. But since then, the growth of mining interests has left that end unsuitable for foxhounds. 1874 also saw a tragedy: the death, in the VWH hunting-field, of that greatly loved soldier, poet and novelist, Major George Whyte Melville, who, as the son of the earlier Master of that name, had been earmarked to join his old friend Col. Anstruther Thomson the following season.

Listening to Adrian Francis, the Fife's new huntsman, now encourage his hounds over a faint line towards Nisbetfield and Whitefield, after leaving that scent-confusing brace at Balmeadow, reminded me of the hunt's tradition of colourful and talented huntsmen. Tom Crane, for example, who saved his commanding officer's life in the Irish rebellion of 1789, learned the huntsman's art in Shropshire, served in the Peninsular campaign, first as a soldier, then as huntsman of the Iron Duke's hounds, and came on to the Fife in 1821.

Crane was followed, in 1830, by John Walker,

whom Nimrod dubbed 'Merry John' and described as 'almost miraculously gifted'. He combined great generosity with a remorseless determination to catch his foxes. 'You ain't a-going, sir, after all this, to kill him, are you?' pleaded Walker's whipper-in, Tom Batters, at one time when their quarry found an earth after a very gallant run. 'Kill him?' Walker exclaimed. 'If my own grandmother ran to ground, why, I'd kill *and eat* her!' In the 1840s the subscribers donated £1000 for 'Merry John' to run the hunt for them and bitterly regretted his departure for Sir Watkin Williams-Wynn's in 1849.

The Smiths of Brocklesby also feature strongly in the Fife's history. Will, who took over the horn from Walker, was the son of Lord Yarborough's Tom. And, more recently, Will Smith, who succeeded as huntsman to the Fife in 1957 and retired last season, is a direct descendant. For half a century, from 1898, the name of Hanley predominated at the Harlswynd kennels. Beginning his career that season, old Will Hanley was joined by his son, Will, as whipper-in in 1917, being succeeded by him as huntsman in 1936. When young Will enlisted, old Will returned at 65 under the Mastership of Major Sir Robert Spencer-Nairn, who also devoted his life to the hunt during the deserted war years. Young Will came back to the Fife in 1945, but soon went on to Ireland, where he was killed hunting the Island hounds in the 1950s.

At 2.00 p.m. hounds ran into calving cows at Whitefield ruins, so Adrian Francis tried Dunbog, and then West Hill Wood again. Here they traced a line that pointed to East Hill and over Collairnie Hill, where, after making a spirited semi-circle, they accounted for their fox in the bracken. It poured with rain at this kill and when the sky cleared, every hue in the landscape intensified, rendering that brilliant mosaic of greens and golds that only the Lowlands know.

(9 February 1974)

Mr Gilmour has hunted hounds since 1977, David Gaylard being his kennel-huntsman and first whipper-in until 1979, when he went to the Radnor and West. Barry Godfrey from the Garth has replaced him. Mr Low-Mitchell, an amateur, has been acting as second whipper-in.

Mr W.J. Turcan formed a triumvirate with Mr Gilmour and Major Hutchinson in 1979.

The Lanarkshire and Renfrewshire

DESCENDED FROM A GLASGOW HUNT

Almost every corner of huntable Scotland boasts a pack of foxhounds. There are half a dozen close to the English border, one in Midlothian, one in Fifeshire, another in Argyllshire and two more against the Firth of Clyde. Of these 11, five were founded before the turn of the nineteenth century. The Duke of Buccleuch's goes back to the days when George Baillie hunted the territory in the 1870s, and the Fife to Wedderburn of Birkhill, to about the same period. The Berwickshire claim to begin in 1740 when a Mr Lumsdaine kept hounds at Blanerne, while the Linlithgow and Stirlingshire boast descent from Lord Erroll's Edinburgh Hunt, which was in existence still earlier. The Lanarkshire and Renfrewshire, who celebrated their bicentenary at the start of the current season, are next in antiquity after the L and S.

On 8 April 1771 as the result of a meeting held at Bothwell Bridge, Lanarkshire, between Capt. Rob-ertson and three sporting friends, it was decided to amalgamate his hunt with the Glasgow Hounds and form a hunt club expressly to provide sport for the landowners and yeomen of the two counties. The L and R were born that day, and enormous trouble was then taken to do everything in efficient and elegant style. It was determined they should have a united hunt and that a treasurer should be chosen annually. A hunt uniform was devised of 'dark brown frock, of hunter's beaver, made without lapells, and lined with white silk shag, both to have plain silver buttons'. The club would have their earthstopper, Thomas Greer, duly adorned (so that keepers and farmers might recognise him) 'with white plaiding breeches, a leather cap, and a green coat and waistcoat, the coat to have a red cape with "Earthstopper to the Roberton Hunt" embroidered on it'. The first 'hunting meeting' of 'The Roberton Hunt', or 'Glasgow Hounds' took place on 14

November 1771, when 'a fox was found at Blantye Whins and killed above ground'. But the hunt records were scanty until the very alarming Viscount Kelburn (afterwards 5th Earl of Glasgow) came on the scene in 1830 with £60,000 a year to spend.

Kelburn's principal claim to fame appears to be as a tyrant. He had been a naval officer from 1807 to 1818 and as a biographer notes: 'The exigencies of his sea-dog education were doubtless partly responsible for his rough manner.' Kelburn hunted his own hounds and the field were 'so frightened of him that if he turned back along the road, they would jump any fence to avoid him'. On one occasion when Jack Harris, a whipper-in, displeased him, Kelburn literally charged him and Harris had to jump a mill lade to get out of his way. According to 'Stringhalt' the place where this happened (rather like the spot where Nelson fell) was on public view. ('But,' said Stringhalt, 'modern improvements have, I think, done away with it.')

Kelburn, however, contained himself for Nimrod's visit in 1834. The sporting scribe records his arrival at baronial Hawkhead with typical unction: '. . . And by the time the first bottle of 1815 claret was finished after dinner, his lordship and myself being tête-à-tête, I felt myself quite at home.' He liked the hounds as well as the wine. 'I thought them to the eye, equal to, if not superior to any other in Scotland. And why should they not be so? They are the blood of the most celebrated in England, the Lambton and the Beaufort.' After a day with them, however, Nimrod decided his lordship was better as a host than a huntsman: 'He erred in letting them get the mastery of him, from motives of kindness and good feeling. I saw Lord Kelburn as a huntsman to disadvantage. His hounds were wild. . . .' Too kind to his hounds, too vehement with his fellow humans? What would the modern psychologist make of this complex Scottish MFH? Anyhow for 13 years Kelburn brought great grandeur to sporting Lanarkshire and Renfrewshire and was probably the first leader of this hunt to apply the science of selective breeding.

He was followed in 1843 by the joint Mastership of Alex Cunningham of Craigends and James Merry (the famous 'cocker' who 'kept thousands of black-breasted reds and whose matches were for 50 guineas a side and 500 the main'). Their successor was Sir David Carrick-Buchanan who transferred the kennels from Craigends to their present situation at Houston, made the L and R a subscription pack, gave up hunting in Lanarkshire in 1870 (because 'there is too much wire and woodlands') and

completed 44 years of Mastership, eventually handing over a 'beautiful pack built on Belvoir, Cheshire and Milton blood' to 'that fine judge of horse and hound', Major Andrew Coats, in 1893. Then came Col. Robertson Aikman, a direct descendant of the hero John Aikman, the 'gude laird o' Cairne'. He kept his own pack of harriers for 22 seasons, 13 of them in Lanarkshire and nine as a very famous Master of Derbyshire's High Peak, before taking over at Houston.

The Victorian Masters of the L and R were fortunate in their huntsmen. The excellent John Dale, who founded a well-known dynasty of hunt servants, carried the horn for Cunninghame and Merry Harrison, who was Sir David Carrick-Buchanan's first huntsman, was succeeded in 1862 by John Squires who, according to 'Tantivy', 'brought with him a high reputation and . . . the country was at this time very bare of foxes, and Squires was chiefly instrumental in bringing about an improvement by laying down vixens in foxless parts'. Foxes never declined in the L and R country after Squires' work. Killed in the hunting field in 1874, he was followed by Pat Bishop (1874–9) and Tom Morgan (1879–82). Then the great Harry Judd took the horn, first for Sir David Carrick-Buchanan and then for Col. Robertson-Aikman, until 1901 when Master and huntsman retired together. Judd, who started as a jockey, came on to this hunt from the North Shropshire, having whipped in first to the Norfolk, then the Atherstone, Quorn, Cottesmore and Lord Leconfield's.

Will Webster, Harry Champstone, Will Hewitt, Ted Molyneux and Will Jacklin were successively huntsmen to Mr George Barclay who was in command till 1921, when he was succeeded by Major W.N. Goff. In 1935 the L and R were lucky enough to secure as Master Lord Inverclyde, who had been hunting the Eglington for the previous three seasons, and all agreed that Will Dickinson, his huntsman, showed outstanding sport. When Lord Inverclyde went to war with the Scots Guards, Dickinson kept the concern going with just the same verve, ultimately completing 27 seasons. In 1949, Brig. J.W.H. Gow took over from Lord Inverclyde, and in 1954 the present Masters, Mr and Mrs F.A. Donaldson, relinquished the duties of hunt secretary to succeed him. They now keep 30 couple in the kennels at Houston, the bulk of which stem from an old line going back to Belvoir Fanny 1793, whose blood first came to Houston with L and R Prudence 1924. The hunt went to Sinnington for their outcrosses in the 1920s and thirties and more

130 The late Bert Stevens. He was huntsman to the Lanarkshire and Renfrewshire from 1952 until his death in the hunting-field in 1975.

recently they have used Middleton, Eglington and Heythrop.

It was on 18 March at Col. Alastair Davie's meet at Grangehill, Ayrshire, that I had the pleasure of seeing them. The 60 followers included a dozen of the Eglington's blue collars (they finished their season on the Tuesday) and there was £100 worth of cap money for the hunt secretaries, Messrs I.H. Stuart Black and H. Couper Brown, to collect. So

that day, it was a big parade that waited at covertside when Bert Stevens, who began his career with the South Notts in 1928 and is now completing his 20th season with the L and R, drew Grangehill Policy. Mr Bob Young, an amateur whipper-in standing in for Nimrod Kennett, who is still out of action from his crippling fall in the cubhunting season, gave an energetic hand, and so did George Orr, huntsman to the Eglington. It was warm and still and foggy, and as hounds dragged their line over the Bigholm and through Brownsmuir, drew the Rashes below and hunted mute to the fox viewed at Auchengrange, it seemed likely that the feeble scent would remain feeble. But on 18 March that was the first of three foxes hunted with infinite perseverance and subsequently marked to ground by these hard-driving hounds; the second being hunted over Cuff Hill from Kirkleegreen Forest to a field above Hoodyard Farm, and a third across Skiff from Castlewalls to Hallhill.

Nobody could have called that a brilliant day's hunting, yet simply to follow hounds in the L and R Saturday country – the hills of Renfrewshire and Ayrshire in contrast to the tight, grazing enclosures to the north that serve for Tuesdays – is a rare privilege. Frequently in the steep and ever-changing terrain, you come across jagged escarpments – like Castlewalls, from which you can normally see Ben Lomond – sparkling lochans, stark marshes and bracken wastes below the moors. It is a joy to watch L and R hounds work out their line over those dramatic hills, for which you need a stocky, well-coupled horse like Gunner, which Mr Houston Shaw-Stewart lent me. Mercifully there should be little change for this wild country, which the L and R have now hunted for just 200 seasons.

(8 March 1972)

Mr J.G. Stewart and Mr H. Shaw-Stewart joined the Mastership in 1974. Mr and Mrs Donaldson and Mr Shaw-Stewart retired in 1979, the Masters for the 1979–80 season being Messrs J.G. Stewart, William Ross and Quinton McKellar.

Bert Stevens, the widely admired houndsman, who went as huntsman to the L and R from the Middleton in 1952, was killed in the hunting-field in 1975. Robin Jackson carried the horn from 1977 and his place was taken, in 1980, by George Orr.

Ireland

Scale
10 0 10 20 30 40 50
miles

Portrush

Londonderry

Larne

L. Neagh

Omagh

Bangor

L. Erne

Dungannon

Lurgan

Enniskillen

Sligo

Monaghan

Upper
L. Erne

East Down

L. Conn

Carrickmacross

Dundalk

Cavan

L. Arrow

Louth

L. Mask

Roscommon

Bally-
macad

L. Corrib

Athlone

L. Ree

West
Meath

Meath

Galway

Co.
Galway
(Blazers)

Dunboyne

Dublin

Tullamore

Cellbridge

East
Galway

Kildare

Shillelagh & District

L. Derg

Portarlington

Ormond

Leix
(Queen's
Co.)

Athy

Ennis

North
Tipperary

Carlow

Wicklow

Kilrush

Thurles

North
Kilkenny

Carlow

Limerick

Tipperary

Island

Listowel

Scarteen

Tipperary

Kilkenny

Wexford

Wexford

Limerick

Tralee

Waterford

Duhallow

Avondhu

West
Waterford

Killarney

Muskerry

United

Macroom

Cork

Carbery

South
Union

Bantry

The Kildare

'BRAVEST OF MEN . . .'

A day in the Kildare's Tuesday country last week impressed on me in no mean terms the increasing difficulties that Irish Masters have to face. Each year the enclosures get more wired up; sheep and cattle are on the increase; and annually, in 30-acre pockets, the Land Commission hand over large expanses to aspiring farmers from the non-agricultural and non-hunting west. While the majority of these are sympathetic to the hunts, many are not; and the proliferation of smallholdings makes a Master's liaison and public relations tasks far more complex and protracted than in the days when the country was in the hands of substantial land owners. (No one owns more than a thousand acres in Kildare now.) All due credit then to Kildare's American Master, Mr Thomas Fields Long, for getting the numerous non-hunting farmers as well as the foxhunters, behind him.

Not that it was all wire and locked gates on the Tuesday of last week. Scenting conditions were fair; and when, after meeting at Calverstown, a little south of the country's centre, we hunted our first fox slowly northwards from Bull Hill covert and over the river by Powell's bridge, it was gorse-strewn heathland, broken up by broad ditches – typical of so much of Ireland's better hunting areas – that we crossed. This was in sparkling sunlight: we could see the tower of the Curragh garrison jabbing the north horizon, the Wicklow Mountains in the east and south towards Carlow. And after that first fox found his earth at 12.30, I wondered how this huge country – 420,000 acres, so they say, now hunted from a palace of a kennels, containing 74 couples, at Jigginstown, near Naas – was kept open in the days before hound-vans and horse-boxes.

Going back 200 years, when the Kildare's colourful story begins, there were three private packs in the country: those of the Kennedys of Johnstown, of William Ponsonby of Bishopscourt and of 'honest Tom Conolly, Castletown's pride', cabinet minister and ancestor of the Kildare's present field Master, Capt. Patrick Conolly-Carew. Squire Conolly, described as a 'pre-eminent sportsman', hunted his Belvoir-bred pack over the largest stretch of the country's three divisions, called his hunt the 'Kildare' and could be claimed as the founder of the present hunt. After his death, in 1804, Sir Fenton Aylmer got the Castletown and Bishopscourt packs

together, and, operating from one clubhouse and kennels and then the next, a fortnight or so in each, hunted the whole county – for two seasons (1810–12) jointly with Mr Arthur Henry – until 1814, when John Kennedy, then aged 29 (he was to be created a baronet by William IV) took over on a £500-a-year subscription basis, increased the number of coverts from 18 to 49 and enjoyed 26 seasons in command.

Sir John was a great houndsman, but it was under his successor, John La Touche (1841–6), 'an exceedingly silent man', that the hunt boasted the 'Killing Kildares, the best pack in Ireland'. According to Lord Mayo, La Touche 'went to practically any lengths to muster it'. When G.S. Foljambe's hounds were sold at Lord Henry Bentinck's kennels by Tattersalls in 1845, this included 'causing the luncheon bell to be rung early just as some lots in which he was especially interested came up, and so evaded competition in the bidding. . . .' La Touche set a standard which the Kildare were determined should never be lowered. But, being in mourning, he himself never hunted again after the day his brother Robert died suddenly in the stands at the Curragh races in 1846. Mr O'Connor Henchy, the 'Pride of Kildare', then had the hounds for the tragic season of 1846–7, that awful potato famine winter, but from all accounts kept a sleek pack hunting three days a week in spite of it.

Lord Clonmel, who followed Sir John Kennedy's son, William, as Master in 1854, put the celebrated Stephen Goodall (brother of Belvoir's Will) on as huntsman and, with La Touche blood still strong in the kennels, he showed some wonderful days. The sporting writer 'Triviata' (O'Connor Morris) wrote that '. . . in Kildare my memory carries me back to Goodall . . . a tall hatchet-faced man sitting on his horse like a pair of tongs intent upon what his hounds were doing and little else . . . his hunters seemed one and all to sympathise with him though he never touched their heads.' He was also said to be idolised by the country people and when he left to take the Bramham Moor horn, Lord Naas (Lord Clonmel's successor) lamented 'there is not a huntsman left in Ireland now'.

Goodall hunted hounds on that famous 26 November 1859, the day of the Laragh run, when 'they never lifted their heads for 18 miles', going deep into

131 Squire Conolly, Master, 1793–1804.

132 Jack Hartigan, kennel-huntsman and first whipper-in from 1946 to 1976.

the Meath country and '. . . so savage were the hounds when the fox was killed that it was with difficulty that he could be got from them, and a lemon-coloured hound, which Will Goodall had sent as a present to his brother, flew at the whip to get the fox from him, and tore his coat to ribbons. . . .' When a number of graziers from Kildare and Meath held a post-mortem on the Laragh run,

one of the Meath men wondered why the fox never went to ground during so long a point. 'Oh, he thought it was the Meath hounds that were hunting him,' put in a Kildare man quickly, 'and knew therefore that his life was safe and there was no need to go to ground. But he made a bad mistake and paid the penalty!'

Besides Conolly, Kennedy, La Touche, Mayo, Clonmel and Naas, other well-known Kildare names are de Robeck, the first of whom came on the Masters' roll in 1862; Mansfield, under whom the kennels at Jigginstown were built; St Leger Moore; Talbot-Ponsonby, Master from 1911 to 1921 and father of the show-jumping trainer; and jovial, bearded, expansive Michael Beaumont, Master between 1948 and 1959, who introduced the 'Hale and Hearty Cup' for the point-to-points ('I got tired of arranging races for little squirts to ride in', he explained, 'and being somewhat large decided I would fix one to suit myself'). And some hunt servants whose names resound in the annals of the chase: Major Mansfield had Will Freeman as first whipper-in, while Frank Goodall, son of Belvoir Will and brother of Pytchley Frank, who hunted hounds for Baron de Robeck, was followed by Fred Champion. But in the hunt's whole history no kennel-huntsman has given such wise, sustained and impeccable service as Jack Hartigan, all-round sportsman and devoted county man, who came to the Kildare in 1927 (and left them only for two seasons to join Sir Thomas Ainsworth, when Sir Thomas gave up in favour of the Tipperary in 1928) and has kept the Kildare kennels in apple-pie order for 43 seasons. Foxhunting is so deep in Hartigan's blood that one imagines him pre-occupied with it as a boy like the Kildare farmer's child who, upon being asked by the school teacher why palms were strewn on the ground during the entry into Jerusalem, replied: 'To tache the ass to lep!'

That is the spirit of Irish foxhunting. The visitor feels this unanimous welcome and that everyone is out to hunt hard and no mistake – except (not always) the point-to-point qualifiers, one of whom on 28 November lost his horse, which went crashing through a thick hedge and three barriers of barbed wire with terrifying results at the start of our second hunt. This ended in a great run up past Hacklow crossroads. They drew Mr Long's property, Martinstown, blank, tried Ballysax Hills and put another fox to ground there.

Then with a rubbish-dump scavenger – one of five – away from the gorse below old Kilcullen, we got well and truly into the birdcage country. A resolute farmer stood sentry with his pitchfork at one gap, but most of the field were already through.

How this dog pack, with its Heythrop, Kilkenny and Portman breeding, flew! But you needed only a brief glimpse of ex-Maryland hunt cup rider Mr Long, Jack Hartigan, Joe Lenehan, and Jack's son Michael, the three whippers-in, to know that thick or thin – they would be up with their hounds at the end:

While the river goes swollen the ocean to meet
With a whisper as soft as a lullaby sweet
We look to our scarlets, our nags and our cords
For a run with the Meaths or a day with the Wards.
Both are good in their way but they cannot surpass,
A brush with the foxhounds across our short grass.
Bravest of men are the men of Kildare
Though fortune prove fickle they never despair
Would you still wear your laurels I'd have you beware
How you ride to our hounds when you come to Kildare.

(28 November 1972)

Mr B.R. Firestone joined Mr Fields Long in the Mastership in 1973, Mr Fields Long retired three seasons later, when Mr J.P.N. Parker came in as joint-Master and amateur huntsman. Joe Lenehan has been kennel-huntsman since the 1976–7 season.

The Kilkenny

IRELAND'S FIRST COUNTY HUNT

Of all the Irish foxhunting traditions, Kilkenny's is the deepest and most consistent. The Earls of Carrick kept hounds at Mount Juliet – now the home of the McCalmonts and headquarters of the Kilkenny Hunt – in the eighteenth century, and hunted fox, as resolutely as they hunted deer and hare. But the country establishment springs from a different source. In the 1790s Sir Wheeler Cuffe, of Leyrath, another dedicated Kilkenny venerer, told his young friend, John Power, about the county's great scenting conditions and foxholding coverts, and so induced him to bring his hounds over from Tipperary, and eventually to settle, first at Derrynahinch, near Ballyhale, then at Kilfane, his wife's home. Unlike his contemporaries, who used harriers, Power bred from the English stud book: the sport he showed soon attracted all the county sportsmen, and in 1797 this brotherhood inspired the Kilkenny Hunt Club,

133 Alf Wright with hounds at Mount Juliet, Co. Kilkenny, on the day of the author's visit. When Major McCalmont's father built the kennels in 1921 they were the largest and most advanced in the world.

the first of its kind in Ireland.

Power, who was created a baronet in 1836, was an influential Whig and Catholic emancipationist, and Daniel O'Connor once said of him, 'no man has seen Ireland, who has not seen John Power'. Major Connellan, author of *Memoir of the Kilkenny Hunt*, described him as 'a delightful man, highly cultivated, a collector of pictures and statuary, and an excellent actor'. (Power founded the Kilkenny Private Theatre, which had a close liaison with the Hunt Club.) He had a sobering influence on the bloods, too: 'Mr Power found existing in the county a state of rowdyism', said the hunting correspondent, 'Maintop' (Commander Forbes); 'duelling and drinking seem to have been the principal recreations of the upper classes, and . . . John Power civilized Kilkenny.'

He had been Master of the County Hounds for 47 years, when he handed over, in 1844, to his son, who had been carrying the horn since 1840, the year in which the veteran Bob Caunt died. Sir John Power

II proved a worthy successor: 'an excellent Irishman', in the opinion of Connellan, 'very observant of the doings of hounds, and very quick when required, but equally patient on a bad scenting day.' Kilkenny sport was soon a legend; this is the county to which English sportsmen first came in large numbers; hundreds of horses were stabled in Kilkenny City and, at the best meets, upwards of 150 scarlet coats were to be seen. R. Frankland sets the jubilant mood after the 1844–5 seasons:

How oft we have stood by the wild bit of gorse,
Expectation alive in each man and each horse –
They've found, they're hard at him, he cannot delay!
Johnny doubles his horn, they're away, they're away!!

Johnny – Sir John Power II – and his father constructed a great many elaborate earths in their fox-preservation campaigns, but now, with hunting slowed up by enclosure, wire, intensive farming, roads and railways, those nineteenth-century drains and caverns are a nuisance, and whenever Major Victor McCalmont, the present Master and huntsman, comes across them, he does not hesitate to fill them in, as I witnessed when he kindly mounted me on The Captain – one of his many brilliant hunters – for the Lukeswell meet, a village on the Dublin-

134 Major Victor McCalmont at Lukesville, Co. Kilkenny. Master and huntsman since 1949, he also fulfilled the same roles with the Wexford from 1965 to 1975.

Waterford road, one Saturday last month. The morning began uneventfully: after drawing half an acre of gorse called Aylwards to no avail, he tried the disused lane from Knockmoylan village down to old Killeen covert, and that was blank, too. Then he crossed the railway to cheer hounds into Springfield (named after Miss Springfield, with whose legacy the covert was bought). An unenterprising fox led them to an earth two fields away; and here Alf Wright, the kennel-huntsman (who went to the Kilkenny from the South Dorset in 1957) and his second whipper-in, Paddy McDonald, spotting two of the old earths, quickly dismounted to fill them up.

These workmanlike, Heythrop-bred hounds – they have been neck-and-neck with the Tipperary as the principal prize-winners at Clonmel for a long time now – were soon on to the drag of another fox, gradually working up to his lair in Mr Frisby's bog.

While they approached the railway line, scent improved, and there was one terrible moment when the Dublin express came straight at them, as they followed their quarry unswervingly down the middle of the track; and, although he veered off at the last moment, it still looked as though there would be a head-on collision, hounds racing on with inches to spare. ('I dread to imagine' said a very anxious Major McCalmont – who has done more for Irish hunting and racing, so I was told, than any man alive – 'how many years it would have taken to breed another pack like that!')

This fox now tried to shake them off by circling Moonroe bog a couple of times. But seeing hounds retain the scent with amazing tenacity right across a field laid with pig manure, I felt quite confident he must find an earth or die: and as he set his mask north for Kilcasy and we twisted past the osier-beds and gorse-clumps, clambered over the rambling walls and jumped the banks, step-up and step-down, that divide that ancient, vivid pasture, I realised how very different conditions must have been when the Powers found it so necessary to put down artificial earths.

A relatively quick change of Masterships followed the Powers: George Bryan (1850–52), a committee (1852–6), Viscount St Lawrence (1856–61), Henry Meredyth (1861–70), Henry Briscoe (1870–76), Col. Frank Chaplin (1876–80), Capt. Hartopp (1880–82), the Earl of Desart (1882–4), Capt. Butson (1884–6), Major R.C. Knox (1886–7), and the author of *Memoir of the Kilkenny Hunt*, Major J.H. Connellan (1887–90). The 1870s and eighties were the evil times for Irish hunting owing to the opposition of the Land League, and to the Kilkenny, in particular for financial reasons.

But now began that era of long and illustrious Masterships which still prevails. Sir Hercules Langrishe, who started his 19-season reign in 1890, was as famous a yachtsman as he was a huntsman, and always studied the wind, nautical fashion, in his casts. He was a considerable judge of hounds, and brilliant on the horn, too. 'Maintop' held that he 'could ring a tune out of a gaspipe'. In 1908 the great American houndsman, Ikey Bell, went to the Kilkenny, and remained as Master and huntsman until 1921. Already known, from his five years with the Galway 'Blazers', as a radical in hound-breeding circles, he had begun to experiment with Welsh blood, Brecon and Curre, and it was probably in the Kilkenny country that the fast, small-coupled hound, of strong nose and cry, approximately the hound we know today, was first seen. It was Bell's

opinion that the Kilkenny was the finest scenting country in the world and, with his reputation, coupled with the walls and banks that were lacking in the Powers' time, I imagine he produced as much excitement as the county had seen.

Since 1921 the tradition has been carried on by the McCalmonts, whose name, with Mount Juliet is synonymous with Kilkenny. The present Master's father, Major Dermot McCalmont, was famous as a breeder of racehorses, such as The Tetrarch, his son, Tetratema, Mr Jinks and many others. But, with the help of Charles Sturman, who had done such wonders as huntsman of the Heythrop, he bred a superb hound, too; and when he inherited Mount Juliet, again with Sturman's advice he built the most efficient and most palatial kennels in the world. It is doubtful if there is one to beat them today. Major Victor McCalmont, who began to help his father as an amateur whipper-in, when he left the Royal Dragoons in 1947, and became joint-Master in 1949 and sole Master in 1968, took on 'a magnificent going concern', as he puts it. Keeping a close liaison with Capt. Wallace, he has perpetuated the Kilkenny blood line – which, through Sturman, was composed of much old Heythrop and Brocklesby blood – by crossing it with the new Heythrop line, and the results show top, both at Clonmel and in the field.

It was 2.00 p.m., and in the difficult conditions of the much-fertilised grassland, hounds had been hunting that railway fox for 75 minutes, with 50 of us still hard behind them, squeezing through the hedge-topped banks and scrambling across the dishevelled walls of this wire-free tract, when a fresh fox got up in a bracken patch and led hounds back towards Moonroe, where their line was confused by several more fresh foxes; and Major McCalmont, not wishing to cross the land of those (albeit willing) farmers, a third time, took out his horn and sounded 'home'. I was received with a blasé laugh on mentioning that it was one of the nicest days I had enjoyed in Ireland. The Kilkennys are indeed fortunate, not to say spoilt. Major McCalmont wrote to me at Christmas: 'We had the best day for 20 years the Monday after you left, a bye day: two hours, very slow, but caught him; and then another, giving us 55 minutes and a five-mile point, and they caught him, too. There were only 15 people out. Such is foxhunting. . . .'

(6 December 1975)

By 1979 Major McCalmont, who still carries the horn, completed 30 years as Master.

The Louth

MR FILGATE'S THOUSANDTH FOX

The killing of Mr William Filgate's 1000th fox on Saturday, 4 March, made this a red-letter day for the Louth; and the event was marked by 'three cheers for our Master and huntsman', an accolade warmly joined by the 30 followers, for all of whom the names Louth and Filgate are synonymous. For not only have this popular family held the Mastership without a break for the past 112 years, but it has been closely involved in the fortunes of the Louth since the seeds of the hunt were sown two centuries and more ago.

County Louth's first Filgate, a Cromwellian officer who settled at Lisrenny on a grant from the Protector, found the Irish to be a people deeply tinged with the love of hounds, horses and hunting. It was said that 'all Rome viewed them with wonder' when a number of Irish wolfhounds were sent there in AD 391; the English were breeding all they could from Irish horses as early as the eleventh century; the Irish kings regarded huntsmen and their staffs as servants of paramount importance, and King Brian Boru who defeated the Danes and was killed at the battle of Clontarf (a place that would be in the Louth country) in 1014, is known to have kept and hunted hounds more or less on the lines prevailing today.

In Louth, the harehunting tradition was as old as anywhere else in Ireland, but there are few records of the sport until the eighteenth century, when several families, including the Filgates of Lisrenny, gave accounts of their harriers and of the sport they enjoyed. These became leading lights of Louth's two hunt clubs: The Northern Rangers which ranks with Cheshire's Tarporley and Northern Ireland's Downe as one of the three oldest in the British Isles, and still thrives as a dining club; and the Ardee, which came into being in 1799 with Col. Filgate at the head of nine founder-members. The Louth Hunt as such was born on 4 February, 1817, after a meeting at Murphy's Inn, Ardee, the harrier packs of Col. Filgate and D.B. Shields, together with a number of other privately owned hounds, becoming 'the property of the country' and being combined in a fresh hunting establishment, with Shields as Master and Billy Kelly as huntsman. The Louth domain soon stretched into five counties, Dublin, Meath, Cavan and Monaghan, as well as the extent of Louth. They hunted their foxes and hares from Belfast down to the capital. Nelson's Pillar, in Dublin, became a famous foxhunter's landmark.

In 1822, Matthew Fortescue, one of the principal subscribers, founded a new pack at his own expense, took over the establishment and was Master for a total of 13 years. But, in 1827, another Filgate founder-member of the Ardee – William Filgate – stepped in. He hunted hounds for only two seasons, but was a stalwart of the hunt and ardent follower for more than half a century. During his brief Mastership the most impressive Louth hunt of the century took place – on a non-hunting day. When one of his farm-workers viewed a fox in a turnip field by Lisrenny, Filgate turned out the pack and quickly notified some of his foxhunting neighbours. For four hours hounds never left the line, eventually marking to ground near Drogheda, making a point of 17 miles, and nearly 30 as hounds ran.

Besides Fortescue, who carried the horn again till 1837, William Filgate, who also hunted a private pack of harriers from 1826 to 1840, saw six Louth Masters out of office before his son, William de Salis Filgate, took over in 1860. From the pen of an Edwardian reporter we have a fair idea of the old sportsman's dedication: 'The Master's father died in 1875 at the age of 94. In 1868 his eager eyes were shrouded in darkness, and yet he did not cease to hunt. The news of his blindness caused widespread sorrow in all the counties where the Grand Old Man had hunted. To the last he came out in pink, attended by a servant, to hear the sweetest music in the world – hounds in full cry – and to receive the greetings of his friends.'

William de Salis Filgate hunted hounds from Lisrenny for 32 seasons before handing over to a huntsman, C. Deao. Supremely proud of his punctilious and unfailing attendance, he wrote in his diary in 1909: 'Providence has been good to me, and I have done my 49 seasons as Master of the Louth hounds without missing a day they have been out, either cubbing or regular hunting, and I have never altered a meet to suit my own convenience.' He was now 74 and during the next few years shared the duties with his son-in-law, Capt. R.A.B. Henry, who changed his name to Filgate on de Salis Filgate's death. Capt. Filgate commanded until 1967. But meanwhile, in 1939, his son, Mr William Filgate, the present Master (joint with Mr D.J. Crerar since 1967) began his long and distinguished career as amateur hunts-

135 Mr William Filgate, Master since 1948. The Filgates have been closely involved in the fortunes of Louth since its foundation.

man. Mr Filgate's hounds' devotion for him is a byword in Louth. They will answer to no-one else. During the 1940s when he was transferred to a motor car after breaking his leg, they refused to leave his side, and it was only when his horse was led in front of them, that they were persuaded away. It was at the Angler's Rest, near Mooretown, that we met him and $16\frac{1}{2}$ couples on 4 March.

The Louth landscape gives the impression of cone-like hillocks, set closely side by side, with an inviting sense of openness and unkemptness overall. The enclosures are irregular and the obstacles unpredictable, there a watery trench, now a bank, and next a double, a low bank, well planted over, with a ditch one side, or both. And when Mr Filgate, very agile for all his 67 years and innumerable falls, led us away in the sunshine that followed the snow on 4 March, I thought how envious many English Masters would be of the profusion of rambling gorse-coverts, such as Mandistown that runs down to the Dee, where farmers complained of lamb-killing foxes and which served as the first draw. A fox (like Mr Filgate's 999th) was promptly killed inside the cover and another hunted to the river. But this was a vixen and while they left her to swim the Dee, we rode up to Shanlis crossroads to find a third in a heap of sticks bulldozed into the side of a stubble-field next to a garden spinney. It was his death that was marked by three cheers for the Master. And Chimer, one of Mr Filgate's favourite stallion hounds, as though appreciating the golden moment, carried the mask jubilantly all the way to the next draw.

More alert, our fourth quarry got clean away after circling from Footstown to Braystown and back to Murtaghs. But the straight-necked fifth provided 20 minutes of Irish hunting at its best. Mr Filgate, a staunch conservative in the world of hound-breeding, co-operates closely and actively with Lord Daresbury (the Limerick's Master since 1947); so it was the hard-driving strains and resounding melody of Belvoir and Brocklesby and Braes of Derwent that showed when they sped from the long-planting at Mooretown and turned swiftly to Corballis, past the sand-holes, with Creedagh Cross on the right, through Meades, and up the big grassy rise at Greenhills, presenting us all the way with barrier after barrier of thorn-tangled ditches and banks to jump, and not an inch of plough in sight.

They thought they had marked their fox to ground at Mentrim. But he found the earth too small, and, in racing on, somehow broke the thread of his scent. This exhilarating three-mile point in cold sparkling sunlight was the climax of the day. For the sixth fox, found in the quarries at Kilpatrick, soon ran to ground in nearby Cusacks. And at 4.30 Mr Filgate took them home to Lisrenny.

There can be few seats of foxhunting that have changed so little as Lisrenny. House and stables and stone-flagged kennels stand much as they stood when Col. Filgate hunted his harriers at the end of the eighteenth century. For most of the last 200 years, three days and more a week during winter months, hounds have trotted (and later been driven) down the drive from tall Lisrenny and, at the end of the day, returned tired and well-contented to the big stone kennels. There was always a sporting Filgate at their head, which makes it doubly sad that William Filgate retires at the end of this season with no Filgate to follow him in command of the Louth. But now he has led his hounds to a thousand kills and he has loved every moment of his 33 years as their Master and huntsman.

(4 March 1972)

Mr R.W. McKeever joined the Mastership in 1973. Mr R. Filgate has turned hounds to Michael McKeever since 1974.

The Scarteen Black-and-Tans

FROM GASCONY TO LIMERICK

'My boy, they were always there', young John Ryan was told in the 1890s on enquiring of his uncle when the Black-and-Tans came into his family. Made in an offhand way, that was a fair answer. For it is believed that the Ryans kept hounds of the native strains as far as the family history can be traced, and no one knows when they first owned Kerry beagles.

But what are these hounds? How did they come to Scarteen? They are of Gascon-Ariègeois stock, that much is certain. Still to be seen in south-west France, small and light-boned, with rather long ears, some black-and-tan, others black-and-white and blue mottled, the Ariègeois are small bloodhound types, prized by the old *veneurs* for their great hunting qualities and more especially for their deep resounding cry, which no less an authority than Sir John

Buchanan-Jardine, who put voice above all other virtues, described as 'absolutely the finest music of any hounds in the world'. Their advent in Ireland is popularly attributed to the 'Wild Geese', those persecuted Catholics who were rallied by King Louis to fight the English on Continental soil. Some of those veterans, soldiers, and sportsmen too, are said to have heard, and been so delighted by, the Ariègeois voice, that they took some home and called them Kerry beagles.

But why Kerry? Mr Thady Ryan, the present owner, joint-Master and huntsman of the Black-and-Tans, proposes a different theory. He believes the Gascon-Ariègeois were also bred in neighbouring Aragon, Catalonia and Navarre, for hounds of that colour and type were remarked upon by Irish

136 Thaddeus ('Tha') Ryan, Master, 1781–1820. He moved the Black-and-Tans from Ballyvistea to Scarteen in 1798.

travellers in Spain and by Irishmen who fought up to the Pyrenees with Franco's army. And Mr Ryan recently saw hound statues in the Canary Islands at Las Palmas, showing identical conformation to his own. He believes they came to Ireland, long before the days of the 'Wild Geese', via the great Spanish-Irish trading island of Valentia, off Kerry.

When crossed with the native Talbot type, the qualities of the dominant Ariègeois blood shone through, albeit in a somewhat taller hound. As for

Kerry 'beagle', in those days the term simply referred to any light-boned hunting dog. The breed were kept, trencher-fed, as they are today, by cliques of farmers over most of south-west Ireland. The Chutes and the O'Connells, the Butlers of Waterville fame, and the Ryans of Co. Limerick, whose eldest sons have alternated through history between a John and a Thaddeus, kept packs of them. But only the Ryans's packs have survived.

John Ryan had them till 1781, then 'Tha', who moved house from Ballyvistea to Scarteen in 1798, so giving the hunt its principal name. Following a Ryan financial collapse, the failure of Sadleir's bank of Tipperary, John Franks, of Ballyscadane, took the family pack on trust for seven years. Then Clement, whose elder brother, Thaddeus, was constantly abroad soldiering, kennelled them at nearby Emly. He got the pick of the Chute and the O'Connell packs, when they broke up, and carried on until 1904, when his nephew, John, whose burning question opens my account, took over.

This John Ryan owned the Black-and-Tans for over 50 years. He hunted them up to the First World War, during which, in rest periods from the front line, he carried the horn for the 'Flanders' hunt. Buried alive for three hours when the Germans mined his regiment's trenches in 1915, Ryan was officially reported killed, but he survived a prisoner-of-war camp to take the Scarteen horn again until 1929 – the year in which they ceased to hunt the carted stag – after which his joint-Masters acted as huntsmen up to the Second World War. These were: Dr McLoughlin and Sir Cecil Walker between 1929 and 1931, Joseph Pickersgill in 1931–32, Capt. Barker for the next two seasons, and then D.E.C. Price from 1934 up to 1938, when John Ryan hunted hounds for one more season before the war. Capt. C.C. Thompson joined him for the duration.

In 1946 Thady Ryan, then aged 23, took the horn; he divided the Mastership with his father until the latter's death in 1955, and was then on his own up to 1971. Since then, while still owning the hounds, he has shared the command with Mrs Dermot McCalmont, widow of the Kilkenny's celebrated Master. She and Thady Ryan are now supported by his sister, Mrs Pearson, a veteran Scarteen hand – who used to whip in to her father, and who went on there from her Suffolk joint-Mastership – and by Mr Percy Harris, as joint-secretaries. Also by Sir Brian Warren, the field Master. Tommy O'Dwyer, who turns hounds to Mr Ryan, has served as kennel-huntsman since 1954, when he succeeded his father, Jack, who held that post for 30 years.

137 The Scarteen hounds in their kennels at the time of the author's visit in December 1973.

Resulting from such solid continuity at the helm and in the kennels, the character of the Black-and-Tan has changed very little. His white markings were bred out long ago; he is jet across the back and flank with head and legs of rich deep tan. He remains a pure Kerry Beagle, possessing the very independent and engaging character of that breed, but with a temperament that is easily upset by insensitive handling.

His conformation, too, is different from FKSB hounds: his shoulder is rather vertical, yet permitting a great stride; he drops away a little on the quarter, but is sufficiently strong at that point to carry it; he compensates for a long back by showing great muscle over the spine and loin; he carries his long-toed feet full on the ground under lengthy pasterns and well let-down hocks; his 'neckcloth' bears evidence of his rich voice, while his French ears reach across amber eyes to the tip of his nose. The dog-hound stands 22–23 inches at the shoulder, the bitch nearly two inches shorter.

How have the Ryans kept the strain pure, and at the same time avoided inbreeding? Mr Ryan once tried a Dumfriesshire cross, but perhaps because the ancestry was so separated the experiment failed. So he goes back for his outcrosses, as his ancestors went, to those Kerry trencher-fed packs that are congregated after Sunday Mass to hunt hare and drag, whose owners revel in the famous song and drive.

138 Mr Thady Ryan. He has been Master or joint-Master, and huntsman since 1946.

South-west Ireland was in flood at the time of my visit earlier this month, and as hunting was cancelled I never heard their famous wild music nor witnessed their unique manner of casting; but other visitors to Scarteen tell me that Joseph Pickersgill's description is as good as any: 'When the leaders are at fault the tail hounds fan round them to left and right, driving on at the same time. If they are still at fault, they will make a big cast all the way round, as a pack – not as individuals, as most fell-hounds do – and most of this at the gallop. . . . I don't think I have ever seen another pack of foxhounds do a really big "all-round-your-hat cast" quite on their own.'

As regards the country, certainly there are hazards and hindrances in the Scarteen's 28 miles by 23: the Cork-Dublin and Waterford-Limerick railway lines, for example, and the great tracts planted by the Forestry Department; but otherwise almost every inch is grass, and where there is wire in the hedge-topped doubles, Limerick and Tipperary horses know how to tackle it. The fame of the Scarteen goes further beyond the shores of Ireland, perhaps, than any other pack in the British Isles. Every year the Masters welcome American and Continental visitors as well as English, and it must be quite a fillip for Thady Ryan to see Frenchmen flocking to south-west Ireland to hear and watch his hounds that stem from Old Gascony.

(1 December 1973)

The Westmeath

AT IRELAND'S WILD CENTRE

If Sam Reynell, 'the father of the Westmeaths', rode with the Westmeaths today, he would be astonished at many things – combustion and classlessness and curious clothes. And yet, in spite of the social and political revolution and national independence that gradually followed, notwithstanding the dispersal of the great estates, he would find the landscape much as he knew it in the 1830s. Mullingar, the county's principal and central town, lies about 50 miles west of Dublin and 80 east of Galway, at the very middle of Ireland. And for a radius of a dozen or 20 miles all around, the busy hub is bordered by a countryside of vivid pasture, gently rolling and gloriously unkempt, providing delectable views on every hand. Most of this grassland is tightly enclosed, here by timber or banks faced with limestone, there by stone walls or palisades of tight blackthorn, with a ditch fore and aft. These are wired, of course, but not everywhere, and Westmeath foxhunters know all the ways over and through.

Returning to ride over this sparkling green in winter, Mr Reynell might find it interrupted, one field in 50, by a square of stubble or a corner of potatoes; he would meet the same broad lakes, with trees reflected in their silver sheen, the same square stone houses at the end of lonely drives; he would come across grey, ramshackle farmyards and rusty antediluvian carts, nettle-covered and up to their axles in peat; he might also see a lorry tipping turnips on a meadow, or, if he was very unlucky, a bulldozer, yellow and elephantine, reclaiming one of the ancient thickets for grassland. But he would not come upon a dual carriageway, a housing estate or even a factory of any account. And he would surely be glad to see how the sporting seeds he planted in Westmeath's north-east corner in the 1830s spread like clover through all the country.

Although he did as much as anyone to kindle the country's sporting fervour, Mr Reynell was not Westmeath's first foxhunter. At the end of the seventeenth century, Bishop Dopping had a private pack at Killucan; 40 years later Thomas Pakenham, the 1st Lord Longford, kept hounds at Pakenham Hall, and we have it from the meticulous diary of Longford's visiting brother, George Edward, that 'the foxhunters here live much after the same manner as in England and drink as hard . . . it is a good hunting country'. At the turn of the nineteenth

century John Fetherstonhaugh hunted the same area, and Henry Murray kept a pack at Mount Murray, west of Lough Owel. But Reynell, with hounds at Clondelever and Archerstown, seems to have been the first to hunt in an organised way with a scientifically bred pack.

During the potato famine, foxes were pursued as strongly as ever in the more firmly established countries. But in Westmeath, whose population was literally halved by the tragedy, the sport petered out in the 1840s. Despairing, Sam Reynell took the Mastership and the horn of the Meath and kept them for 20 years. But he had shown the squires of Westmeath what fine sport could be had over their grassland. They wanted a county pack and, in 1854, this was given to them on a subscription basis by Sir Richard Levinge of Knockadrin, a hunting base much closer to Mullingar. He got in drafts from the Oakley, Lord Southampton's and Sir Richard Sutton's, found Jack Ransom, formerly of the Duke of Rutland's, to hunt them, and received a £400-a-year guarantee for two days a week. Now the Westmeaths gathered identity: from Levinge the hunt button, with shamrock surrounded by a garter, inscribed with the hunt's name, and from his successor, Mr George Rochford Boyd, the famous black collar.

With the advent of the railways, the hunt's fame spread and soon the whole country was opened up. 'Hunt specials' were run, hounds were herded into goods vans, meets were organised at the stations; and on other lines, engine drivers, when they saw a fox which the hunt could not see, slowed down to give a bloodcurdling *holloa* before puffing on to Connaught, or wherever.

Up to 1860 the Westmeath Hunt Club consisted largely of the Master's friends – who invited him to stop overnight to draw their coverts – and officers from the Mullingar garrison. But between 1860–68 the hunt moved one step closer to its present character when Capt. Gerald Dease, who had enjoyed long experience with harriers, became Master. His nephew, Edmund Dease, the hunt's Victorian chronicler, wrote, 'by his tact and good taste, Capt. Dease got all classes to join the common good cause of foxhunting'. This meant increased popularity for the hunt and more money, too. But right through to Ireland's independence there were

139 A scene at Knockdrin Castle in 1913. Mr Harry Worcester Smith, the American Master, with (*middle*) Sir Richard Levinge, and Lady Levinge and her son (afterwards 11th Baronet).

contretemps more sinister than mere squabbles, such as that with the Meath over the ownership of coverts: 'agrarian outrage and intimidation', political attempts to stop hunting, dissidents sometimes being sent in train-loads from Dublin for the purpose, and violent demonstrations against fox-hunting magistrates and clerics, who were accused of shirking their duties in favour of sport. The appalling poverty was thrown sharply into relief by the exoticism of meets of the county's hounds. Yet, in spite of the agitators, the country people, many of whom could not afford a loaf of bread, let alone a horse, loved the hunt. Their descendants help to run it today.

After Dease's resignation there was constant difficulty in finding conscientious Masters who would stay for more than a season or two: among the longest innings were those of Sir Montagu Chapman (1876–82), Lord Greville (1886–93), who bred from Berkeley sires, the much-respected Earl of Longford and his brother Edward Pakenham (1894–1900), whose joint-Mastership ended when their regiments set sail for South Africa, and Mr Frank Barbour (1908–12) who secured that talented huntsman, Jack Brown, from Lord Willoughby de Broke.

There is in Ireland a strong tradition of American Masterships, and nowhere more than in Westmeath. Mr Harry Worcester Smith, of Worcester, Massachusetts, disembarked at Dublin from the *Lusitania* in 1912 with a 'fabulous retinue', said a newspaperman, 'of seven niggers, a string of 17 horses, one big game-cock, one motor car, three Yankee four-wheel buggies and a two-wheel sulkie used for the limbering up of trotters. . . .' With the help of Jack Brown he hunted first the county pack, then his own Grafton hounds, once he had got them fit after nine months' quarantine. Showing dashing sport his regime was welcome – once the locals became accustomed to the 'Yankee bizarre' (Oh, glory be to God, the poor man, and d'ye think he'll ever get over it?' exclaimed one cottager as she slammed her door on seeing a coloured second horseman for the first time). In 1924 another American of great charm and generosity, Mr Norman Field, took over for three seasons, after Mr E.E. Hope-Johnstone (1913–24) had steered the Westmeath through the war years and the worst period of the troubles. And in 1950 Miss Joy Hansel, from Virginia, who was described as having 'light hands, light weight and light heart', and was originally only visiting for a single day's hunting, joined Lt-Col. Denis Purdon during his Mastership, until 1952.

With the exception of Lt-Col. Purdon and his brother Lt-Col. Purdon-Winter, who shared the Mastership for 29 years between 1927 and 1966, the twentieth-century pattern, too, has been one of short reigns. So it is hoped that Major Patrick Tandy, who has just returned to the helm after three seasons' absence, will settle for a long command. He shares it with the Hon. Kieran Guinness, fresh from the Oxford University Drag and a son of Lady Moyne, joint Master of the Tedworth. Mr Guinness hunts the dog-hounds, while John Smith, the kennel-huntsman who came in from the neighbouring Ballymeads nine seasons ago, hunts the bitches.

Sam Reynell would be amazed at many things. He would find a level pack of Kilkenny and Tipperary breeding, Welsh-blooded hounds, faster, lower-scenting and with a louder song than his own; he would meet descendants of his old friends – Kellys, Nugents, Vandeleurs and Purdons; and a few years ago he would have met his descendant – Sam Reynell, too – a distinguished hunt secretary; yet he would find the field composed, not of the squirarchy, but of a preponderance of farmers and their families (more women than men), at least half a dozen vets, and a priest – the chairman, Father Dunne.

He would find the members stoutly jealous of their country. The Dublin weekenders go mostly to the Kildares, Meaths, Louths and Wards. But the tantalising pastures and fences and buoyant spirit of the less accessible Westmeath also act as a magnet for sporting outsiders. If any encouragement is given, it is for love, not money. Being essentially a farmer's country, the outsider is only made welcome if he follows as one of them. (No visitor may bring his own horse; he hires in Westmeath.)

Surely Sam Reynell would share one's own impression of this thriving county pack at the heart of Ireland; that if and when foxhunting ends everywhere else in the world, the Westmeath will still gallop on, oblivious.

(6 October 1973)

When Mr Guinness resigned in 1976, Major H. Hesse and Mr J.C. Beveridge joined Major Tandy in the Mastership, but he retired in 1978. Mr Beveridge was then joined by two young brothers, Messrs Gerry and John Delamere, members of a celebrated Westmeath sporting family. In 1979 Mr Guinness returned to the fold and has since carried the horn again.

Mr Laurie Woollard has given up the secretaryship and his place has been filled, since 1978, by Col. William Harvey Kelly, of Clonhugh, and Mr L.M. Gavin.

British Army of the Rhine

The Weser Vale Bloodhounds

SOLDIER QUARRY IN WESTPHALIA

Jagd. No word rolls off the German sportsman's tongue with greater relish than this one, especially when the hunting implies following hounds, as distinct from shooting. It conjures the sound of those great brass horns looped around the body, the sight of green-coated horsemen galloping down the rides of gigantic pine forests, and of the scent of venison that marked the feast at the end of their day.

Jagd: it is rhapsody in German ears. Yet the hunting of live quarry died there between the wars. The first socialist governments, seeing it, in the 1920s, as one of the symbols of the despotic power of the landlords (but daring to condemn it openly only on allegations of hunting's disservice to conservation) imposed as much restriction on the sport as they could. It was finally banned in the 1930s under the Nazis. The trouble was that, in contrast to the British hunting *milieu*, it had always been a rich man's game; neither the farmers, nor scarcely even the yeomen, were encouraged to take part. In the revolutionary spirit of the Fatherland of those post-Great War years such an exclusive pursuit could not endure. So hunting men and women of the Third Reich, and their successors, were reduced to the aniseed trail. There are now five drag hunts in the Federal Republic, and their members can still pronounce *Jagd* with some of the fervour of their grandfathers, who entered their hounds to pig and fox and deer.

When the Royal Horse Guards (The Blues) were stationed in Westphalia with the post-Second World War army of occupation, German field sports as a whole were moribund. The law was the law of the Allies and only they had the right and the means to hunt and shoot. No regiment has a stronger reputation for the production of devoted hunting men than the Blues. (The tradition persists: the current edition of *Baily's Directory* shows a dozen former officers of this regiment as Masters of Foxhounds.) In 1949 they built up a pack of hounds intended for hare, but which spent much time in pursuit of roe deer. Whichever they chose it made a fine diversion.

During their second tour of duty in the 1960s, many Blues spent Saturday afternoons following the drag packs. Then, faced with a third stint of Rhine Army soldiering in 1969, immediately prior to the amalgamation with The Royal Dragoons (the second regiment of Household Cavalry now being the Blues and Royals), they were determined to do a bit more about those somewhat cheerless winter weekends.

When stationed in Wiltshire for their conversion training from armoured cars to tanks, they witnessed the delightful spectacle of the Master of the Savernake Forest, Lady Rosemary Brudenell-Bruce, hunting one of her keepers with four couples of bloodhounds. These, they decided, were the answer for Westphalia. This way a human quarry could be given a general direction in which to run, with a view to the most enjoyable crosscountry riding for the followers; but, as against the rigid certainty of the aniseed and animal urine trails, hounds could be seen to work out their line 'clean boot', that is to say, not from anything carried or trailed by the quarry, but rather from the scent of the man himself. (A live quarry it might be, they argued, but the Germans would scarcely object, on the grounds of conservation, to the tracking of a Household Cavalry trooper?)

So they approached Mr Eric Furness of the Peak bloodhounds, securing Chary, Charity and Bannister; Mr R.R. Wright of the North Warwickshire, who sold them Doubtful and Dainty, and Heer Frederick Majoie, Master of Holland's Ralley ma Joie, who produced Xenophon. Of these only Bannister is pure-bred bloodhound, the remainder being all Dumfriesshire foxhound – Peak bloodhound crosses. By March 1969, the nucleus of the pack was kennelled at the Blues and Royals barracks at Detmold (midway between Hannover and Dortmund) and the first opening meet of this new hunt, the Weser Vale, the only British pack in Germany, was held there on 1 September that year.

Last season there were 42 meets, the final one being held at Schloss Neuhaus-im-Solling, near Paderborn, on 17 April. Since the Life Guards – with Capt. T.M. Hickman, the present field Master, and Capt. C.N. Haworth-Booth, a former Master of the Eton Beagles, as joint-Master and huntsman of the Weser Vale – take over at the Detmold barracks next September, 17 April marked, not only the close of the present season, but the last of this hunt under its founders, the Blues and Royals. It was as poignant a day for the German landowners and farmers as it was for the regiment. On this occasion, the three quarry hunts into which the afternoon was divided were jointly organised by a group of the

140 The quarry greeting the last hound to reach him after the final hunt of the 1970–71 season. The leading horseman is Capt. C.N. Haworth-Booth, who hunted hounds when the Life Guards relieved the Blues and Royals in Germany later that year.

hunt's staunchest supporters: Prince and Princess von Preussen, Herr von Meyer and Herr Christian von Loesch, Master of the Niedersachsenmeute, who hunt their draglines between Hannover and Bremen.

Effecting the moral transition from army of occupation to NATO garrison this last quarter of a century has been neither swift nor easy, and such spontaneous co-operation by Germans highlights a quite fresh mark in the *entente* between the Army of the Rhine and the landowners of the Federal Republic. On both sides it is readily admitted that the Weser Vale has done much to foster the growing warmth. Formation commanders, weary of complaints of damage from German farmers, have gone so far as to send for the hunt to perform in scarred manoeuvre areas, soon resolving disharmony. Neither British soldier nor German countryman would deny that the chief inspiration behind all this cordiality comes from Capt. W.A. Stringer, the Blues and Royals Quartermaster, a modern Surteesian hero if ever there was one, who is joint-Master and huntsman.

Many of the 15 Germans out on 17 April are regular mounted followers, and as always a host of Westphalians watched from car and foot. Frederick Majoie, the Dutch Master of bloodhounds, was also riding. Of the 30-strong British contingent eight were mounted on Household Cavalry blacks. Sixteen of these are allotted to the regiment to train volunteers for mounted duty, and also for Rhine Army equitation courses; they are an almost essential asset for the hunt.

The British in traditional silk or bowler hat orders of dress, the Germans wearing white collars and ties with their velvet caps and scarlet coats, the Weser Vale cavalcade now hacked three kilometres from Schloss Neuhaus to the head of a wooded valley. Here Capt. Stringer, assisted by Corporal-of-Horse

Burton-Johnson, the whipper-in, laid hounds on to the smell, consisting of a piece of rag which had been regularly handled by the quarry during the previous week. Winding it, they gave their sudden deep baying chorus and, with a terrific spurt, away they swept down the grassy vale on a line that was one hour cold. There had been snow and sleet at Schloss Neuhaus and now the sun was shining; it was a weak scenting day, one affording many opportunities to watch hounds cast and seek as they missed the human smell. Then their great loose-skinned heads sank closer to the grass, the folds of brow and cheek and jowl pouring against the muzzle to produce that extra nose capacity that renders them the most powerful scenting creatures in the canine world. (And also among the most short-sighted.) There were only four and a half couples out. Bloodhounds are independent; by comparison they do not work well as a pack, and a larger number would certainly be very difficult to control, a factor made especially important by the presence of large numbers of deer, which are stringently protected by the German game laws.

Meanwhile the field were getting their share of timber-jumping over sound pasture which, in those parts, is largely free of cattle until later in April. When the quarry turned in at the end of his first three-kilometre line, we had a fine view of hounds romping home with baritone tongue to greet him. On the second line, up the foothills of the Neuhaus Forest, the emphasis changed from timber to stone walls, and here Major Crawford, the regiment's equitation officer, going very boldly, if well collected, at four and a half feet of boulders, took a most spectacular toss. The third hunt switched back towards the *Schloss*. Scent had not improved, hounds had still to work out their line with snuffling vigour, and it was amusing, at this point, to hear a regular German follower explaining in English, with painstaking detail, the niceties of houndwork to a visiting compatriot who was only familiar with the straight drag. For them this was more like the sound of *Jagd*, pronounced full-blooded.

(17 April 1971)

Index